From the Library of
David S. Norris

Philip's Daughters

Princeton Theological Monograph Series

K. C. Hanson, Charles M. Collier, and
D. Christopher Spinks, Series Editors

Recent volumes in the series

Kevin Twain Lowery
Salvaging Wesley's Agenda: A New Paradigm for Wesleyan Virtue Ethics

Matthew J. Marohl
Faithfulness and the Purpose of Hebrews: A Social Identity Approach

D. Seiple and Frederick W. Weidmann, editors
*Enigmas and Powers: Engaging the Work of Walter Wink
for Classroom, Church, and World*

Stanley D. Walters
Go Figure!: Figuration in Biblical Interpretation

Paul S. Chung
Martin Luther and Buddhism: Aesthetics of Suffering, Second Edition

Ralph M. Wiltgen
*The Founding of the Roman Catholic Church in Melanesia
and Micronesia, 1850–1875*

Steven B. Sherman
*Revitalizing Theological Epistemology: Holistic Evangelical
Approaches to the Knowledge of God*

David Hein
Geoffrey Fisher: Archbishop of Canterbury, 1945–1961

Mary Clark Moschella
*Living Devotions: Reflections on Immigration, Identity,
and Religious Imagination*

Philip's Daughters

Women in Pentecostal-Charismatic Leadership

Edited by

ESTRELDA ALEXANDER AND AMOS YONG

PICKWICK *Publications* · Eugene, Oregon

PHILIP'S DAUGHTERS
Women in Pentecostal-Charismatic Leadership

Princeton Theological Monograph Series 104

Pickwick Publications
A Division of Wipf and Stock Publishers
199 W. 8th Ave., Suite 3
Eugene, OR 97401

ISBN 13: 978-1-55635-832-6

Cataloging-in-Publication data:

Philip's Daughters.

    Philip's daughters : women in pentecostal-charismatic leadership / Edited by Estrelda Alexander and Amos Yong.

    ISBN 13: 978-1-55635-832-6

    viii + 252 p. ; 23 cm. Includes bibliographic references and indexes.

    Princeton Theological Monograph Series 104

    1. Pentecostal churches — United States. 2. Women clergy. 3. Pentecostalism. I. Alexander, Estrelda. II. Yong, Amos. III. Title. IV. Series.

BV676 P60 2009

Contents

Preface

I JOINED THE FACULTY AT REGENT UNIVERSITY SCHOOL OF DIVINITY during the summer of 2005. Early that fall semester, I began conversations with my new colleague, Dr. Estrelda Alexander, about having a series of colloquia at the Divinity School to engage crucial issues for Renewal Christianity. We decided to focus on the topic of women in Pentecostal and charismatic leadership, and began planning what turned out to be the "Women in Pentecostal-Charismatic Leadership" colloquium which was held over three weekends during the academic year 2006–2007. The papers collected in this volume are revisions of drafts originally presented at this event, and it has been my joy and privilege to have had her as a collaborator and co-editor for this project.

There are many people who need to be thanked for their help in planning and then carrying out the colloquium, and then with transforming the papers into this volume. To begin, we are grateful to Randall Pannell, Vinson Synan, Donald Tucker, and Michael Palmer, who have each served in various top leadership capacities at the University and School of Divinity over the last three plus years, and have supported this project in various ways, not the least of which is financially. Thanks also to those who have worked hard on the marketing end to promote the colloquium and on the audio-visual production end during the events: Joy Brathwaite, Misty Martin, Julia Jennette, David Massey, Brian J. McLean, Mark Stevenson, and Chris Decker. Every academic conference involves organization, administration, and just plain hard work; for these, we have to express gratitude to Libby Hightower, Pidge Bannin, Leila Fry, Doc Hughes, and William Catoe.

Of course, books are composed by writers, and we as editors are honored to have worked with the contributors to this volume. Each essay has also benefited from personal responses delivered at the colloquium. For that thankless task, we are beholden to the four respondents, who each responded to three papers over the course of the colloquium: J. Lyle Story, Professor of Biblical Languages and New Testament at the Regent

University School of Divinity; Mara Crabtree, Associate Professor of Spiritual Formation and Women's Studies; Bramwell Osula, Assistant Professor of Leadership Studies at the Regent University School of Global Leadership and Entrepreneurship; and Rosemarie S. Hughes, Dean of the Regent University School of Psychology and Counseling.

We also appreciate Sophronia Vachon, my graduate assistant, for help with copyediting the entire manuscript, and to Timothy Lim Teck Ngern, my doctoral student, for help with the indexes.

Finally, thanks to K. C. Hanson at Wipf and Stock Publishers for seeing the promise of this book. Diane Farley and Patrick Harrison at the press has also been a great help in moving the book through the production process.

—Amos Yong
Chesapeake, Virginia
August 2007

1

Introduction

Estrelda Alexander

> On the next day we who were Paul's companions departed and came to Caesarea, and entered the house of Philip the evangelist, who was one of the seven, and stayed with him. Now this man had four virgin daughters who prophesied.
>
> —Acts 21:8–9[1]

THIS SHORT PASSAGE IN THE BOOK OF ACTS IS EASILY PASSED OVER AMID all the miraculous encounters and evangelistic activity that is the focus of Luke's writing. We know very little about these four women— Philip's daughters—for they remain unnamed as individuals. Despite the cultural restrictions of the time, they could not be completely left out of the narrative; they were recognized as prophets. We know nothing else about them, except that they were unmarried virgins who still resided in their father's home. We do not know what they said, but what they said made enough of an impression on the writer that he noted that they were prophetesses—individuals set apart by divine impartation and recognition of the church to speak on God's behalf.

The identification of their ministry as prophetesses begins a legacy of ministry of Spirit-empowered women and, at the same time, a history of suppression of that ministry by the church. Generally, as within the patriarchal setting of the New Testament, such suppression has been in line with the cultural setting in which women have found themselves.

---

1. All Scripture quotations are from the New King James Version.

Historically, women were prohibited from leadership not only in the church but also in most other arenas of society.

Throughout the last half of the twentieth century, however, women's roles have changed dramatically. Women lead some of the nation's most successful corporations, and head some of the most prestigious academic institutions in the country and the world. They hold major political offices at every level, and for the first time in the United States a woman was a serious contender and a front-runner for the nation's highest office. Yet, one of the most challenging issues facing the Pentecostal-Charismatic movement into the twenty-first century concerns the role of women in the ministry and leadership of the church.

Many Christian communities have taken the challenge of women's leadership to heart and have involved women in ever increasing levels of ecclesial authority. Most mainline denominations ordain women with full clergy rights.[2] A number of these have elected several women to the office of bishop. The United Methodist Church has fifteen active women bishops among the sixty-nine in its ranks, and presently a woman, Janice Riggle Huie, serves as the president of its Council of Bishops. The African Methodist Episcopal Church has three women among its twenty-one bishops and the Episcopal Church now has a woman, Katharine Jefferts Schori, as its presiding bishop. Yet Evangelical churches, especially the classical Pentecostal movement, have been resistant to any genuine elevation of the status of women within their ranks.

The irony in this turn of events is evident when one notes that some observers have characterized Pentecostalism as essentially "women's religion" because of the greater proportion of women than men who have historically participated in the movement. It is even more ironic when one explores women's involvement in the unfolding of this movement which has come to be the fastest growing segment of global Christianity. Like its antecedent nineteenth century Holiness movement, the attraction of women to the nascent Pentecostal movement was partly because of its promise of greater freedom to participate in ministry. In the earli-

2. In *Ordaining Women: Culture and Conflict in Religious Organization* (Cambridge: Harvard University Press, 1997), 2–3, Mark Chaves defines "full clergy rights" as ordination, and all the rights and privileges that come with it. According to Chavez, denominations that grant full clergy rights are those in which there is "formally open access [to women] to all religious positions." He distinguishes that from denominations which ordain or credential women for ministry but bar them from holding institutional leadership.

est stages of the movement, Pentecostal women took on more roles and enjoyed a greater degree of freedom than was true for their counterparts in most other branches of the Christian church.

In those earliest years, there appeared to be almost absolute freedom for women to pursue whatever course they felt God was leading them to follow. Women pastored churches, served as missionaries, preached, taught, exhorted, and held governing positions in the church. As the movement grew and attempted to gain respectability, women's roles were curtailed by a number of formal and informal restrictions in most Pentecostal bodies. Women still had freedom to preach and exhort, but governing roles became more limited and these bodies grew to more closely reflect the gender-stratified hierarchy they once denounced in mainline bodies.

Even where official dogma was egalitarian, unofficial tradition concerning "male-only" leadership was often very palpable. While official polity may have opened all levels of ministry to called and qualified persons, unofficial tradition saw only men holding top positions, such as presiding elder, district overseer or superintendent, bishop, or other denominational head. Furthermore, within this unofficial tradition, women could not hope to be appointed as pastor of congregations of any substantial size.

The original freedom given to women in the Pentecostal movement—even when limited—derived from several factors. First, Pentecostal eschatology supported the premillennial understanding that saw the revival as a fulfillment of the biblical prophecy of Joel 2:28a: "And it shall come to pass afterward that I will pour out My Spirit on all flesh; your sons and your daughters shall prophesy." Early Pentecostals understood themselves as living in those last days, before the return of Christ, when he would establish his millennial kingdom on earth. As such, they felt an urgent need to involve everyone in the task of winning as many souls into this kingdom as possible. Therefore, women as well as men were enlisted to preach the gospel.

Secondly, these early Pentecostals held that individuals were empowered through Holy Spirit baptism to do ministry as the Spirit willed. They believed God supernaturally anointed individuals, without regard to social constriction, education, or other formal preparation. Proof of one's call lay in the person's own testimony to such a call and in the perceived fruit of a Spirit-empowered ministry, rather than in a formal ecclesiastical system of selection or promotion. Men or women who demonstrated preaching skill and ability to convey a convincing gospel message, and who displayed charismatic ministry gifts and evangelistic ability were urged into action. This radical egalitarianism was coupled with a general disdain for hierarchical church structures and denominationalism.

Yet competing theologies complicated the status of women ministers. Preaching women modeled themselves after their Holiness predecessors, who also took their authority from the Joel 2:28 passage, and held to a radical concept of the equality of the sexes in ministry. However, restorationist elements within Pentecostalism sought to return the church to "New Testament simplicity and purity." While for some, an essential rudiment of this restoration was the full empowerment of all believers for service, for a substantial number of others it involved the felt need to follow Pauline restrictions on the ministry of women within the church, despite the witnesses of passages such as that found in Acts and the testimony of Jesus' inclusion of women found in the Gospels.

These competing understandings and values were played out in a number of interesting ways. Under Charles Fox Parham's leadership, a woman is credited by many with ushering in the entire modern Pentecostal movement when shortly after midnight on January 1, 1901, Agnes Ozman became the first reported person to speak in tongues publicly with the explicit understanding that it was the initial evidence of Holy Spirit baptism. Parham organized his Bible School in Topeka Kansas to "fit men and women to go to the ends of the earth to preach."[3] He ordained women, as well as men, and commissioned both to ministry. Many of these women and men assisted Parham in the later evangelistic campaigns that he conducted throughout the country.

Names like Lucy Farrow, Florence Crawford, Clara Lum, and Jennie Evans Seymour are representative of the significant contribution women made to the Azusa Street Revival. Additionally, several outstanding women were among the many evangelists and missionaries who went out from Azusa Street to take the message of Pentecostalism across the country and around the world. In much of the historiography of Pentecostalism, these women's names and legacies have been all

---

3. David G. Roebuck, "Loose the Women," *Christian History* 17:2 (1998) 38.

but forgotten. Since male leaders have dominated the historical record, the roles of these women have been basically ignored, and, like Philip's daughters, they have largely remained unnamed.[4]

Further, despite these auspicious beginnings, evidence of erosion of women's leadership opportunities runs through the breadth of the movement. From the outset, the Church of God in Christ (COGIC), arguably the largest Pentecostal denomination, and certainly the largest black Pentecostal denomination in the United States, placed restrictions on women's ministry that have remained in place during its entire history. Within COGIC, women are not ordained, but can be licensed as "evangelists" or "missionaries" to preach and teach primarily other women and work in what the COGIC leadership has termed "vital" roles.[5] In these roles, women raise funds for local congregations and the national denomination; direct local, regional, and national women's programs; and provide material support for the pastor and his family.

Several early Pentecostal denominations granted women "limited ordination" or ministerial credentialing without giving them governing authority. For example, in the early United Holy Church of America, another African American denomination, women were licensed or ordained to ministry, but received little material or spiritual support from male colleagues who only tolerated them.[6] Practical restrictions on women's ministry in the Assemblies of God were cleared in 1935 when they were granted full ordination. Yet this concession has not materially improved the opportunity for ordained ministry of most women or reduced the predominance of male congregational and administrative leadership. Within the Church of God (Cleveland, Tennessee), however, women are still only allowed to attain two of the three ranks of ministry, and remain restricted from voting in the Assembly, from governance in the local congregation, and from holding regional and national offices. So by the end of the twentieth century, Pentecostal women find them-

---

4. I have attempted to set some of the record straight in Estrelda Alexander, *The Women of Azusa Street* (Cleveland: Pilgrim, 2006).

5. For a discussion of the COGIC context, see Ithiel Clemmons, *Bishop C H Mason and the Roots of the Church of God in Christ* (Bakersfield, CA: Pneuma Life, 2001), 101–9.

6. Yet the United Holy Church has perhaps shown the greatest growth on the issue. Presently women have full clergy rights, several women pastor substantial congregations and at least three have been elevated to the office of bishop.

selves in a place where their position has been reversed and they enjoy less freedom than their sisters in mainline denominations. Indeed, the current status of women within Pentecostalism is one of ambivalence.

Just as the limited freedom of women in early Pentecostalism resulted from several factors, other forces have contributed to the gradual decline of opportunities for women's leadership. First, the eschatological, premillennial hope of the imminent return of Christ faded with the realization that several years had passed and Jesus had not yet returned. With this, the sectarian, anti-denominational, anti-structural bias of the Pentecostal movement gave way to the sense that some sort of organization was needed if the movement were going to endure. Loosely tied sects began to form denominations with written polity and doctrine. From the beginning, some level of restrictions on the ministry and leadership of women was generally incorporated amid these developments.

Second, Pentecostals sought to distance themselves from any association with modernity and "worldliness," including ideas of the "new woman" that were coming into fashion by the middle of the century. They sought by dress codes, rhetoric, and social constraints to ensure there was a distinction between the modern, "unsaved" world and themselves. They also saw the modern women's movement as representing rebellion against God and threatening the God-ordained social order prescribed in Scripture.

Third, the conservative understanding of women's role within the family and society among Pentecostals only deepened when the movement sought to align itself more closely with the broader Evangelical community. Evangelicals believed that the proper place for women was in the home. Like Philip's daughters, unmarried women were expected to remain under the protection of their fathers, and married women were expected to be submissive to their husbands and supportive of their work and/or ministry. Yet evangelicals, along with Pentecostals, made a place for those few, exceptional women whom God chose to use in extraordinary ways.[7] For, again, like Philip's daughters, it was impossible to ignore the prophetic witness of their lives and ministries.

7. Women such as Catherine Boothe, who alongside her husband, William, co-founded the Salvation Army; faith healer Kathryn Kuhlmann; and Roberta Hestenes, an ordained Presbyterian USA minister who served as president of Eastern University from 1987–1996, are but three examples of such extraordinary women.

Fourth, in some Pentecostal denominations, women who sought pastoral placements encountered another unofficial limitation. Leaders willingly allowed them to "dig out" or plant new congregations and nurture them to the point of viability. They also encouraged them to take on congregations that were at the point of failing and to use their gifts for preaching, evangelism, and administration to rebuild them to viability. Once these congregations had grown to the point that they could economically sustain the salary of a full-time pastor, the woman would be replaced with a new, male, pastor. Leaders then sent the woman to dig out another new work or repair another failing congregation. Over several decades, a woman might start or renew several congregations in this manner, but would never be allowed to take any of them past the point of viability.[8]

Along with more pronounced structures came a growing "professionalization" of the ministry. This professionalization was characterized by differing criteria for credentialing men and women for ministry, hierarchical ranks of ministry, dual tracks for women and men seeking to pursue God's call to ministry in their lives, and the shift of ministry from a primarily voluntary vocation to a paid occupation—at least for men. With these structures in place, women were very cognizant that there were limits on their ministries. Yet they persisted in entering the ministry in large numbers and seeking leadership roles during those early years. Eventually however, with increased restrictions came the decline of the actual numbers of women who answered the call and pursued public ministry and leadership or attempted to move beyond the limited roles prescribed for them. So today, many Pentecostal bodies see a declining rather than increasing number of women entering the ministry; on the other side, there is also a pronounced increase in the number of women leaving Pentecostal churches to pursue ministry within mainline or non-denominational bodies.

The above discussion highlights the intricacies of the issue of women's ministry and leadership in the Holiness/Pentecostal/Charismatic movement. For the most part, Pentecostal women have been allowed no voice in determining their roles because in many bodies they are excluded from the higher levels of leadership where the decision

---

8. See, for example, David Grant Roebuck, "Limiting Liberty: The Church of God and Women Ministers, 1886–1996" (Ph.D. dissertation, Vanderbilt University, 1997).

making conversations occur, and/or they are denied the privilege of voting in the very bodies which deliberate these issues.

Yet, while it is true that women have limited direct voice in deliberations regarding their leadership in Pentecostal bodies, contemporary church leaders continue to look to the academy for theological guidance on issues that are vital to the church, its life, and ministry. This volume allows women (and men) to speak to this issue in ways that can inform such a discussion and help shape the Pentecostal/ Charismatic movement into the twenty-first century. We have gathered scholars from a variety of traditions and cultures within the Holiness/ Pentecostal/Charismatic community and invited their prophetic voices and expertise to assist in unraveling the myriad of historical, biblical, and theological issues that have influenced the ministry and leadership of Pentecostal women.

The papers collected here were originally presented in a three-session symposium held over the 2006–2007 academic year at Regent University School of Divinity in Virginia Beach. Amos Yong and I approached this project with three particular goals in mind:

1. To expose our own students in the School of Divinity to cutting edge scholarship regarding a contemporary issue with which they will wrestle throughout the course of their professional careers.

2. To provide a public forum for Pentecostal women scholars to be in dialogue together and to critically explore the biblical, historical, theological, sociological, ethical, and ecclesial dimensions of a major issue that is facing the church in the twenty-first century.

3. To add to the growing volume of work within Pentecostal/ Charismatic scholarship by producing an edited volume of Pentecostal perspectives on the subject of women in American religion—an area that remains largely untapped.

The multicultural and multidisciplinary essays in this volume explore the breadth of the academic span of the issue, with scholars from the disciplines of biblical studies, theology, history, sociology, and ethics from a range of classical Pentecostal and Charismatic traditions. We have organized the set of twelve essays into two sections: Historical and Biblical/Theological perspectives.

The first essay in Part One—Historical Perspective, "Wesleyan/ Holiness and Pentecostal Women Preachers: Pentecost as the Pattern for Primitivism," by church historian Susie C. Stanley, explores the role of the Wesleyan/Holiness Movement's affirmation of women preachers among Pentecostals, and asks if Pentecostal women would have preached in such large numbers if converts to Pentecostalism had been primarily from mainline Protestant denominations. Stanley shows how the Wesleyan/Holiness movement provided a theological rationale for women preachers and, perhaps even more importantly, the witness of women preachers themselves. The essay highlights the calling and ministry of some of the many Pentecostal women preachers who came directly from holiness affiliations.

In "'Cause He's My Chief Employer': Hearing Women's Voices in a Classical Pentecostal Denomination," historian David G. Roebuck asserts that Christians have historically claimed the Bible as their source of authority regarding the role of women in ministry. Yet, he insists that both the Spirit and culture have been and continue to be influential in our interpretation of Scripture. His essay attempts to hear the voices of women ministers in the classical Pentecostal movement by examining textual sources and providing oral history interviews. These reveal how Pentecostal women have used Word, Spirit, and culture to justify, locate, and describe their ministries.

Historian Karen Kossie-Chernyshev lays out in her essay, "Looking Beyond the Pulpit: Social Ministries and African-American Pentecostal-Charismatic Women in Leadership," how the pastorate and pulpit have been the most highly contested spaces among African American Pentecostals since the advent of Pentecostalism. She outlines how Pentecostal women who felt compelled by the Spirit to preach, pastor, or form fellowships or denominations embraced their respective callings despite the criticism. Further, she gives evidence of how some women established successful ministries that have continued to function for generations after their death. Even while twenty-first century black Pentecostal women leaders continue to interrogate traditionally contested spaces, Kossie-Chernyshev uses a variety of sources, including interviews with black Pentecostal women leaders, to argue that in our post-modern, post-denominational age, the organizations they have founded are relevant loci of spiritual leadership. She demonstrates how these organizations directly and systematically address the complex problems of our time—teen pregnancy, homelessness, substance abuse, domestic and community violence, and AIDS—and sees the collective commitment of these women to faith-in-action as a vibrant reflection of spiritual leadership at its best. Her essay signals the need to broaden the traditional definition of leadership within the African American Pentecostal church.

Deidre Helen Crumbley uses the language and techniques of anthropology to explore the interplay of cultural legacy, social history, and human agency in the formation of women's roles in two spiritual church contexts—an African and an African Diaspora congregation. She draws on a global approach to Christianity practiced by Africans and people of African descent to examine these roles in a Nigerian indigenous church and an African American sanctified church as windows into dynamics of gender, religion, and power. Crumbley defines "spiritual churches" as faith communities in which (1) biblical literalism forms the theological foundation, (2) revelation is on-going and demonstrated through charismatic adepts, and (3) divine power is experienced as imminent, accessible, and expressed through the body of believers in the forms including glossolalia, religious dance, healing, and revelation. While both churches Crumbley examines share these religious features, in one, women have held both ritual and political power as doctrinal arbiter and administrative decision-maker; in the other, women may not speak in the congregation or approach holy places when menstruating. Her essay explores how gender practices in spiritual churches can range so widely, from arenas of unfettered female leadership to religious institutions which exclude women from both holy office and holy space.

Gastón Espinosa's essay adds to previous scholarship on Latinas in religion that has been almost exclusively focused on the contemporary struggles of Catholic and mainline Protestant women from a decidedly feminist and/or liberationist perspective. Though his scholarship fills an important gap in the literature, the stories of millions of non-feminist Latina still remain largely untold. His essay attempts to partially fill this gap by focusing on the contributions of Hispanic Pentecostal women to the Latino Pentecostal movement in the United States that now numbers more than 4.5 million adherents. Espinosa challenges Charles H. Barfoot and Gerald T. Sheppard's thesis, as applicable to all

Pentecostal women, insisting that there was no great reversal of power or the right to ordination for early twentieth-century Latinas as there was in Anglo-American Pentecostalism. Instead, he insists, the history of Latino Pentecostal clergywomen has been long and checkered, with Latinas facing an uphill struggle against gender discrimination and the right to full ordination. Espinosa's essay shows how they have practiced a kind of paradoxical domesticity in which they were exhorted to be end-times prophetesses in the public sphere and devoted mothers and good wives in the private sphere. He further insists that, in the last analysis, despite their seemingly paradoxical lives, Latina Pentecostal women are, by their own accounts, "liberated."

Barbara L. Cavaness' essay, "Leadership Attitudes and the Ministry of Single Women in Assembly of God Missions," the final essay in Part One, examines how many first-generation Pentecostal leaders encouraged and empowered women in ministry during a period of initial excitement over the Spirit's outpouring. She specifically examines the women affirmed by three such leaders: Charles Parham; Thomas Barratt, founder of the Norwegian Pentecostal movement; and William Seymour. As a missiologist, she then surveys one early Pentecostal movement—the Assemblies of God—to assess how and to what extent leadership attitudes impacted the ministry of women (particularly single missionaries) as revival fires waned.

Whereas essays in part one are more historically oriented, those in part two draw on Scripture, the major resource for Pentecostal spirituality, to reflect theologically on the critical issues related to our topic. In the first of these, "Pentecostalism 101: Your Daughters Shall Prophesy," New Testament scholar Janet Everts Powers asserts that when early Pentecostals read Acts 2:16–17, they saw a promise that the Spirit of prophecy would be poured out on all who received the baptism of the Holy Spirit, and understood clearly that the church was meant to be constituted as a prophetic community. In this understanding, prophetic leadership encompassed all aspects of ministry of the Word including preaching, teaching, evangelizing, and giving of prophetic words. All who received the baptism of the Holy Spirit—including women— were potential ministers of the Word. However, over the next century this definition of prophecy was eroded and women were increasingly barred from various aspects of word ministry, especially teaching and preaching. Powers' essay traces the narrowing definition of prophecy

and argues for the restoration of a biblical and truly Pentecostal view of
prophetic ministry that will again empower women for the full ministry of the Word.

An American Baptist and sociologist, Cheryl Townsend Gilkes
brings the perspective of someone who has stood outside the
Pentecostal and charismatic movements but yet consistently given it
critical attention. In "'You've Got a Right to the Tree of Life': The Biblical
Foundations of an Empowered Attitude among Black Women in the
Sanctified Church," Gilkes contends that debates over the interpretation
of the Bible have been central to forming the "sanctified church" traditions, and women in these churches have shaped powerful positions
for themselves in spite of the patriarchal background. Gilkes sees the
conflicts in which these women are engaged as part of the larger world
of the black church and its diverse approaches to women's participation
and leadership, which have been partly shaped through debates over
the roles of women in the Bible. She pays particular attention to the important witness of women in ancient Israel and in the New Testament
that sanctified women have employed to challenge Christian patriarchy, and details how these discourses are part of an historic, trans-
denominational ethos traceable to slave religion that has enabled wom-
en to shape and seek opportunities for participation and leadership in
multiple spaces throughout the black church. She contends that what
some characterize as Black women's "holy boldness" in the use of the
Bible demonstrates the conflict and order in a religious world of the
black church.

Within Pentecostalism, the authentication of women in ministry
vocation is often conveyed with images of anointing and Spirit empowerment. Quite often Joel 2:28–29 has been the reference text for
women in ministry within the tradition. Theologian Cheryl Bridges
Johns agrees with Powers that in the early years of the movement,
when the dominant image of ministry was the prophetic, men, as well
as women, saw themselves as anointed prophets. The turn comes for
Johns, however, as ranks of ordination were quickly established, and by
the mid-twentieth century, Pentecostal ministry contained both priestly
and prophetic elements. Her essay, "Spirited Vestments: Or, Why the
Anointing Is Not Enough," shows how women were relegated to the
prophetic corner, where they were consigned to the roles of evangelists
and church planters. Johns is insistent that in many classical Pentecostal

denominations the prophetic image and language of Spirit anointing continues as the dominant or only image and is used to maintain a fa-çade of empowerment for ministry, all the while giving little external validation to the callings of women. She further insists that women in the twenty-first century want more external validation of ministry. For her, it is important that Pentecostal/Charismatic churches look beyond Joel 2:28 (while continuing to acknowledge the prophetic anointing), and develop a more holistic image of ministry. Her essay attempts to provide a paradigm for a "new relatedness" grounded in a trinitarian model of human relationships. It revisits the meaning of *imago dei* and its implications for defining the priestly vocation of women and men, and calls for a Pentecostal option for women not unlike the liberationist "preferential option for the poor."

In "The Spirit, Nature, and Canadian Pentecostal Women: A Con-versation with Critical Theory," Pamela Holmes provides a Canadian perspective through the lens of critical theorists from the early Frankfurt School in Germany, who were analyzing the political revolutions going on around them and advocating for further counter-revolutions and revolt. Holmes sees the Pentecostal revival that broke out among the de-scendents of slaves and others like them as a revolution of sorts against former owners and current oppressors within both Christian churches and society. For her, this revolution that began at Azusa Street was spurred on by the efforts of women and men of various ethnic back-grounds. As an emerging Pentecostal feminist theologian, Holmes ex-amines the decline of women's involvement in Canadian Pentecostalism using the insights of critical theorists and the feminist scholars who draw upon them. She asserts that Pentecostalism contains rhetorically and symbolically significant ideas and practices that hold emancipatory potential for women's lived realities within an ecologically and envi-ronmentally sustainable framework. Her essay places these ideas and practices in a self-reflective, critical dialogue that attempts to illuminate this emancipatory potential for women in Canada as well as the rest of the world.

Julie C. Ma looks at how societies in different countries have rec-ognized the significance and capability of women, particularly in social settings. She sees this recognition as an indication of the growing aware-ness of women's ability to lead in cultures where such leadership has not always been valued or even permitted. Ma's essay, "Changing Images:

Women in Asian Pentecostalism," calls on churches and Christian institutions to look at the changes in the social fabric of their societies and begin to investigate ways in which they can change their attitudes and practices to include women in their ranks.

Finally, in "Spiritual Egalitarianism, Ecclesial Pragmatism, and the Status of Women in Ordained Ministry," theologian Frederick L. Ware provides a critical examination of what he calls the "spiritual egalitarianism" and "ecclesial pragmatism" that have influenced the status of women in ordained Pentecostal ministry. Ware defines spiritual egalitarianism as a theological distinctive of Pentecostalism, and ecclesial pragmatism as an accommodation to prevalent social and cultural norms. He argues that ecclesial pragmatism is inconsistent with values established at the outset of the Pentecostal movement. The Azusa Street Revival exemplifies the early Pentecostal vision of unity, and the free, equal, and meaningful participation of all persons in Christ, which Ware says was in stark contrast to existing social practices. This embrace of spiritual egalitarianism as an authoritative tradition requires Pentecostals to abandon policies prohibiting women's ordination. For Ware, God's reign of justice which is "not yet" can function "now" as the present moral guide for human action, including the full recognition of the ministry of women.

This volume does not attempt to provide the definitive answer to all the remaining questions regarding the position of women within the Pentecostal and Charismatic movements. Even with their combined multi-disciplinary approach, these twelve essays only provide a starting point for a deeper conversation that needs to take place within the movement to rescue this vital, yet volatile issue from the knee-jerk application of proof texts. They also point the way toward such a conversation, taking advantage of the rich deposit of historical, biblical, and theological evidence that is available for engaging such a conversation.

It will take courage from both men and women within the movement to deal with the legacy of Philip's daughters. Though they remained unnamed as individuals, they could not be completely ignored; and despite the cultural restrictions of the time, they boldly prophesied in the power of the Spirit. We do not know what they said, but what they said made enough impact on the writer of the book of Acts that he noted they were prophetesses. Even though their story is barely an aside, handled in two short verses, a hermeneutic of recovery instructs us to glean from that aside that women have always had a strong, if often muted voice, among God's people and to continue to look for places in our own traditions where the faint yet prophetic voice of women can be discerned among the many stories that have consistently taken the limelight. Perhaps it is in the telling of these stories that we can point the way to a different, inclusive future for the tradition.

PART I

Historical Perspectives

2

Wesleyan/Holiness and Pentecostal Women Preachers

Pentecost as the Pattern for Primitivism

Susie C. Stanley

Introduction

THREE GROUPS OF WOMEN MANIFESTED VARIOUS UNDERSTANDINGS OF the baptism of the Holy Ghost: Wesleyan/Holiness women, Wesleyan/Holiness women who embraced Pentecostalism, and other Pentecostal women who primarily ministered in the United States. Generally, their hermeneutic of Pentecost evidenced a primitivist emphasis. Without the theological groundwork and the model set by Wesleyan/Holiness women preachers and those who embraced Pentecostalism, it is doubtful that Pentecostalism would have affirmed women preachers.

It can be argued that the theological context of the Wesleyan/Holiness movement, particularly its emphasis on the baptism of the Holy Spirit or sanctification, provided the basis for its affirmation of women preachers.[1] The doctrinal emphasis on sanctification provided a positive theological context for women in ministry. Women preachers did not minister in a vacuum. Their ministries illustrated the consequences of the doctrine of sanctification. The theology of sanctification

---

1. For examples, see the following: Susie C. Stanley, *Holy Boldness: Women Preachers' Autobiographies and the Sanctified Self* (Knoxville: University of Tennessee Press, 2002); and Susie Stanley, "Women Evangelists in the Church of God [Anderson, Indiana] at the Beginning of the Twentieth Century," in Juanita Evans Leonard, ed., *Called to Minister: Empowered to Serve: Women in Ministry* (Anderson, IN: Warner, 1989), 35–55.

had a direct impact not only on their interpretation of Pentecost itself but on their actions as evangelists, pastors, and church leaders.

Holiness Categories

Holiness categories in the United States are difficult to determine precisely because of the large overlap among individuals and groups. So a brief comment on my use of "Wesleyan/Holiness" is essential. Wesleyan/Holiness doctrine, as the name suggests, originated with John Wesley, the founder of Methodism. It denotes one of the paths to holiness. It would be easiest to use the more generic term "holiness" to encompass all the paths, but affirmation of women preachers was most evident in the Wesleyan/Holiness movement. Hundreds of women on this path to holiness ministered with the blessing of Wesleyan/Holiness adherents. However, some women followed more than one path to holiness. It is like a road near my house that actually crosses itself. Holiness paths intertwined. Whatever the ultimate path, each one branched off the Wesleyan/Holiness movement.

An excellent case in point is Carrie Judd Montgomery. Raised an Episcopalian, she came in contact with holiness believers through her involvement with others who advocated faith healing. One such individual was William Boardman, who followed the higher life path of holiness, a phrase which Calvinists such as Boardman preferred. Boardman's introduction to holiness, though, came from attending Methodist Phoebe Palmer's Tuesday Meetings for the Promotion of Holiness.[2] Palmer is the mother of the Wesleyan/Holiness movement because of her role in articulating and disseminating Wesleyan/Holiness doctrine.[3] Montgomery testified at a non-denominational holiness service, probably modeled after Palmer's meetings.[4] Montgomery ministered both in the Christian Alliance founded by A. B. Simpson and The Salvation Army which split from Methodism. Obviously, she saw no tension between the two groups, even though The Salvation Army was Arminian and the Christian Alliance, while non-denominational,

2. In contrast to Calvinists, Methodists are Arminian, believing in free will rather than predestination.

3. Melvin E. Dieter, *The Holiness Revival of the Nineteenth Century*, 2d ed. (Lanham, MD: Scarecrow, 1996), 30, 113.

4. Carrie Judd Montgomery, *"Under His Wings": The Story of My Life* (Oakland, CA: Office of Triumph of Faith, 1936), 68–69.

reflected Simpson's Presbyterian background. Montgomery observed: "During my early ministry in the Lord's work I had sweet fellowship with many other leaders and workers in the Lord's vineyard. Among these were many who were active in the Holiness movement. It seemed as though all the deeply spiritual people were drawn together in those days, no matter by what name they were called."[5] Here, she is aware of various categories but she refuses to acknowledge them as being in conflict. The label or the name of the path was not important. While some scholars have placed Montgomery in the higher life movement, I believe her exposure to Wesleyan/Holiness groups and individuals allows me to locate her on the Wesleyan/Holiness path as well. A key difference between the two groups is their understanding of sin. Higher life doctrine held that inbred sin is suppressed while the Wesleyan/Holiness view was that sanctification eradicated inbred sin. No holiness believer, to my knowledge, ever refused to work with another Christian who believed in the suppression of sin rather than the eradication of sin. Probably like many others, Montgomery was a hybrid, blending two understandings of holiness without being preoccupied with the differences.[6]

Montgomery's ministries ignored doctrinal boundaries. Significant friendships she developed with Wesleyan/Holiness women ministers surely influenced Montgomery's theology as she walked the path of holiness with them. Most frequently, she mentioned Anna Prosser, a Methodist, calling her a "dear friend" who worked with her at a gospel mission sponsored by the Woman's Christian Temperance Union

5. Montgomery, *"Under His Wings,"* 114.

6. Edith L. Blumhofer, *"Pentecost in My Soul": Explorations in the Meaning of Pentecostal Experience in the Early Assemblies of God* (Springfield, MO: Gospel Publishing House, 1989), 66. Daniel E. Albrecht places the young Montgomery in the "Reformed" or "Keswick" category (Albrecht, "The Life and Ministry of Carrie Judd Montgomery" [M.A. thesis, Western Evangelical Seminary, 1984], 186). However, he undermines his own labeling by his discussion of Montgomery's emphasis on love which is a one-word summary of Wesleyan/Holiness doctrine (142, 149). When writing about her ministry, Albrecht concludes: "Her vision of the effects of holiness was well within the scope of Wesleyan pietism as represented in the holiness movement" (199). His observations illustrate the hybrid nature of Montgomery's understanding of holiness.

(W.C.T.U.) in Buffalo.[7] Other Wesleyan/Holiness friends active in ministry were Emma Whittemore, Dora Dudley, and Jennie Smith.[8]

Hannah Whitall Smith's holiness walk, likewise, led her to a merger of several paths. She wrote that Presbyterians used the term "The Higher Life" or "the Life of Faith" to speak of holiness, but she maintained that "by whatever name it may be called, the truth at the bottom of each name is the same, and can be expressed in four little words, 'Not I, but Christ.'"[9] Although she became acquainted with the doctrine of sanctification at Methodist meetings, she preferred the term "The Life of Faith."[10] Commissioned as lay evangelists of the National Camp Meeting Association for the Promotion of Holiness, a Wesleyan/Holiness organization, Hannah and her husband Robert Pearsall Smith visited England, paving the way for what became known as the Keswick Convention for the Promotion of Holiness which promoted the higher life path to holiness.[11] The Smiths were key figures along with Mary and William Boardman in this Calvinist movement which held its first con-

---

7. Montgomery, *"Under His Wings,"* 68, 82, 89. The W.C.T.U. had Wesleyan/Holiness roots. Frances Willard described the Woman's Crusade and its culmination in the W.C.T.U. in Pentecostal terms: "Born of such a visitation of God's Spirit as the world has not known since tongues of fire sat upon the wondering group at Pentecost . . . and baptized in the beauty of holiness," Frances Willard, "Work of the W.C.T.U.," in Annie Nathan Meyer, ed., *Women's Work in America* [1881; reprint, New York: Arno, 1972], 408.

Prosser mentioned Judd Montgomery several times in her autobiography (see Anna W. Prosser, *From Death to Life: An Autobiography* [Buffalo: McGerald, 1901]), 47, 92, 140, 155). They shared a belief and ministry in divine healing. Prosser also led a Christian Alliance mission for five years (138).

8. Montgomery, *"Under His Wings,"* 106, 118, 125–26. Speaking of Jennie Smith, Montgomery wrote: "What precious times of fellowship and prayer we had together! A fragrant aroma arises in my heart whenever I think of this beloved sister" (125–26).

9. Hannah Whitall Smith, *My Spiritual Autobiography or How I Discovered the Unselfishness of God* (New York: Revell, 1903), 261.

10. For documentation of her attendance at Methodist holiness meetings, see Meg A. Meneghel, "Becoming a 'Heretic': Hannah Whitall Smith, Quakerism, and the Nineteenth-Century Holiness Movement," (Ph.D. dissertation, Indiana University, 2000), 163, 165, 167–68, 175. Hannah also read William Boardman's *Higher Christian Life* (148). The two paths converged.

11. Melvin E. Dieter, "Wesleyan-Holiness Aspects of Pentecostal Origins As Mediated through the Nineteenth-Century Holiness Revival," in Vinson Synan, ed., *Aspects of Pentecostal-Charismatic Origins* (Plainfield, NJ: Logos International, 1975), 61–62.

vention in England in 1875.[12] Like Carrie Judd Montgomery, Hannah Whitall Smith's footprints appeared on several holiness paths.

The Baptism of the Holy Spirit

The baptism of the Holy Spirit is a Wesleyan/Holiness synonym for holiness or sanctification. Phoebe Palmer identified three phases of the sanctification experience—consecration, faith, and the necessity of public testimony describing the experience. Palmer appropriated Hester Ann Rogers' use of "altar" language when speaking of the consecration required prior to sanctification.[13] Pentecostal Zelma Argue used "altar" terminology as well but she, like many others, may not have been aware of her indebtedness to Palmer's theology. Argue wrote of her quest for the baptism of the Holy Ghost in terms of consecration: "Everything as well as I knew, was laid upon the altar of sacrifice" followed by an increasing faith that led to the fulfillment of her desire.[14]

Some attribute the emotionalism sometimes associated with the Wesleyan/Holiness movement or Pentecostalism's emotional response accompanying the baptism of the Holy Ghost to Phoebe Palmer. This definitely is not the case. In fact, it was difficult for Palmer to accept the

12. Like his wife, Robert Pearsall Smith's understanding of holiness was informed by a Wesleyan/Holiness perspective (Edith Waldvogel, "The 'Overcoming Life': A Study in the Reformed Evangelical Origins of Pentecostalism" [Ph.D. dissertation, Harvard Divinity School, 1977], 116). Along with the different understanding of sin, Keswick believers generally emphasized dispensationalism. Dwight L. Moody promoted Keswick doctrine in the United States through his conferences at Northfield, Massachusetts. Edith Blumhofer acknowledged: "Wesleyan doctrines had directly influenced some Reformed 'higher life' advocates" (Waldvogel [Blumhofer], "The 'Overcoming Life,'" 78–79). This was true for D. L. Moody as well as Boardman. Wesleyan/Holiness women introduced Moody to the doctrine of holiness. Free Methodists Sarah Cooke and Sister Hawxhurst talked with him several times about sanctification and, at his request, met with him on a number of occasions to pray for his "Pentecost" or "fullness of the Spirit" (Sarah A. Cooke, *The Handmaiden of the Lord, or Wayside Sketches* [Chicago: Arnold, 1896], 42).

13. Harold E. Raser, *Phoebe Palmer: Her Life and Thought* (Lewiston, NY: Mellen, 1987), 247. Likewise, Palmer's emphasis on faith and testimony as crucial components of holiness also reflect the influence of Rogers (Charles Edward White, *The Beauty of Holiness: Phoebe Palmer as Theologian, Revivalist, Feminist, and Humanitarian* [Grand Rapids: Asbury / Zondervan, 1986], 123; and Raser, *Phoebe Palmer*, 247–48).

14. Zelma E. Argue, "My Personal Story," in Blumhofer, *"Pentecost in my Soul,"* 158–59. She was ordained in 1920: "It was a confirmation of what God Himself had already done!"(161).

baptism of the Holy Ghost by faith since she did not feel any emotion initially. She concluded that emotion was not essential to indicate that sanctification had taken place. Instead, faith alone resulted in sanctification.[15] Montgomery echoed Palmer's theology: "Our part is simply to reckon our prayer as answered, and God's part is to make faith's reckonings real. This is by no means a question of feeling faith, but of acting faith."[16] Anna Prosser agreed that faith rather than emotion was essential to sanctification.[17]

Pentecostal women who came from a Wesleyan/Holiness background spoke of three works of grace, viewing the third work as a logical extension of their beliefs. Montgomery, who became a Pentecostal, listed faith as the only criteria for receiving all three works of grace: salvation, sanctification and speaking in tongues.[18] Florence Crawford clearly enumerated three works of grace in the doctrines of The Apostolic Faith Church which she founded in Portland, Oregon. First, she listed justification and regeneration "whereby one receives remission of sins and stands before God as though he had never sinned." Entire sanctification (holiness) "is the act of God's grace by which one is made holy. It is the *second, definite* work wrought by the Blood of Jesus through faith, and subsequent to salvation and regeneration." Last, "The baptism of the Holy Ghost is the enduement of power from on High upon the clean sanctified life . . . . When one receives the gift of the Holy Ghost, it is accompanied by the same sign as the disciples had on the Day of Pentecost, viz., speaking with tongues as the Spirit gives utterance."[19] Crawford had experienced both sanctification and Spirit

15. Phoebe Palmer, *The Way of Holiness with Notes by the Way: Being a Narrative of Religious Experience Resulting from a Determination to Be a Bible Christian* (New York: Piercy and Reed, 1843; reprint, Salem, OH: Schmul, 1988), 28.

16. Quoted in Donald Dayton, *Theological Roots of Pentecostalism* (Grand Rapids: Francis Asbury Press of Zondervan, 1987), 126. Florence Crawford also incorporated altar language in her quest for sanctification: "I knew that the fire of God had never fallen on the altar of my heart" (quoted in Cecil M. Robeck, Jr., "Florence Crawford: Apostolic Faith Pioneer," in James R. Goff, Jr., and Grant Wacker, eds., *Portraits of a Generation: Early Pentecostal Leaders* [Fayetteville: University of Arkansas Press, 2002], 223).

17. Prosser, *From Death to Life*, 97.

18. Jeannette Storms, "Carrie Judd Montgomery: The Little General," in Goff and Wacker, eds., *Portraits of a Generation*, 283.

19. *A Historical Account of The Apostolic Faith: A Trinitarian-Fundamental Evangelistic Organization: Its Origin, Functions, Doctrinal Heritage and Departmental Activities of Evangelism* (Portland, OR: The Apostolic Faith Mission, 1965), 48; italicized words are emphasized in the original.

baptism at Azusa Street. Pentecostal women who did not come from a Wesleyan/Holiness background affirmed two works of grace: salvation and the baptism of the Holy Ghost.

Born Methodist, Mrs. W. H. McGowan became a Christian at a holiness meeting and experienced sanctification. After meeting William Seymour, she confessed: "We Holiness people believe we had the Holy Ghost. Well, we did have the Holy Ghost, for the Bible says we are sanctified by the Holy Ghost. But I found out later we did not have the mighty Power of the Holy Ghost as they got it on the Day of Pentecost."[20] Differing from the testimonies of other Wesleyan/Holiness women, Montgomery and McGowan attributed the "mighty" power of the Holy Ghost to a third work of grace instead of identifying it with sanctification or the second work of grace. Rather than eliminating the role of power in the second work of grace, women such as Agnes (Ozman) LaBerge and Carrie Judd Montgomery understood the third blessing as supplying more power for service.[21]

Palmer contributed theological language to Pentecostalism. Her "altar" terminology offers one example. Melvin Dieter traced her use of "Pentecostal" language to her reports of an 1857 revival she conducted in Canada,[22] which then ignited the lay revival of 1858–59 in the United States. Agnes (Ozman) LaBerge supports Dieter's thesis because she could have been quoting Palmer in the following account of her testimony as she sought the experience of speaking in tongues. LaBerge prayed for the promise of the Father and longed for the baptism of the Holy Ghost. Palmer had used "promise of the Father" as the title of one of her books.[23] The result of this longing, however, was very different

20. Mrs. W. H. McGowan, *Another Echo from Azusa: Personal Testimony of Mrs. W. H. McGowan* (Springfield, MO: Flower Pentecostal Heritage Center, Assemblies of God Archives), 6.

21. Agnes N. O. LaBerge, *What God Hath Wrought: Life and Work of Mrs. Agnes N. O. LaBerge* (Chicago: Herald, n.d.), 38; and Storms, "Carrie Judd Montgomery," 286.

22. Dieter, "Wesleyan-Holiness Aspects of Pentecostal Origins," 65. Palmer, however, was not unique in using "Pentecostal" with reference to sanctification. She reflected her Wesleyan heritage because she was following the lead of Hester Ann Rogers and Mary Bosenquet Fletcher, contemporaries of John Wesley, who frequently employed Pentecostal language in their spiritual writings.

23. Phoebe Palmer, *The Promise of the Father* (Boston: Degen, 1859; reprint, Salem, OH: Schmul, n.d.).

from Palmer's. LaBerge spoke in tongues on the evening of 1 January 1901.[24]

Florence Roberts, a worker in Wesleyan/Holiness mission homes, defined sanctification: "Briefly, it refers to a second blessing, following justification, or the forgiveness of sins; a second work of grace, whereby the nature becomes purified and kept free from sin by the operation and power of God's Holy Spirit—now the indwelling presence."[25] Roberts' reference to purification reflected the belief that the second work of grace eradicated sin. She also highlighted the crucial role of the Holy Spirit in sanctification. Roberts' definition followed Palmer's emphasis on purity and power. Palmer's claim that "holiness is power" equated the two. Palmer insisted that "heart holiness and the gift of power should ever be regarded as identical."[26] Alma White, founder of the Pillar of Fire, a Wesleyan/Holiness denomination, echoed Palmer when she wrote about "holiness of heart which brings the enduement of power."[27] Prior to her sanctification, Almira Losee, too, was "waiting for the baptism of the Holy Ghost, with power."[28]

The Wesleyan/Holiness movement and Pentecostalism shared the emphasis on the power of the Holy Spirit. However, the manifestation of this power differed. Pentecostals believe that speaking in tongues evidenced the baptism of the Holy Spirit. However, even this statement was not universally accepted. Elizabeth Baker, founder and superintendent of Elim Faith Home, a Wesleyan/Holiness believer who became a Pentecostal, wrote: "What is the meaning of this new and strange movement that is breaking out all over the earth in these days? Much

24. LaBerge, *What God Hath Wrought*, 29.

25. Florence Roberts, *Fifteen Years with the Outcast* (Anderson, IN: Gospel Trumpet, 1912), 50.

26. Palmer, *Promise of the Father*, 206; see also Phoebe Palmer, *Four Years in the Old World* (New York: Foster & Palmer, Jr., 1865), 33. While Palmer stressed the equivalence of purity and power, she used "power" more frequently in her writings. For instance, in *The Promise of the Father* "power" appeared 90 times and "purity" or "cleansing" 21 times. *Four Years in the Old World*, a chronicle of her preaching tour of Great Britain, contained "power" 38 times and "purity" or "cleansing" 6 times.

27. Alma White, *The Story of My Life and the Pillar of Fire*, 5 vols. (Zarephath, NJ: Pillar of Fire, 1935–43), 5:196. White initially called her group the Pentecostal Union, causing several scholars to misidentify her as a Pentecostal.

28. Almira Losee, *Life Sketches: Being Narrations of Scenes Occurring in the Labours of Almira Losee* (New York: By the author, 1880), 74.

harm has been done by some of its friends through trying to formulate a doctrine, trying to label and pigeon-hole the experience, dogmatizing about what other Christians have, or have not. Many teach that no one has the Holy Spirit till they speak in tongues. The experience of God's devoted servants throughout the centuries past disproves this statement."[29] Based on her personal experience, Montgomery joined those who did not believe that speaking in tongues was the initial evidence of the baptism of the Holy Spirit.[30]

Palmer associated fire with the baptism of the Holy Ghost: "'The question now before us is,' she concluded, 'May we ask in faith . . . that we may be endued with power from on high, baptized with the Holy Ghost and with fire?' Palmer testified that one meeting closed with many receiving 'the baptism of fire' and the rest 'in expectation of receiving a Pentecostal Baptism.'"[31] Prior to her sanctification, Susan Fitkin, a Wesleyan/holiness pastor, spoke of her desire "to be baptized with the Holy Ghost and fire."[32] If readers did not know otherwise, it would seem that Palmer and Fitkin were speaking as proponents of Pentecostalism who used the same language in reference to speaking in tongues.

Montgomery was initially puzzled regarding a third work of grace. She had experienced sanctification as a second work of grace and had been empowered to testify. She had understood this as the baptism of the Holy Ghost, so she was wary about the need for a third work. However, she testified: "I came to understand that I was not to depreciate His precious work in the past, but to follow on to receive the fullness of the same Spirit." She used the term "fullness of the Holy Ghost" to refer to the third blessing. She offered a scriptural foundation for her conviction: "Before Pentecost, Jesus 'breathed' on His disciples to receive the fullness of the same Spirit. And said unto them 'Receive ye the Holy

29. Elizabeth V. Baker and Co-workers, *Chronicles of a Faith Life* (N.p., 1910), 141.

30. Storms, "Carrie Judd Montgomery," 283.

31. Quoted in Dieter, "Wesleyan-Holiness Aspects of Pentecostal Origins," 65. Palmer is referring to the tongues of fire that fell of Jesus' followers at Pentecost (Acts 2:3).

32. Susan Fitkin, *Grace Much More Abounding: A Story of the Triumphs of Redeeming Grace During Two Score Years in the Master's Service* (Kansas City, MO: Nazarene Publishing House, n.d.), 34–35.

Ghost' (John 20:22). I believe they then received a foretaste, or earnest, of what they afterwards received in fullness at Pentecost."[33]

Hermeneutic of Pentecost—Women Preachers and Power

The emphasis on Pentecost (Acts 1–2) among both Pentecostals and Wesleyan/Holiness believers, as illustrated above, reflected a restorationist perspective with the goal of restoring the practices of the early church. Richard T. Hughes defined primitivists or restorationists as those who "place supreme value on the founding age and seek to recover specific dimensions of that age in their own time."[34] As discussed above, Wesleyan/Holiness advocates sought to duplicate the experience of sanctification or the baptism of the Holy Spirit which they believed occurred at Pentecost. Phoebe Palmer identified with Jesus' disciples prior to her sanctification when she wrote of "waiting at Jerusalem for the promise of the Father."[35] Pentecostals, on the other hand, sought the experience of speaking in tongues which took place at Pentecost. This was Pentecostal Clara Lum's meaning when she wrote: "He [God] is pouring out Pentecost in old time power."[36]

For Wesleyan/Holiness believers, the baptism of the Holy Spirit resulted in purity and power for service. Using Pentecost to identify sanctification with the baptism of the Holy Ghost linked sanctification and power. The experience of Pentecost confirmed that the baptism of the Holy Ghost provided power for Jesus' followers to spread the gospel.

Wesleyan/Holiness evangelist and mission worker Sarah Cooke compared her experience of power to Pentecost, where Jesus' promised his followers that they would be empowered to evangelize throughout the world (Acts 1:8). Cooke explained: "The power that came to the early disciples is the same that comes to us to-day, and comes in the

33. Montgomery, "*Under His Wing,*" 166, 167.

34. Richard T. Hughes, "The Meaning of the Restoration Vision," in Richard T. Hughes, ed., *The Primitive Church in the Modern World* (Urbana: University of Illinois Press, 1995), xii. Restorationism and Primitivism are often used as synonyms. Hughes' typology of primitivism included ethical, ecclesiastical and experiential primitivism. He identified Pentecostalism as experiential primitivism.

35. Palmer, *Way of Holiness*, 77.

36. Clara Lum, letter to *The Missionary World*, August 1906, in the Assemblies of God Archives, Flower Pentecostal Heritage Center (Springfield, MO).

same way."[37] Abbie Mills was another Wesleyan/Holiness preacher who referenced Pentecost in her discussion of the power of the Holy Spirit.[38]

The account of Pentecost was the primary basis for support-ing women in ministry among Pentecostals. LaBerge acknowledged women who preached at Pentecost, concluding: "That is a great encour-agement to us women today."[39] Wesleyan/Holiness defenses for women in ministry always included Pentecost but incorporated other biblical texts as well to bolster their case.[40] For instance, the Wesleyan/Holiness church planter and a founder of the Church of the Nazarene, Mary Lee Cagle, painted with a broader restorationist brush when she preached: "I am persuaded that what [women] were allowed to do when the New Testament was written will be all right for them to do now."[41] Rather than restricting her restorationist vision to Pentecost, she incorporated the entire New Testament in her argument supporting women in min-istry. My focus, however, will be on references to the experience of Jesus' female followers at Pentecost.

Both groups recognized that the Holy Spirit empowered women to preach at Pentecost. I have added egalitarian primitivism to Hughes' categories to designate those restorationist impulses that acknowledged and encouraged women's involvement in ministry.[42]

37. Cooke, *Handmaiden of the Lord,* 115; see also 257.

38. Abbie C. Mills, *Grace and Glory* (Los Angeles: By the author, 1907), 208.

39. LaBerge, *What God Hath Wrought,* 49. Pentecostal Marie Brown in her article "The Meaning of Pentecost" wrote of the "enduement of power to carry out the great commission" but did not mention the women who were present at Pentecost (Marie Brown, "The Meaning of Pentecost," 213–17). It is impossible to know if LaBerge's understanding came from her exposure to Wesleyan/Holiness doctrine as opposed to Brown who was not Wesleyan/Holiness.

40. David G. Roebuck, "Limiting Liberty: The Church of God [Cleveland, Tenn.] and Women Ministers, 1886–1996" (Ph.D. dissertation, Vanderbilt University, 1997), 39–40.

41. Mary Lee Cagle, *Life and Work of Mary Lee Cagle: An Autobiography* (Kansas City, MO: Nazarene Publishing House, 1928), 161.

42. Susie C. Stanley, "'Bumping' into Modernity: Primitive/Modern Tensions in the Wesleyan/Holiness Movement," in Richard T. Hughes, ed., *Primitive Church in the Modern World* (Urbana: University of Illinois Press, 1995), 129. While the focus on Acts reflects the positive role of restorationism in terms of affirming women preachers, restorationism has also been employed to restrict women's freedom to preach. Using a couple verses from the Epistles, people have claimed, despite overwhelming evidence to the contrary, that the early church did not recognize or authorize women to preach or serve as leaders.

Wesleyan/Holiness women understood Pentecost as setting the precedent for women preachers. They were quick to note that Acts 1:14 mentioned women who were present in the upper room. Cagle preached that Mary, Jesus' mother, was among those listed and concluded: "I don't believe that she would have been there if it was wrong."[43] Cagle offered a unique interpretation of the number of men and women in the upper room. She studied Acts 1:13–15 and did the math:

> Now, we will see if we can find out how many women there were in the upper room, in Acts 1:15, "And in those days, Peter stood up in the midst of the disciples, ... (The number of names together were about an hundred and twenty)." The men and the women all composed the 120. The names of the men are given and we can count for ourselves and see how many there were. There were eleven men. Subtract eleven from 120, and you find how many women there were: 109. It seems that the women were largely in the majority. They only gave the names of eleven and if there had been more men it is reasonable to suppose that their names would have been given. There were so many women that there was no attempt made to give their names, only Mary, the mother of our Lord.[44]

Was Cagle being facetious in her estimate of the women who were present in the upper room? Based on the text she does seem to have a case!

When the Holy Spirit descended at Pentecost, there was no selection process based on sex. Wesleyan/Holiness evangelist Mary Cole pointedly asked: "According to Acts 2:4, they all spake as the Spirit gave them utterance. Does not the 'all' include the women present? Was not their speaking as the Spirit gave utterance the act of a minister in preaching?"[45] It was obvious to Cole that the answer to these questions was "yes."

Acts 2:16–18 recorded Peter's sermon on the day of Pentecost in which he declared the fulfillment of Joel's prophecy: "But this is that

---

43. Cagle, *Life and Work*, 161. Cagle included her standard sermon in her autobiography (160–76) as did Maggie Newton Van Cott; see Cott's "Shall Women Preach?" in *The Harvest and the Reaper: Reminiscences of Revival Work of Mrs. Maggie N. Van Cott: The First Lady Licensed to Preach in the Methodist Episcopal Church in the United States* (New York: Tibbals & Sons, 1876), 326–37.

44. Cagle, *Life and Work*, 171.

45. Mary Cole, *Trials and Triumphs of Faith* (Anderson, IN: Gospel Trumpet, 1914), 86.

which is spoken by the Prophet Joel; And it shall come to pass in the last days, saith God, I will pour out of my Spirit upon all flesh: and your sons and daughters shall prophesy, and your young men shall see visions and your old men shall dream dreams. And on my servants and on my handmaidens I will pour out in those days of my Spirit; and they shall prophesy." Again, it was clear that the Holy Spirit did not discriminate. Cooke explicitly revealed her restorationist approach based on this passage when she chose the title *The Handmaiden of the Lord* for her autobiography. Almira Losee and Lela McConnell also saw themselves as God's handmaidens.[46] Losee was an evangelist and established mission homes while McConnell founded the Kentucky Mountain Holiness Association.

Pentecost often served as a paradigm for sanctification and also the subsequent call to preach. Self-identified as God's "handmaidens," women used the term as a synonym for preacher. Wesleyan/Holiness evangelist Mary Still Adams believed sanctification was a prerequisite for preaching: "I did not want to go out without being wholly equipped for warfare." Quoting Acts 1:4, she followed the example of Jesus' disciples by tarrying until she was baptized with the Holy Spirit. Her wait was rewarded when she received "the joy and power of the Holy Spirit."[47] Adams credited the experience of sanctification and the subsequent power of the Holy Spirit with giving her the ability to fulfill her calling.

In some cases, women attributed their call to preach directly to their sanctification experience. Cagle had been called to preach when she was a girl but dismissed it. However, with sanctification her call "was stronger than ever before."[48] Jonnie Jernigan, another Nazarene preacher, was initially dissuaded from answering her call to preach by claims that it "was masculine and unladylike." For her the order of sanctification and call was reversed. As an adult, she experienced sanctification when she yielded to God's call to ministry.[49]

---

46. Losee, *Life Sketches*, 210; and Lela McConnell, *The Pauline Ministry in the Kentucky Mountains or A Brief Account of the Kentucky Mountain Holiness Association* (Louisville, KY: Pentecostal Publishing [1942]), 40.

47. Mary Still Adams, *Autobiography of Mary Still Adams or, "In God We Trust"* (Los Angeles: Buckingham Bros., Printers, 1893), 66–67, and 5.

48. Cagle, *Life and Work*, 21.

49. Jonnie Jernigan, *Redeemed through the Blood or the Power of God to Save the Fallen* (Louisville, KY: Pentecostal Herald Print, 1904), 6, 8. She ministered among the poor and built a home for former prostitutes in Peniel, Texas.

Like other Wesleyan/Holiness women, Maria Woodworth-Etter initially resisted God's call on her life. Her excuse was that she was not educated. Despite her hesitancy, she answered God's call to preach. This call coincided with her baptism of the Holy Spirit which to her was evidenced by speaking in tongues. She credited the power of the Holy Spirit for her ability to preach before crowds of thousands.[50] Woodworth-Etter was one of the most prominent early Pentecostal preachers.

When Wesleyan/Holiness believers Lizzie Miller and Lucy Drake Osborn were called to preach, they had another hurdle to surmount since they were personally opposed to women preaching.[51] They had to overcome their opposition before inaugurating their own ministries.

Likewise, Pentecostal Elizabeth Baker, a sanctified woman with a Methodist background, resisted the call to preach because she was a woman. She recounted the struggle: "Then [the Lord] asked, 'Will you go into pulpits and preach for Me?' I had a great aversion to women in a pulpit. I had always felt that they were out of place, and that the many other spheres of usefulness in home, schools and church were quite sufficient but now the Lord was asking me to do the thing I had so disliked in others. 'O, I cannot, I cannot,' I cried. But the Spirit was unmoved by my human logic, and again repeated the same question, 'Will you go into pulpits and preach for Me?'" For Baker, preaching did not include ordination. After building Elim Tabernacle, she and the workers prayed for a man to serve as pastor but none came forward. Baker recounted: "We had not believed in women as pastors, or occupying any official position in the church, but here we were in a position wholly unsought by us, and from which only real cowardice and disobedience to plain leading could free us. Not believing in ordination for women, we went on as we were. . . . A board of deacons was formed, who officiated at the Communion service, until regular ordained elders were provided, so

50. Wayne E. Warner, "Maria B. Woodworth-Etter: Prophet of Equality," in Goff and Wacker, eds., *Portraits of a Generation*, 202.

51. Lizzie E. Miller, *The True Way: Life and Evangelical Work of Lizzie E. Miller (of Fairview, West Va.) Written by Herself* (Los Angeles: By the author, 1895), 23–24; and Lucy Drake Osborn, *Heavenly Pearls Set in a Life: A Record of Experiences and Labors in America, India and Australia* (New York: Revell, 1893), 108. Unfortunately, it is unknown whether Miller approved women's ordination or if she was ordained herself. Likewise, Osborn's position on women's ordination is undetermined.

that all the ordinances are properly administered and the needs thus supplied."[52]

Despite her Wesleyan/Holiness background, she did not believe ordination was an option for women. However, she pastored the church in all respects except for administering communion which was done by deacons, presumably males. This is a fascinating resolution to the dilemma since it appears that the men were not ordained either. This was prior to the Pentecostal revival at Elim. Baker did not comment on her view of ordaining women following this revival. For her, the power of the Holy Spirit extended to the prophetic function of preaching but not the priestly function of serving communion.

Palmer and other Wesleyan/Holiness adherents believed that sanctification resulted in a heart free of sin and the power of the Holy Spirit that enabled a Christian to be useful.[53] Empowerment led to action. Prior to her sanctification, Anna Prosser "sighed for an unction and power in service, which as yet I did not possess." Her desire was granted according to her testimony following her sanctification: "My anxiety as to the matter of power for service was now forever at an end. I saw that the Holy Ghost Himself, would be my power day by day, quite equal to any service to which He called me."[54] Montgomery likewise spoke of the power promised in Acts 1:8 as a power to witness.[55] Individuals from Palmer to Prosser to Montgomery understood the causal relationship between sanctification and power for service.

Wesleyan/Holiness women acknowledged the presence of the power of the Holy Spirit when they preached.[56] Quaker Huldah Rees reported preaching "in the power of the Spirit" after experiencing sanctification.[57] McConnell related that "it takes holy courage and unflinching holy boldness to conduct revivals." Like others, she traced power to

52. Baker, *Chronicles of a Faith Life*, 21, 129. Despite Baker's opposition to women's ordination, she also founded the Elim Faith Home, Elim Publishing House, and the Rochester Bible Training School, making Rochester "an important center for early Pentecostalism" (3–5, 12, 16).

53. Palmer, *Promise of the Father*, 248.

54. Prosser, *From Death to Life*, 84, 106.

55. Albrecht, "The Life and Ministry of Carrie Judd Montgomery," 144, 151.

56. Miller, *The True Way*, 126; and Cagle, *Life and Work*, 59.

57. Byron J. Rees, *Hulda, The Pentecostal Prophetess or a Sketch of the Life and Triumph of Mrs. Hulda A. Rees, Together with Seventeen of Her Sermons* (Philadelphia: Christian Standard, 1898), 20.

Pentecost which fulfilled Jesus' promise to his followers that they would receive power or the promise of the Father after tarrying in Jerusalem.[58]

The power that resulted from sanctification enabled women to overcome timidity. This was the case for Losee, who testified: "Yet I can say that for thirty years past I have been constantly, fully saved from all fear."[59] Alma White, speaking of her experience, found that sanctification helped her overcome her timidity and fear.[60] While some rose above shyness, others spoke of a "man-fearing spirit" that had prevented them from preaching.[61] Sanctification enabled Wesleyan/Holiness preacher Lillian Pool to overcome a man-fearing spirit and answer the call to preach.[62] Woodworth-Etter also relied on God's power to overcome a man-fearing spirit.[63]

It is impossible to ascertain how many women were ordained in Wesleyan/Holiness or Pentecostal churches. The Salvation Army alone had over 1,000 women officers.[64] Most other Wesleyan/Holiness denominations ordained women with full clergy rights. On the other hand, the Assemblies of God initially limited women's ordination to evangelism or missionary service while the Church of God (Cleveland, Tennessee) recognized women evangelists but did not ordain women. The Church of God's reluctance to ordain women is surprising since it began as a Wesleyan/Holiness denomination and then adopted Pentecostal doctrine. However, the group also had Baptist roots that may have influenced its position.

Mary Anna Arthur was a member of the Methodist Episcopal Church when introduced to Pentecostalism through the ministry of Charles Parham. She was a leader in the Apostolic Faith mission in

58. Lela McConnell, *Hitherto and Henceforth in the Kentucky Mountains* (Lawson, KY: n.p., 1949), 92. She was quoting Luke 24:49. Likewise, Prosser wrote of being filled with a holy boldness (Prosser, *From Death to Life*, 48).

59. Losee, *Life Sketches*, 122.

60. White, *Story of My Life*, 1:354.

61. Palmer, *Way of Holiness*, 88.

62. Lillian Pool, "Experience and Call to the Ministry," in Fannie McDowell Hunter, ed., *Women Preachers* (Dallas: Berachah, 1905), 67–68.

63. Wayne E. Warner, *Woman Evangelist: The Life and Times of Charismatic Evangelist Maria B. Woodworth-Etter* (Metuchen, NJ: Scarecrow, 1986), 14.

64. Norman H. Murdock, "Female Ministry in the Thought and Work of Catherine Booth," *Church History* 53 (1984): 349. This statistic is for 1896. Most old line Protestant churches decided to ordain women between the 1950s and the 1970s.

Galena, Kansas, when evangelist Frank Anderson ordained her in 1910. Ordinations in the early decades of the Wesleyan/Holiness movement often were this informal as well, which explains why precise numbers are impossible to determine. Arthur obtained ministerial credentials with the Assemblies of God in 1915 and continued her involvement in the renamed Galena Pentecostal Mission. Her roles included assistant pastor, minister and pastor, and evangelist.[65]

Arthur also held the designation of "Mother Arthur" no doubt based on Deborah, an Old Testament leader who was called a mother in Israel in recognition of her leadership.[66] Florence Crawford was known as Mother Crawford.[67] Sarah Smith, a Church of God (Anderson, Indiana) evangelist, also was called Mother Smith as an indication of respect for her spiritual maturity and authority.[68]

Based on a limited sample, it appears that Pentecostal women preachers saw themselves as more passive than most Wesleyan/Holiness women when they preached, perceiving themselves as empty vessels through which God spoke. It is impossible to determine why this was the case. Pentecostal McGowan testified that God "preached a sermon, using my lips and tongue."[69] On another occasion, again referring to herself, she claimed: "There He [God] preached a sermon on that scripture."[70] Aimee Semple McPherson likewise believed God used her as a passive instrument when she received her call to ministry. She reported that God promised to "send the power of the Holy Ghost" and then described her role as "the mouthpiece of the telephone," "the key on the typewriter," and the "mouth through which the Holy Ghost can speak."[71]

65. Blumhofer, *"Pentecost in My Soul,"* 121–22.

66. Ibid., 122.

67. Estrelda Alexander, *The Women of Azusa Street* (Cleveland, OH: Pilgrim, 2005), 69.

68. "Mother Smith Goes Home to Rest," *Gospel Trumpet*, (12 March 1908): 8.

69. McGowan, *Another Echo from Azusa*, 13.

70. Ibid., 16. It is not clear whether the sermon was preached in tongues or in English.

71. *Aimee: Life Story of Aimee Semple McPherson* (Los Angeles: Foursquare Publications, 1979), 223.

R. M. Riss has noted the lack of Pentecostal literature that advocated women in ministry.[72] Perhaps this is related to the passive posture of women preachers. Carrie Judd Montgomery and Maria Woodworth-Etter were among the few Pentecostal women who addressed women's right to preach explicitly. Montgomery published "Should Women Prophesy?" in her magazine *Triumph of Faith*.[73] Woodworth-Etter's published sermon "Women's Privilege in the Gospel," though, did not extend that privilege to performing the rite of baptism since she relied on men to baptize her converts.[74] In another sermon, "Women's Rights in the Gospel," she listed women throughout the Bible who were called to ministry. Speaking in the third person, she used her own experience as evidence: "and that she had been successful in winning souls to Christ."[75] Aimee Semple McPherson rarely addressed women's right to preach. Estrelda Alexander discovered two minor exceptions, one when McPherson taught on the book of Acts and noted the prophecy of Joel which Peter referenced in Acts 2:17–18. On another occasion, she also quoted the Joel 2:28 passage.[76]

The crucial influence of Wesleyan/Holiness women is evident in the broader context of the earliest phase of the Pentecostal movement. Wesleyan/Holiness women helped set the stage for the Pentecostal revival. At least fifteen of the nineteen women Alexander considered in *The Women of Azusa Street* were Wesleyan/Holiness.[77] William Seymour first heard the Pentecostal message from Lucy Farrow, the pastor of his holiness mission church in Houston. He never would have come to Los Angeles if Neely Terry had not approached him about leaving Houston

72. R. M. Riss, "Women, Role of," in Stanley M. Burgess, Gary B. McGee, and Patrick H. Alexander, eds., *Dictionary of Pentecostal and Charismatic Movements* (Grand Rapids: Zondervan, 1988), 898.

73. The article appeared in the December 1886 issue (Albrecht, "Life and Ministry of Carrie Judd Montgomery," 51).

74. Warner, "Maria B. Woodworth-Etter," 203; and Warner, *Woman Evangelist*, 50, 59.

75. Warner, "Maria B. Woodworth-Etter," 209.

76. Estrelda Y. Alexander, "Gender and Leadership in the Theology and Practice of Three Pentecostal Women Pioneers" (Ph.D. dissertation, The Catholic University of America, 2002), 157. Based on the lack of documentation, Alexander concluded this topic was not important enough to McPherson to address in writing (244, 252).

77. Alexander, *Women of Azusa Street*. R. M. Riss also discussed the influence of the Holiness Movement (Riss, "Women, Role of," 898).

to serve as associate pastor at a Nazarene church in Los Angeles pastored by Julia Hutchins. On his way to Los Angeles, he experienced the hospitality of Alma White.[78] Hutchins initially rejected Seymour's preaching of a third work of grace and locked him out of her church. Subsequently, she accepted his teaching and became a Pentecostal preacher, spreading the message as far as Africa.

My focus has been on the impact of Wesleyan/Holiness women on the affirmation of women preachers in the Pentecostal movement. The involvement of Wesleyan/Holiness women prior to and during the initial phase of the Pentecostal movement illustrates the extraordinary influence of Wesleyan/Holiness women. Their ministries were crucial also as a model for other Pentecostal women. In addition, their theology of the baptism of the Holy Spirit and their hermeneutic of Pentecost formed the basis for endorsing women preachers among Pentecostals. Without the precedent provided by Wesleyan/Holiness women and Wesleyan/Holiness women who became Pentecostals, the number of Pentecostal women preachers would undoubtedly have been much smaller.

78. Susie C. Stanley, "Alma White: The Politics of Dissent," in Goff and Wacker, eds., *Portraits of a Generation*, 75. Her subsequent negative view of Pentecostalism extended to Seymour.

3

"Cause He's My Chief Employer"

Hearing Women's Voices in a Classical Pentecostal Denomination

David G. Roebuck

Introduction

DURING 1990, I CONDUCTED INTERVIEWS WITH TWELVE WOMEN MINIS-
ters who had been active in ministry during the middle of the twentieth
century.[1] These interviews were part of my dissertation research, and
my purpose was to document their ministries and to explore why there
had been a decline in the percentage of women ministers in the Church
of God [COG] (Cleveland, Tennessee). One of the ministers I interviewed was Lucille Turner, a sixty-eight-year-old retired missionary
and widow, who had spent twenty-five years as a missionary in India.
When I asked Turner if she had given any thought to why there had
been a decline in the percentage of women who were ministers, she
spoke candidly about the difficulties of being a female minister in the

---

1. These interviewees were Zoe Brown, Mary Graves, Mary Howard, Pauline
Lambert, Amanda Miller, Odine Morse, Dorothy Murphy, Tilda Oxendine, Ruth Staples,
Lucille Turner, Lucille Walker, and Bernice Woodard. Mary McClintock Fulkerson later
transcribed these interviews while doing research for her book *Changing the Subject:
Women's Discourse and Feminist Theology* (Minneapolis: Fortress, 1994). The quota-
tions used in this paper were drawn from McClintock's transcripts rather than from
the video tapes. Both the video tapes and the transcriptions are available at the Dixon
Pentecostal Research Center, Cleveland, TN.

COG. Whether or not she had given previous thought to the question, she related her own attitude:

> I've never stuck my foot in the door. I've never made one tele-
> phone call and asked anyone for any kind of meeting. If God
> doesn't open up the door, Lucille Turner's not going to be there.
> But if he opens the door, you better believe, I'm gonna be there.
> And I'm going to be prayed up, packed up and ready to preach
> or teach. I'm going to do that thing and nothing's going to stop
> me. And it's not who the congregation is or where it's located, it's
> where a need is. Let me in there, Lord. And he designates that.
> And I'm not bitter, but I'll tell you now, it's because God is faith-
> ful. And I count it a privilege of being a member of the COG.
> I count it a privilege to be a minister, a licensed minister, in the
> church. It's a great privilege. But it is a limited privilege as [far
> as] organization is concerned. If my resources, if my inspira-
> tion, if my encouragement, if my nurture had to have its source
> in a body here or there or wherever, I would be depleted. I can't
> answer those questions. I just know that [there's] organization
> and God's not like that. See? That's a contrast. Cause he's my
> chief employer. . . .[2]

Turner's response revealed a life of tension between her call to ministry and her relationship to the institution within which she ministered. She considered herself to be privileged to be a part of the Church of God, but she recognized that it was a privilege limited by a human organization. Despite those limitations, she was confident that the God that called her to ministry would open doors for that ministry. She did not view herself as dependent on a human organization in order to fulfill the call of God in her life, and her voice could not be silenced by the limitations of the institution.

The primary purpose of this essay is to hear the voices of Turner and women like her as they integrated their call to speak within an institution that had specific restrictions on their voices. Much of my previous work as well as that of other historians of women in the Pentecostal movement has focused on Pentecostal denominations and depended largely on the traditional types of documents these denominations produced. But women have often been left out of institutional leadership,

---

2. Lucille Turner, interview by author, 26 July 1990, transcript, 20. I have taken the liberty of eliminating some of the repetitions and starts and stops that naturally occur in conversation in order to make quotations more readable.

and thus rarely appear in the official documents of denominations. This essay is an effort to move beyond that silence and to hear the voices of women ministers. Turner and the other women interviewed help us to do that through the method of oral history.

Oral history is now being used widely by historians and especially practitioners of women's history. Although much of human knowledge was first passed on orally, the rise of the printing press and the modern emphasis on empirical evidence led to the preference of archival evidence among historians. As an historical method, oral history's recent emergence can be traced to the post-World War Two era with an increased interest in the history of "common people" and the development of widely accessible tape recorders.[3] Oral history helps to bring to the fore individuals and groups who otherwise might be left out of the historical record because there are few written documents related to their lives. Regrettably the lives and work of women have often been considered secondary to that of men within many of society's leading institutions, so that women's work is often absent from the public record.[4] Janice Dilg has written regarding oral history and women's studies, "oral history remains an essential methodology that moves women out of obscurity, past the peripheral position they have often been relegated to, and situates them more centrally in the historical record where they belong."[5]

Oral history as an historical method has its own set of challenges, however. The memory is subject to error, and information gained from interviews must be carefully compared to other sources. The interview is usually separated by time from the events being discussed, and there are often discrepancies between the perceived truth of a situation and documented facts regarding that situation. While all sources are subject to the perspective of the producer and what she or he desires to communicate, part of what make these realities more problematic for

3. Alistair Thomson, "Four Paradigm Transformations in Oral History," *The Oral History Review* 34:1 (2007): 49–71.

4. For discussions of these issues see Katrine Barber and Janice Dilg, "Documenting Women's History: Using Oral History and the Collaborative Process (Research Files)," *Oregon Historical Quarterly* 103 (2002): 530-40.

5. Janice Dilg, "Expanding Historical Perspectives," in Barber and Dilg, "Documenting Women's History," 536-40; quotation from 540.

the oral historian is the relationship with the narrator that inevitably develops during the interview process.

Today's oral historians move beyond a sense of "naïve realism," and see oral history as more than simply access to facts not available elsewhere. Indeed the relationship between the narrator's life story and history is a complicated one in which the form of the narrative has as much significance as the facts revealed in the narrative, so that the form as well as the narrative tells the ethnographic and cultural story of the narrator. As a consequence the narrator becomes a collaborator along with the historian, and together they create a new text.[6] Despite these complexities, oral history both provides access to information outside the institutional record and helps us to interpret those written documents that we already have. Oral history adds a richness and texture to lived experiences that cannot be gained from paper alone. It has added benefit in a movement such as Pentecostalism that is highly oral and places a premium value on the individual's personal journey and testimony. But before we turn to the stories of COG women ministers, let's review the development of the COG and women leaders in this particular denomination.

Development of a Classical Pentecostal Denomination

The COG is a classical Pentecostal denomination of almost one million members in the USA and another six million members internationally. The denomination began as a Baptist restoration movement, was swept into the Holiness movement in the late nineteenth century, and then into the Pentecostal movement shortly after the Azusa Street revival.

The COG dates its origin to the work of a Baptist minister by the name of R. G. Spurling, and his father Richard Spurling, who opposed an exclusive Baptist theology being taught by James R. Graves and the Landmark Baptist movement. As an alternative to this ecclesiology the

6. For an example of this discussion see Daniel James, "'Tales Told Out on the Borderlands': Doña María's Story, Oral History, and Issues of Gender," in John D. French and Daniel, James, eds., *The Gendered Worlds of Latin American Women Workers: From Household and Factory to the Union Hall and Ballot Box* (Durham, NC: Duke University Press, 1997), 31–32. See also Paul Thompson, *The Voice of the Past: Oral History*, 3rd ed. (Oxford: Oxford University Press, 2000); Valerie Raleigh Yow, *Recording Oral History: A Guide for the Humanities and Social Sciences*, 2nd ed. (Walnut Creek, CA: AltaMira, 2005); and Gwyn Prins, "Oral History," in Peter Burke, ed., *New Perspectives on Historical Writing* (University Park: University of Pennsylvania Press, 1994), 114–39.

Spurlings established the Christian Union in 1886 at a grist mill they ran on Barney Creek in Monroe County, Tennessee. They contended that all who are in Christ and take the New Testament as their rule are eligible to covenant with a local congregation as the church of God.[7]

Over the next few years R.G. Spurling organized other congregations and was instrumental in forming the Holiness Church at Camp Creek in Cherokee County, North Carolina, in 1902. This congregation was a remnant of people who had been together since an 1896 community revival. Held at Shearer Schoolhouse, that revival introduced the doctrine of sanctification as a second work of grace. These new converts to the Holiness movement met for several years in homes and log meeting houses. Their emphasis on holiness led to their expulsion from their Baptist churches and severe persecution. As with many in the late nineteenth century, their turn toward holiness likely led to an increased emphasis on the language of Acts 2. There is some evidence that they were swept up into B. H. Irwin's Fire-Baptized Movement as well.

As in other places around the world, they experienced numerous spiritual manifestations including speaking in tongues. Although there are no extant records, according to a later account by A. J. Tomlinson, "The people earnestly sought God, and the interest increased until unexpectedly, like a cloud from a clear sky, the Holy Ghost began to fall on the honest, humble, sincere seekers after God. While the meetings were in progress one after another fell under the power of God, and soon quite a number were speaking in other tongues as the Spirit gave them utterance."[8] Yet their isolation hindered them from

7. For histories of the COG see Charles W. Conn, *Like a Mighty Army: A History of the Church of God*, Definitive edition (Cleveland, TN: Pathway, 1996); and David G Roebuck, "Restorationism and a Vision for World Harvest: A Brief History of the Church of God (Cleveland, TN)," *Cyberjournal for Pentecostal-Charismatic Research* 5 (1999) [http://www.pctii.org/cyberj/cyber5.html].

8. A. J. Tomlinson, *The Last Great Conflict* (Cleveland, TN: Rodgers, 1913; reprint, New York: Garland Publishing, 1985), 188–91. Tomlinson introduced the idea that error and fanaticism followed this spiritual outpouring. Although he does not describe the nature of the error and fanaticism, there are tantalizing clues that the group may have been involved in Irwin's Fire Baptized Movement. Certainly the many baptisms and esthetic practices noted by Charles W. Conn resemble the Fire Baptized Movement and Harold D. Hunter noted likely connections as well. See Conn, *Like a Mighty Army*, 47–52; and Hunter, "Beniah at the Apostolic Crossroads: Little Noticed Crosscurrents of B. H. Irwin, Charles Fox Parham, Frank Sandford, A. J. Tomlinson," *Cyberjournal for Pentecostal Charismatic Research* 1 (1997) [http://www.pctii.org/cyberj/cyber1.html].

connecting with other people and events, and it was only after the outpouring of the Holy Spirit at Azusa Street that they developed a Pentecostal pneumatology.[9]

A. J. Tomlinson joined the fledgling group the next year, and with some success planting churches in east Tennessee he moved to nearby Cleveland. In 1906, the congregations had their first General Assembly. Over time the General Assembly became the primary decision making body and the place where the roles of women in the COG has frequently been discussed, even as late as August 2008.

Women in Leadership

The Baptist womb from which the COG emerged gave the movement an early model for ministry, a clear conviction that the New Testament is the basis for all decisions, and a tendency toward limiting women in ministry. Typically Baptist congregations would grant a license to preach to qualified men who testified of a call to ministry. They would then "ordain" those who were "called" by a local congregation to serve as pastor or in some other specific ministry such as the deaconate.[10] Due to their interpretation of biblical passages related to women and ministry, most Baptists did not recognize women as either preachers or pastors. This was not a universal exclusion, however, and the independence of each Baptist congregation allowed for some variation. Perhaps influenced by the Holiness movement, R. G. Spurling licensed women ministers to preach including Dorcas Louiza Freeman, who was likely the first female minister in the COG.[11]

Thus, from the time of Spurling the COG has licensed women to preach. This was formalized in 1909 when the Assembly advised "that the women who engage in the ministry of the Word be acknowledged by the church and supplied with a certificate or license showing the

---

9. David G. Roebuck, "From Azusa Street to Cleveland: The Amazing Journey of G. B. Cashwell and the Spread of Pentecostalism," in Cecil M. Robeck Jr. and Harold D. Hunter, eds., *The Azusa Street Revival and Its Legacy* (Cleveland, TN: Pathway, 2004), 111–24.

10. Bill J. Leonard, "Ordination, Baptist Views," in Bill J. Leonard, ed., *Dictionary of Baptists in America* (Downers Grove, IL: InterVarsity, 1994), 213–14.

11. See Wade H. Phillips, "Photo Caption," *Church of God History and Heritage* (Fall 1997): 2.

date of appointment and by what church."[12] In 1913 the first published list of ministers divided them into the categories of bishops, deacons, and evangelists, with women listed among the evangelists. Just over 12 percent of the ministers in that list were women. The percentage of ministers who were women reached a high of just over 18 percent following World War Two, but fell into single digits in the latter part of the twentieth century.[13]

Although the COG licensed women to preach as evangelists, it prohibited their ordination. In 1909 the Assembly reversed its previous year's decision that women could serve as deaconesses, because it viewed the deaconate as an ordained position.[14] The rational for that action served as the justification for not using ordination language for women until 2000. The 1909 minutes recorded that "for lack of precept or example in the New Testament for ordination the assembly advised for the present, that the wives of the deacons be considered and appointed deaconesses by virtue of the position and ordination of their husbands."[15] Because of this interpretation of the Scriptures, COG women could preach but could not hold any office of leadership that required ordination.

After serving as a licensed evangelist, male ministers could be ordained as a deacon or bishop. It was preferred that pastors be bishops, and the fact that women could not be ordained implied that they should

12. *General Assembly Minutes 1906–1914: Photographic Reproductions of the First Ten General Assembly Minutes* (Cleveland, TN: White Wing, 1992), 63.

13. For the first published list of ministers see COG, *Echoes from the Eighth General Assembly of the Churches of God* (n.p: n.p., [1913]), 91–94. For a survey of the percentage of ministers who were women from 1913 to 1994 see David G. Roebuck, "Limiting Liberty: The Church of God and Women Ministers, 1886–1996" (Ph.D. dissertation, Vanderbilt University, 1997), 60. My report of the percentage of ministers who were women is considerably less than the high of 29 percent that Carolyn Dirksen reported in her article "Let Your Women Keep Silence." As discussed in my dissertation, Dirksen's statistics are based on licensed and ordained ministers. I chose to include deacons in my statistics because the deaconate was an ordained order of ministry from which Church of God women were specifically excluded. Several scholars such as Mickey Crews have used Dirksen's statistics. See Carolyn Rowland Dirksen, "Let Your Women Keep Silence," in Donald N. Bowdle, ed., *The Promise and the Power: Essays on the Motivations, Developments, and Prospects of the Ministries of the Church of God* (Cleveland, TN: Pathway, 1980), 165–96; and Mickey Crews, *The Church of God: A Social History* (Knoxville: University of Tennessee Press, 1990), 92–107.

14. *General Assembly Minutes, 1906–1914*, 49.

15. Ibid., 63.

not serve as pastors of local churches. But the reality was that there were never enough male pastors to meet the needs of the movement. Frequently women served as pastors of churches that they planted, and often they were willing to go places and serve churches that men were unwilling to serve. In such cases they were considered helpers rather than pastors in their own right. The 1927 *Book of General Instructions for the Ministry and Membership* stated "It is not expected that women shall pastor churches, but only act as helpers in connection with the District Overseer. She, according to the Word of God[,] cannot take care of the business of the Church such as holding conferences, receiving or expelling members [,] etc."[16]

Along with the restriction on ordination, the COG placed other restrictions on women including prohibitions from serving in any governmental or sacerdotal role. By 1910 women were excluded from government at any level in the denomination. This exclusion was particularly stressed in the teaching of the first general overseer, A. J. Tomlinson. Tomlinson interpreted Paul's statement about women keeping silent in the church in a way that prohibited women from church government while allowing them to preach. Tomlinson equated Paul's use of the word "church" with "government." According to Tomlinson, "Church then means government. Christ's government. His Church. Here is where women are to keep silence. 1 Cor. 14:34 ... There were no women speaking in the council at Jerusalem."[17] Later Tomlinson wrote, "Let the good sisters feel at perfect liberty to preach the gospel, pray for the sick or well, testify, exhort, etc., but humbly hold themselves aloof from taking charge of the governmental affairs. This is Paul's meaning by the expression, 'Let your women keep silent in the churches; for it is not permitted unto them to speak.'"[18] Although women had participated in the discussion of at least the first two General Assemblies, Tomlinson's definition resulted in the denomination excluding women

16. COG, *Book of General Instructions for the Ministry and Membership* (Cleveland, TN: Church of God Publishing House, [ca. 1927]), 10.

17. A. J. Tomlinson, "Christ Our Law–Giver and King," *The Evening Light and Church of God Evangel* (I November 1910): 2. Tomlinson's definition was repeated in his book *The Last Great Conflict* (71) and became a frequently repeated rationale for the exclusion of women from church business.

18. A. J. Tomlinson, "Paul's Statements Considered," *Church of God Evangel* (18 September 1915): 5.

from participating in both the General Assembly and local church business meetings.

Women with an "Evangelist License" could preach but could not perform sacerdotal responsibilities. Although the first female evangelists were granted the same license as men, there is no evidence that they administered the Lord's Supper, baptized in water, or received members into the church. While early licenses had authorized the evangelist to "publish, preach and defend the gospel of Jesus Christ, to baptize, to administer the Lord's Supper and the washing of the Saints feet," by 1914 church officials had developed a new license for women. This new license specifically provided women with the authority to "publish, preach, and defend the Gospel of Jesus Christ; and do all the work that may devolve on her as a prophetess or female minister of the Gospel."[19] This differing language between evangelist licenses for men and women was codified in 1931 when editors added it to the "Supplement" to the *Minutes of the General Assembly*.[20]

When the General Assembly revised categories of ministry in 1948, it eliminated the office of deacon, designated the office of male evangelist as "licensed minister," and changed the office of male bishop to "ordained minister." Regarding women, the Assembly specifically stated that "the ministerial status of lady evangelists remains unchanged,"[21] and the "Supplement" was expanded to create a separate section for women ministers under the heading "Female." Women were effectively moved outside the offices for male ministers and practically limited to the roles of helper and evangelist.[22]

This reference to women as "lady evangelists" was likely an expression of politeness, but it soon became the common way of referring to women ministers. In addition to signaling respect, the term "lady" also signaled a cultural understanding that the female minister was in

19. See as an example the evangelist license of Rachel J. Brackett (25 December 1914) in the Rachel J. Brackett ministerial file, COG Office of Business and Records, Cleveland, TN.

20. The "Supplement" was a compilation of "all acts and teachings now in vogue . . ." See COG, *Minutes of the Twenty–Sixth Annual Assembly of the Churches of God* (Cleveland, TN: Church of God Publishing House, [1931]), 90.

21. COG, *Minutes of the 42nd General Assembly of the Church of God* (Cleveland, TN: Church of God Publishing House, [1948]), 27.

22. Ibid., 197.

a category distinct from those of male ministers. The fact that this was more than an expression of politeness is revealed by the fact that a male minister was not casually or officially referred to as a "gentleman minister." In 1964 the Supplement heading "Female" was changed to "Lady Minister,"[23] and by 1972, without any official action, the denomination began to use the title "Lady Evangelist" on credentials.[24]

Despite these boundaries regarding women ministers, women continued to respond to the call of God and the COG to proclaim the gospel through pulpit ministry. By 1950 women comprised over 18 percent of COG ministers. In the second half of the twentieth century the percentage gradually declined to under 10 percent, however. This essay attempts to allow women ministers to tell their stories about how they experienced their call to ministry, and how they lived and ministered within these COG limitations.

Hearing the Voices of Church of God Women

As an historian my goal is modest. My small sample does not have comparative interviews of male ministers, and my original interviews had a somewhat different agenda than is the focus of this essay. I particularly wanted to interview women involved in ministry during the period within the COG in which the percentage of women ministers began to decline. I hoped to gain clues about what was happening to cause this decline and how women ministers perceived these changes. What I discovered were powerful stories of women who persevered in ministry within a system that included very specific boundaries for their ministry. Their stories revealed their integration of their ministries within these boundaries. At the core of that integration was a distinct sense of God's call to ministry.

Experiencing God's Call

Most of the COG women that I interviewed experienced dramatic life events and struggles associated with their call to ministry. In some

---

23. COG, *Minutes of the 50th General Assembly of the Church of God* (Cleveland, TN: Church of God Publishing House, [1964]), 73.

24. As an example see the certificate of Dixie Chambers. Her certificate was dated 31 February 1932, but was actually a replacement issued after 1971. Special Collections Box 260, Dixon Pentecostal Research Center, Cleveland, TN.

cases, but not always, these struggles were directly related to their being a woman. Most of these women had the support of key people in their lives to help them make sense of God's call. In almost every case there was the perception of an immediate action of the Holy Spirit in their lives.

Lucille Walker's call was with little fanfare. She reported, "It was while I was in high school that the Lord spoke to me in a Wednesday night service and called me to be a worker . . . I remember saying to my aunt the Lord wants me to work for him. And she said, 'well stand up and tell the church.' So I gave my testimony, and the church invited me up to the altar, and they all prayed for me until I was filled with the Spirit."[25]

Although she was somewhat frightened because of the public speaking aspect of God's call,[26] Walker's personal challenge came as a senior in high school when she experienced the Lord speaking to her again—this time to conduct her first revival in a nearby Baptist church. For her the experience was unforgettable, "But the Lord spoke to me that I was to go to that place for a revival. And I can remember it wasn't a voice, but it was clearer, and it was like you could forget a voice, but you couldn't forget that. I had remembered reading in the Scripture; it was like somebody writing on your heart with a pen made of a diamond cutting, cutting into your spirit. So I couldn't get away from it. And I started talking with the Lord, 'Lord you know I'm a girl and that's a Baptist church, and I don't think they have women preachers. And Lord you know I'm Pentecostal.'"

In the midst of her fears Walker seemed to realize that this was the test of a lifetime. "And I just made all these excuses to the Lord, but it was something, it was like my door to the future. I would either pass through it, or I would be stopped in my life."[27] Despite all of her excuses, she felt God's response was simple, "He said, that's the way I'm walking if you want to walk with me. And I said Lord I want to walk with you . . . You're my life. I'm totally lost without you."[28] Walker's revival was successful, and she went on to have a very diverse ministry in the COG

---

25. Lucille Walker interview by author, 21 June 1990, Cleveland, TN, transcript, 2.

26. Walker, 3.

27. Ibid., 2.

28. Ibid.

including youth camps, community service, inner city drug rehabilitation, nursing, college administration, editing, and writing.

Pentecostal history is full of testimonies of children who claim the call of God on their lives. Ruth Staples was five when she first felt the call of God. At that young age she preached at home the sermons she recalled her pastor preaching. According to Staples, a passerby heard her preaching and committed his life to the Lord. From that point on she envisioned she would be a missionary. But as the got older her childhood experiences faded into the background.[29] Born in 1915, like so many women by World War II she was working in a government job, but she was also living a life that she was not proud of.

Staples could not get away from her call, however. "I felt this calling and I would cry at night . . . it seemed the Lord would speak to me and remind me of my calling. However, at this period, stage of the game, you know, I thought well, I won't do that. That's not for me. But I never got away from it. I guess there wasn't a night when I laid down that I didn't think of that."[30] After struggling with God, Staples found herself in an Assemblies of God church, singing with a trio and getting invitations to speak to youth groups and in jails, nursing homes, and street services. She still did not consider herself a preacher.[31] "I was speaking, and even in my home church I was speaking, but I didn't call myself a minister. And I kept saying 'God, you've got to give me a sign, if you really want me to come out and be a fulltime minister.' And in the meantime, at that very time, I was trying to satisfy myself with helping to build churches in foreign countries . . ."[32]

But still not satisfied, Staples kept asking God for a sign. "One night just as I came into the church, there was one of the elderly ladies that belonged to the church. I had a lot of confidence in her. She walked up to me and she said, 'God has called you to preach the Gospel.' But it was just like electricity. And you see it was a confirmation. Now I'm a person that don't believe in telling somebody God told me to tell you this and that. Because it works both ways, He speaks to us first. But that was a confirmation. And I knew, I knew that I had the calling. From

29. Ruth Staples interview by author, 26 June 1990, Atlanta, GA, transcript, 6, 8.
30. Ibid., 9.
31. Ibid., 12.
32. Ibid., 13.

then I went to Milledgeville, Georgia, to preach in a tent."[33] Within a short period of time Staples had planted a COG in Milledgeville, where she served as pastor from 1950 to 1955. For much of the rest of her life she served as an evangelist and short-term missionary preacher and teacher.

Lucille Turner experienced her call initially through a word of prophecy in a Pentecostal home prayer meeting. As a young girl she was both awed and frightened. She recollected the words of the prophecy and her response, "God's hand is on you. And He has something for you to do for Him in His Kingdom, and you were born for this purpose. He has chosen you . . . I see you now. You are in a foreign country . . . God's hand is leading you to be a foreign missionary . . ." Although Turner was frightened and had no desire to go to a foreign country, that small prayer group blessed her and assured her that God had a great future for her.[34] Her wise mother counseled her to wait and see.

Later as a young adult Turner took a bookkeeping job that she found very unsatisfying. She remembered, "But when I tried it alone with God in that bookkeeping department, He never let me go. He said, 'Lucille, you've never been satisfied with this bookkeeping. Numbers like this will not count . . .' And I realized this business will never satisfy me."[35] Meanwhile Turner's husband found himself stationed in India during World War Two and desired to return there as a missionary. For Turner this was a confirmation of the prophecy that had taken place in that Pentecostal home prayer meeting.

Serving first with the Congregational Holiness Church, her husband was the one given the appointment, and Turner ended up working as his secretary. It was both frustrating and unsatisfying for her. As they left India at the conclusion of four years of service, she had a frank conversation with her husband. "'Lovell, I'm going to tell you this much. If ever we come back to this country, don't you think I'm going to be your secretary, cause I'm not going to do it. If I don't work with people, I'm not coming. It's people—I want to win some souls to Jesus, I want to be responsible to help them to pray and learn how to pray . . . I will never be another secretary. . . you just got the wrong woman if that's what

33. Ibid., 14.
34. Turner, 6.
35. Ibid., 9.

you think I'm for.' He said, 'well that's OK. We can use you somewhere. I have to find out the somewhere.'"[36] When they later returned as COG missionaries, Turner had the responsibility of planning and organizing the curriculum of a Bible school along with teaching English and Bible classes.

Other women had more intense struggles with their calls. Pauline Lambert experienced a great deal of resistance to the idea of a woman preaching the gospel. Lambert did not have an appreciation of women preachers, yet she felt a call of God on her life. She said, "I really felt the call of God to carry the gospel. But I was a woman. And I finally, I talked to my husband and he said, 'well, what if you do have to preach.'"[37] During her struggle Lambert was seeking the baptism of the Holy Spirit. "There in my heart, I think I was willing, but I had a lot of things to pray through and pray over . . . Because before I could receive the baptism, I had to get willing to either preach or be a missionary."[38]

Not only did Lambert face the difficulties of an unsupportive husband and the responsibilities of children, she found plenty of people who assured her that God did not call women to preach, especially in her husband's Baptist church. She found herself agreeing with that assessment. She recalled, "since I was a woman, I just didn't feel like that a woman should be in the pulpit."[39]

What changed Lambert's mind to believe that God might in fact call women to preach? As Lambert struggled, her three-year old daughter Bonnie became ill. Lambert's report of the events are challenging even today, "But then when she took very ill, it seemed that the Lord spoke (not in an audible voice), but the Lord spoke to me and said, 'I'll take your baby daughter and you will carry my gospel . . . heaven [will] be sweeter if I take your daughter, and then you will carry my gospel.' And then I got down to business with the Lord."[40] In response Lambert not only prayed for her daughter's healing, but she rededicated her own life and began to prepare for the ministry.[41] Her formal ministry lasted

36. Ibid., 15.
37. Pauline Lambert, interview by author, 21 June 1990, transcript, 4.
38. Ibid., 5.
39. Ibid., 6–7.
40. Ibid., 14.
41. Ibid., 13.

from 1948 to 1968, and her husband eventually came around to supporting her. Following retirement, she administered a local telephone counseling service in Cleveland, Tennessee.

In the lives of those I interviewed, it was not unusual for the call of God to be tied to a life crisis event. Mary Howard was personally opposed to women ministers even though she was saved at a revival preached by her future mother-in-law.[42] According to Howard, "But I had the feeling, you know, about women preachers. I don't know what it was. I just felt like that it was usurping the authority over a man—that a man was supposed to do all that."[43] Howard continued, "God called me to preach in 1950. I said, no, no, no."[44]

Howard's call came while, as a widow and single mom, she was working at the COG orphanage in Sevierville, Tennessee. There she experienced a number of personal difficulties including a broken arm that was miraculously healed. Howard remembered, "I knew what God was calling me to do, but I would not say yes. I still had that old background [of opposition to women ministers] in me, you know."[45] Continuing to resist God's call, she experienced a tragic accident in the laundry and suffered another broken arm and life-threatening burns. After three months in the hospital, Howard, known at the time as Mary Black, had settled the matter of calling with God.[46] Perhaps hoping for one last out, she visited the orphanage director with the intention of telling him of her call and being willing to listen to his advice if he discouraged her from ministry. His simple affirmation was "Sister Black, I know God had called you."[47]

These voices are representative of the call of God on the lives of ordinary COG women. All of them are within the realm of common Pentecostal experience. In most cases the call came within their Pentecostal communities and they were supported by those communities. Often an older relative or supervisor confirmed the call, and their local congregation supported them in prayer. Most of these women

42. Mary Howard, interview by author, Cleveland, TN, transcript, 14.

43. Ibid., 21.

44. Ibid., 22.

45. Ibid.

46. Ibid., 23–25.

47. Ibid., 27.

realized that being a woman and a minister was unusual in someway. Several such as Staples, Turner and Howard delayed responding to their call. Strikingly, these women did not usually appeal to Scripture to support or to describe their call experiences. But all of them were convinced that they had heard from God and would be outside of the will of God if they failed to heed the call. Despite this certainty regarding their calls, how were they to fulfill their ministries within COG limitations?

Living within the Boundaries

As a child of the late twentieth-century, I was surprised that many of these women not only lived with restrictions placed on their ministries but agreed with those restrictions. Most of them affirmed the church's traditional position that God appointed men to lead both church and home. Tilda Oxendine served most of her ministry as an evangelist, often alongside her brother. In her early days they were designated to "carry the state tent" in order to hold revivals and plant churches in communities without a COG. During her ministry she served as a district youth director and for a brief period as pastor when the state overseer assigned her to a church that was about to be closed. When asked about limitations she responded, "I didn't think nothing about it. It didn't bother me. I thought, we'll let the men do what they're supposed to do, and I'll do what I'm supposed to do."[48] Oxendine expressed no desire to baptize converts under her ministry, and there had been no need for the Lord's Supper or water baptism during her brief tenure as pastor.[49]

Bernice Woodard agreed, "I never felt that the women preachers in the COG w[ere] out of their place because we have always worked under the administration of the man as the head of the church, and I never felt that I was ever doing wrong or any of the ladies, because they have always worked under the supervision and the guidance of the men of the church which are to be the head over the church."[50] Woodard repeated Tomlinson's interpretation of Paul's admonition for women to

48. Tilda Anders Oxendine, interview by author, 25 June 1990, Charlotte, NC, transcript, 14.

49. Ibid., 6.

50. Bernice Woodard, interview by author, 22 June 1990, Cleveland, TN, transcript, 7.

keep silent in the church as meaning that men are to form the governing body of the church and take care of the business. Woodard believed that while it was perfectly appropriate for women to express themselves in Sunday school, women were not to be part of the General Assembly or the General Council. Woodard was convinced that these limitations were the result of the General Council searching the Word, and she was content to serve under the supervision of district and state overseers.[51] She wondered if those women who want to do more were acting out of a spirit of rebellion.[52] And although women sometimes must do things because men do not do them, she insisted that man is to be head and high priest of the home.[53]

Other women disagreed with the limitations, but had come to terms with the fact that they had willingly aligned themselves with the COG and thus were committed to abiding by its polity. Perhaps the most vocal example of this attitude was Mary Graves. Graves had grown up in the household of a mother who preached and had participated in ministry opportunities as a child, including preaching at an early age. She had accepted her own call to ministry with very little struggle. But she did not agree with the limitations the COG placed on women. Graves admitted, "Well, I knew what it was like when I committed to it, when I came into this church. After those many years . . . I knew exactly what to expect . . . I would not be the one to speak against it because I accepted it . . . I think that much of it's a political thing, I really do . . . I've had many young men say to me, 'You know, if you were a man . . .' And immediately, before I hear the rest of it, I say, but I'm not. I'm not a man, and I don't wish I were. I like being a woman. That's what God made me. I tease them. I say, if you could be a woman for 24 hours, you'd never want to be anything else."[54]

But when asked about her views regarding the scriptural basis for these limitations, Graves clearly saw no biblical reasons for distinctions. She commented, "I don't' believe he made one above the other. I believe that in Genesis he gave dominion to both the male and the female."[55]

51. Ibid., 17.

52. Ibid., 19.

53. Ibid., 8.

54. Mary Elizabeth Graves, interview by author, 26 June 1990, Birmingham, AL, transcript, 14.

55. Ibid., 15.

When asked about distinct roles for men and women in Scripture she replied, "I don't know how to answer that. In what way is this distinction defined? I don't see that one supersedes the other. I don't see that one is elevated above the other. You don't either. I don't believe that anybody really does. I think it's just sort of a safeguard that we build."[56] And when asked about COG restrictions she concluded,

> Well I think that some of the restrictions, perhaps, have come from our culture ... in the COG, a woman minister doesn't even get to vote at the General Assembly. Now everybody can vote for a pastor in a local church. But I have put in years—I've put in over 50. I've put in over 35 in the COG. And I go to the Assembly, and I have to sit up [there] in the top of the house and watch what goes on down there with young men that have not even finished school. And they can vote and make decisions. I can't vote! I don't particularly resent it, I accept it cause that's the way it is. But I feel like that we should have more expression. I feel like that we should be heard more, because what we say doesn't amount to a whole lot .... But I don't think that it'll ever change, and we're not the only church .... I think that our church needs to look at it. But my mother taught me, don't [quarrel]—you'll waste time struggling with it. So I don't deal with it."[57]

Interestingly, Mary Graves' situation forced the COG to deal with the restrictions placed on women ministers in very practical ways. While serving as pastor in Wyoming, she found herself 200 miles away from the nearest ordained minister who could perform those sacerdotal ministries that the church prohibited women from performing. The COG determined that the best course of action would be to ordain her husband. At first he rejected the idea, but she persuaded him of its value. She reported, "But we prayed about it, and finally I said to him, now, when you need a secretary, I help you [in] your business. So let's make my ministry a team ministry. He's an ordained minister so I don't have to borrow any preachers to come in, we both do it. And so we both marry the young people. We both do what needs to be done. But he's the ordained minister ... I'm the preacher ... He's the official. That's COG polity."[58]

56. Ibid.
57. Ibid.
58. Ibid., 14.

Although most of the women interviewed either agreed with COG polity or at least agreed to abide by it, Lucille Walker actively attempted to change that polity. Married to J. Herbert Walker Jr., a son of a former general overseer and a well-known COG minister in his own right, Walker was part of a family that understood the COG's history and structure as well as how decisions are made and changes are inaugurated. Walker attributed her willingness to attempt to change the status quo to her father who was involved in local politics. On more than one occasion she wrote letters and had conversations with COG officers calling for changes in policies and practices. Concerned that the Department of Women's Ministries was not treated equally with other departments, she reported,

> I wrote a letter to the Executive Council. I really sought the Lord, and I said, Lord, should I put this in writing. And the Lord gave me a scripture in Ezekiel that I wasn't even aware of. In this scripture it says, God [told] them to measure the temple. Measure every room of the temple, every room must be holy. Every room is holy. Put it in writing. I said, Thank you Lord, I know I asked you should I put it in writing. Right there it is. Put it in writing. And in there it says and if they see and are ashamed, then people will fix it right . . .[59]

Although there is no evidence that her request produced any immediate response, Walker's action revealed a keen ability to attempt to expand women's opportunities within COG practices and polity. She clearly understood that in COG polity the General Assembly was empowered to make changes and that the Executive Council was the initial starting place for the General Assembly agenda. Rather than appealing strictly to reason and cultural expectations, she referred to a Biblical text for support; since every room in Ezekiel's temple was holy then there should be no "structural" distinction regarding COG departments due to gender. Finally, she was empowered by a sense of divine direction as to what her actions should be.

On another occasion Walker wrote in support of allowing women to be part of the General Assembly and invoked the historical past as an appropriate model. Realizing that women participated in the earliest Assemblies, she recalled, "Now I wrote the Executive Committee

59. Walker, 12.

and asked them to please tell me when that was decided and how. They never did answer me cause I don't think anybody knows where the word male got inserted . . . So I did a proposal once to the Council and Herbert [her husband] signed on this, for them to discuss reinstating that every member of the COG would be part of the General Assembly."[60] Although the written record does not record cause and effect, by 1994 the General Assembly agreed with Walker and women became full participants in the Assembly.

For this small sample of women there was a clear continuum regarding acceptance of restrictions. All clearly had thought about and were conversant with the scriptures regarding the roles of women in church and home. Some, such as Woodard, were convinced that the COG's interpretation of those scriptures was correct. Others, such as Graves, questioned the interpretation but were content to live with their personal commitment to the denomination. At least one woman, Lucille Walker, understood how changes were made in the COG and actively worked to make those changes on behalf of women.

Although this sample is small, there are hints that social location may have played a role in these attitudes and actions. Many of these women were born and raised on farms, but the outspoken Graves was the daughter of a doctor and woman preacher, and Walker's father had been involved in local politics. Thus Graves and Walker had a broader sense of possibilities for women, of how to work within the structures for the benefit of their ministries, and even how to work for changes in the restrictions on their ministries.[61]

Conclusion

Women ministers in the Church of God faced challenge and opportunity. The denomination was historically open to women preaching but not to women in leadership roles. Elsewhere I have shown that the aftermath of World War Two included a renewed emphasis on women in the home and contributed to an environment that discouraged

60. Walker, 18.

61. Not all gave clear indications of their families' occupations, but most were poor. Lambert, Murphy, Oxendine, Turner, and Woodard were from farm families. Miller's father was a grocer.

women from entering into public ministry[62] In this essay we see that a distinct sense of call was key to women who persevered as ministers. Additionally that call was often encouraged by local congregations and significant persons as well.

For some Church of God women the appropriate response to boundaries they faced was to accept them as the will of God mandated through biblical and natural circumscription and expressed through separate spheres within the church. This was especially true of women who grew up in traditional situations and whose ministries were inaugurated prior to World War Two. Speaking from this place in life Tilda Oxendine comfortably reported, "We'll let the men do what they're supposed to do, and I'll do what I'm supposed to do."

Lucile Walker and Mary Graves revealed that not all women were content to be passive in their relationship with the Church of God and its limitations. They sought ways to be faithful to their call and to their denomination. Yet Walker and Graves also actively expanded the ways in which women ministers lived within their denominational boundaries. Although research has not been done to determine the reception of Walker's letters, it is likely that she and women like her have slowly influenced changes in the COG. At the 1990 General Assembly, held after all but one of these interviews, the COG changed the title of "lady minister" to "licensed minister" and agreed to allow women the same sacerdotal rights as male ministers including receiving members into the local church, officiating in the Lord's Supper, and baptizing the saints.[63] Except for the right of ordination, this put women in the same ministerial category as male licensed ministers. It also moved the COG away from the culturally grounded and gender specific language of the term "lady" when referring to women clergy.

Two years later, the Assembly agreed to give women the right to vote in the General Assembly.[64] This did not make women full participants in the government of the COG because the International General Assembly can only debate an agenda previously approved by two bodies of ordained bishops from which women are excluded: the International Executive Council and the International General Council. But it did

62. Roebuck, "Limiting Liberty," 170–250.

63. COG, *Minutes of the 63rd General Assembly of the Church of God* (Cleveland, TN: Pathway, 1990), 79.

64. *Minutes of the 64th General Assembly*, 73.

make women full participants in the highest governing body of the denomination—a body that can at least reject motions brought by the other bodies even if it cannot initiate change itself. It is likely that a poll of women today would continue to show varying opinions as to whether or not women should participate in these other governing bodies. Yet within time, it is probable that changes will continue and will come here as well.

The most recent change regarding women in ministry came in 2000 when the nomenclature of ministerial ranks was modified so that the former rank of "licensed minister" became "ordained minister" and the former rank of "ordained minister" became "ordained bishop."[65] The effect of this change was to eliminate ninety-one years of restricting women from using the term ordination to describe their ministries. This may not be a clear line of progression for women in the COG, however. The fact that women are now considered "ordained ministers" does not give them any additional rights or responsibilities. Further, changing the name of the highest rank of ministry to that of "ordained bishop" could potentially make it more difficult for women to advance to that rank in the future. With the COG steeped in a tradition of separate spheres and a literal interpretation of Scriptures that seemingly prohibit women from serving as bishops and from usurping authority over men, there remains continued resistance to the idea of women serving as bishops or in governmental roles in the denomination. A motion before ordained bishops to allow women to serve on local Church and Pastor's Councils, seen to be a governmental role in the local church, was defeated in 2004 and 2008, and a 2006 study of whether or not women should be permitted to serve as ordained bishops was presented to the International General Council without recommendation.[66]

65. *Minutes of the 68th General Assembly*, 81.

66. At the request of the International General Council, the International Executive Council directed the Doctrine and Polity Committee to study the question of whether or not women should serve as bishops. The initial proposal for the study came via a single person's motion to the International General Council's Motions Committee, and in my observation passed only so that the ordained bishops could move on to a matter they considered more important. The results of the study produced a booklet with two position papers supporting and two papers opposing women serving as bishops, but neither the Doctrine and Polity Committee nor the International Executive Council made any recommendation. Rather than supporting or opposing the question of women serving as bishops, they distributed the report to the International General

Although COG women now have more rights as ministers, their exclusion from the ministerial rank of bishop continues to prevent those rights from being translated into leadership opportunities. The situation is further complicated if it is true that we now live in a post-denominational and post-modern age. There is at least anecdotal evidence that younger women may not be as willing to live within denominational restrictions as were the women whose voices were heard in this essay. Although the certainty that God is their chief employer may still empower women to minister, it remains to be seen if it will continue to be a sufficient bond to this classical Pentecostal denomination.

Council without discussion. See "A Study of the Issue of Women Serving as Ordained Bishops," Personal files of author, Cleveland, TN.

4

Looking Beyond the Pulpit

Social Ministries and African American Pentecostal-Charismatic Women in Leadership

Karen Kossie-Chernyshev

Introduction

IN RECENT YEARS, SCHOLARS OF PENTECOSTALISM IN GENERAL AND African American Pentecostalism in particular have begun to examine the social engagement of early Pentecostals.[1] Such undertakings are particularly relevant for scholars and students in the social sciences where intellectual inquiry necessarily intersects with societal concerns. This essay provides an overview of African American Pentecostal women leaders and their sustained commitment to social uplift and discusses how expressions of that commitment evolved over time. It engages a variety of sources but relies heavily on Sherry Sherrod DuPree's groundbreaking work *African American Holiness Pentecostal Movements: An Annotated Bibliography* (1996), a partial but portable form of the DuPree collection now housed at the Schomburg Center for Research in Black Culture in New York City.[2]

1. See Grant Wacker, *Heaven Below: Early Pentecostals and American Culture* (Cambridge: Harvard University Press, 2003); and Wallace Best, *Passionately Human, No Less Divine: Religion and Culture in Black Chicago, 1915–1952* (Princeton: Princeton University Press, 2005).

2. Sherry Sherrod DuPree, *African–American Holiness Pentecostal Movement: An Annotated Bibliography* (New York: Garland, 1996); and DuPree, "African American Pentecostal and Holiness Collection, 1876–86," Schomburg Center for Research in Black

Research to date has shown that social ministries among African American Pentecostals of Trinitarian, Oneness, Evangelical, or Neo-Pentecostal theological bents fall into two basic categories: those that function as auxiliaries to established churches or denominations and those launched independently of established churches or denominations. Historically, such ministries have followed the basic blueprint for social outreach outlined in the New Testament: to feed the hungry, clothe the naked, pray for the sick, and visit the imprisoned. They have relied on the contemporaneous needs of given conversion populations to determine the shape of the ministry established. Regardless of the target population, such ministries have placed great emphasis on the salvation/sanctification message, which requires radical life changes among converts expressly related to what converts are purportedly "saved" or "delivered" from. The initial conversion experience might have happened instantaneously, but sustaining the fruit of the experience was believed to require transforming not only the converts' philosophies of life but also their manner of dress, where they lived, with whom they lived, and even their vocation. For the dual outward and inward transformation was expected to reflect the tenets of scripture.

The breadth, scope, and relevance of social ministries, particularly those directly affiliated with established churches, have depended on the following: the importance and range of the service provided, the size of the ministry, its location, and the ministry's ability to amass sufficient material and human resources to address the needs in question. As "the finances of the local black church often reflect the economic condition of its members," one can safely assume that the complexity of a given social ministry will often mirror the educational, social, and economic profiles of the founders, staff, and volunteers.[3]

It is impossible to know the number of social ministries established and sustained over the course of African American Pentecostal history, as the recording and archiving of such data by governing bodies, con-

Culture, New York Public Library, New York. See http://digilib.nypl.org/dynaweb/ead/scm/scdupree/@Generic__BookTextView/142;pt=132 (last accessed 24 April 2007).

3. See C. Eric Lincoln and Lawrence H. Mamiya, *The Black Church in the American Experience* (Durham, NC: Duke University Press, 1990), 236–73, quote from 253. See also Hans A. Baer and Merrill Singer, *African–American Religion in the Twentieth Century: Varieties of Protest and Accommodation* (Knoxville: University of Tennessee Press, 1992).

gregations, and ministries has been neither uniform nor systematic. The available evidence nonetheless permits categorizing the kind and nature of the social ministries established, determining the degree to which such ministries responded to the needs of selected communities within a given historical framework, and examining the role that African American Pentecostal women have played in their implementation and continuation.

Historical Overview

African American Pentecostal women leaders have been committed to social ministry since the advent of the modern Pentecostal movement, when women electrified by the Azusa Street Revival set out to change the world with their message of hope.[4] Those women leaders affiliated with established Pentecostal denominations were well positioned to found and steer the growth of social ministries within their organizations at local, state, and national levels given the shared theological bent and modus operandi of the bodies they served. This is particularly true of Church of God in Christ (COGIC) church mothers, who had ready access to the creative energies of women affiliated with the COGIC jurisdictions and auxiliaries. The bulk of the social ministries established by COGIC women leaders aimed to meet basic needs for food, clothing, and shelter, and granted special attention to the young and elderly. COGIC women leaders were also engaged in the universal quest among African Americans for education and civil rights.

Lizzie Woods Robinson (1860–1946), first International Supervisor of COGIC Women's Work, helped frame the social consciousness of COGIC women. Robinson was born a slave on April 5, 1860, in Phillips County, Arkansas, five years before the Civil War ended. In the early 1900's, when women's suffrage lay hidden in the future and poor African American women were marginalized, Robinson distinguished herself as a gifted leader by setting the precedent for the national leadership role of women in the Church of God in Christ. She worked within one of the premiere Pentecostal denominations in the United States in the early twentieth century to forward a philosophy of self-help among women throughout the country.

---

4. Estrelda Alexander, *The Women of Azusa Street* (Cleveland: Pilgrim, 2005).

Robinson began her tenure in 1911, when Charles Harrison Mason, founder of the reorganized Church of God in Christ (1907), appointed her to head "Women's Work," one of the first four departments established for COGIC governance. Robinson began to raise a national army of women who impacted the social, economic, and religious outlook of urban and rural African Americans. Robinson created a number of programs, including the Sewing Circle, Sunshine Band, and Home and Foreign Missions that encouraged self-reliance, entrepreneurship, and humanitarianism. In Sewing Circles, women learned needlework to make clothing for their children, as well as to earn income for their families. In Sunshine Bands established throughout the United States, women were trained in home economics, health care, personal management, parenting skills, and family relationships. Robinson also raised money through her national travels to support African American women missionaries in Trinidad; Cristobal; Canal Zone; Haiti; Costa Rica; British West Indies; Cape Palmas, Africa; Monrovia, Africa; Wisseka Station, Africa; and Tubake Station, Africa. In addition to her work in COGIC, Robinson kept close contact with Mary McCleod Bethune, a renowned African American educator and advocate of women's rights in the early twentieth century.

Following closely in Robinson's footsteps, Lillian Brooks Coffey (1896–1964), second International Supervisor of COGIC women's department, established the Lillian B. Coffey Rest Home in Detroit, Michigan, where she was commissioned to establish COGIC presence and Women's Work.[5] She and other COGIC women in Michigan "labored and sacrificed, in district meetings and convocations, cooking, serving, preparing, doing whatever good things their hand found to do for the establishment of a better and bigger Church of God in Christ."[6] Coffey also founded the International Women's Convention of the COGIC six years after Robinson's death. The first of its kind in American religious history, the convention attracts some 25,000 women and remains an important place for COGIC women to hone their leadership skills for spiritual and communal use.

Native Texan, Dr. Mattie McGlothen, fourth International Supervisor of COGIC Women's Work (1976–94), continued to empha-

---

5. DuPree, *African–American Holiness Pentecostal Movement*, 182, Entry 1349.

6. Ibid., 181, Entry 1349.

size the dual spiritual and social mission of the COGIC's International Women's Department established by her predecessors. McGlothen oversaw the construction of a pavilion in Port-au-Prince, Haiti, for senior citizens and unwed mothers.[7] In 1992, a facility for battered women and the homeless in Richmond, California, was named after McGlothen, and a Senior Housing facility was constructed in the California Northwest Jurisdiction of the COGIC in Oakland, California.[8]

COGIC women leaders provided a model for church mothers of regional and local jurisdictions who also created social ministries. Mother Mary Davis purchased a home for women in Northern Illinois.[9] Charleszetta Waddles-Campbell established Perpetual Mission for Saving Souls of All Nations, Inc., in Detroit, in a four-story warehouse. By 1972, when the *Kalamazoo Gazette* covered her story, the mission was serving more than 75,000 meals per year and distributing tons of free clothing and furniture and other services such as tutoring programs, legal aid, job placement, and medical care.[10]

Other socially engaged COGIC women leaders focused on education and played key roles in the founding and governance of three COGIC schools located in the US South: Page Normal Industrial Institute, located in Hearne, Texas;[11] Saints Industrial and Literacy School, in Lexington, Mississippi;[12] and a Bible College in Little Rock, Arkansas. Emma F. Bradley served as principal of the Page school where students were given civic and moral lessons as well as instruction in reading, writing, and mathematics. The daughter of a teacher, Bradley graduated from Prairie View A & M University in 1915 and taught in the Hillsboro school system. She was invited to serve as the first principal of the Page Normal when COGIC leaders in Texas de-

7. Emma J. Clark, *Dr. Mattie McGlothen: A Virtuous Woman* (Richmond, CA: Library/Museum, 1995), 13. Cited in Karen Kossie-Chernyshev, "A 'Grand' Old Church Rose in the East: The Church of God in Christ (COGIC) in East Texas," *East Texas Historical Journal* 41 (2003): 26–36, esp. 34.

8. DuPree, *African–American Holiness Pentecostal Movement*, 534, Entry 3003.

9. Ibid., 192, Entry 1368.

10. Ibid., 448, Entry 2534.

11. Bobby Dean, *This is the Church of God in Christ* (Atlanta: Underground Epics, 2001), 55.

12. Charles H. Pleas, *Fifty Years of Achievement—From 1906–1956: A Period in History of the Church of God in Christ* (1956; reprint, Memphis, TN: COGIC Public Relations, 1991), 47.

cided to establish an academic, industrial, and Bible-training institute.[13] Page Normal Institute made "rapid progress" for fifteen years because of the "jurisdictional system" established to raise funds for the institute.[14] Bishop C. H. Mason affirmed the school's importance to the national organization by sending his son to study there.[15]

Similarly, Arenia C. Mallory helped establish Saints Industrial and Literacy School in Lexington, Mississippi.[16] Mallory earned a bachelor's degree from Simmons College in Louisville (1927), a master's degree from Jackson State University, a master's degree from the University of Illinois (1950), and a doctorate of law from Bethune-Cookman College in Daytona Beach, Florida (1951).[17] Mallory's tenure as president of the school spanned from 1926 to 1983, approximately 57 years. The school was renamed Saints Junior College in 1954, and in the 1970s became Saints Academy, a private secondary school for grades one through twelve. As a graduate of Bethune-Cookman, Mallory was inspired by college founder Mary McCleod Bethune, and introduced Bethune to another of her mentors, Lizzie Robinson.[18] The introduction may have reinforced Bethune's effort to establish the National Council of Negro Women in 1935 as COGIC women were formally acquainted with the organization's focus. Mallory also acted as an international spokesperson for Bethune. She effectively drew on the examples of both Bethune and Robinson and became a trailblazer among black women founders of educational institutions in the early twentieth century.

The list of socially engaged COGIC women would not be complete without Mamie Till-Mobley, a woman whose life circumstances propelled her into civil rights history. Till-Mobley was the mother of Emmett J. Till, the COGIC youth whose murder galvanized the civil rights movement. Till-Mobley noted in an interview that while the

13. Funeral Program, Mother Emma Bradley (1894–1996), Saintsville COGIC, Dallas, TX.

14. Williams Goodson, Email to Karen Kossie–Chernyshev, Tuesday, March 26, 2002.

15. Ibid.

16. Pleas, *Fifty Years of Achievement*, 47.

17. Susan L. Smith, "Arenia C. Mallory," http://www.olemiss.edu/depts/south/ms_encyclopedia/areniamallorysample.htm (last accessed 24 April 2007).

18. Elijah Hill, *Women Come Alive: The Biography of Lizzie Robinson* (Charleston, SC: Book Surge, 2005).

COGIC organization did not take a public position on her son's death, she deemed it her personal responsibility to expose the horrors of racism.[19] Till-Mobley did so by granting *Jet* magazine the right to publish a picture of Emmett Till's mutilated remains. Till-Mobley's commitment to social justice continued throughout her life. She obtained a Master's degree and dedicated the rest of her life to educating children and others about racial tolerance and reconciliation. Till-Mobley was featured in *Emmett Till's Murder*, a PBS documentary examining her son's death and her role in its remembrance.[20]

Similar to COGIC women, African American Pentecostal women of Apostolic traditions embraced social ministry as well even though adherents of the "Oneness" doctrine preferred decentralization to the gender-restrictive hierarchical governance characteristic of COGIC.[21] Apostolic women participated in various levels of church governance; they served as missionaries, ministers, and bishops. Black Apostolics established a variety of social ministries from the 1930s onwards, including schools, senior citizens' homes, tutoring programs, and other community outreaches.[22] But the explicit involvement of women is most evident in The National Woman's Council of the Church of Our Lord Jesus Christ organized in October 1952 and "composed of all women of the Church of Our Lord Jesus Christ."[23] The council outlined its dual spiritual and social mission during the umbrella organization's 57th National Convocation held in San Francisco, California: "The aim and objective of the council is to support home and foreign mission for the extension of the gospel, the building of schools and the care of the sick."[24] The organization also established churches, schools, and a clinic in Africa.

Social ministries were also established by women founders of African American Pentecostal, Evangelical, Charismatic, or Neo-

19. Karen Kossie, Telephone Interview with Mamie Till–Mobley, Texas Southern University, 2000.

20. *The Murder of Emmett Till: The American Experience*, PBS Home Video, 2003. See http://www.pbs.org/wgbh/amex/till/index.html (last accessed 24 April 2007).

21. DuPree, *African-American Holiness Pentecostal Movement*, 245.

22. Ibid., 265, Entry 1756; 256, Entry 1726; 250–52, Entry 1713; 255, Entry 1723; 267, Entry 1763; and 157, Entry 1223.

23. Ibid., 276, Entry 1784.

24. Ibid., 276, Entry 1784.

Pentecostal churches. Bishop Annie Lizzee Brownlee (1910–84) of Triumph the Church in Righteousness (Trinitarian), Fort Lauderdale, Florida, established five churches, the growth of which stemmed from the mission Brownlee had established for children, the poor, the old, and the mentally ill.[25] The True Church of God (Apostolic) was founded in 1910 in New York by Mother Susan Gertrude Lightfoot. The first black woman to establish a large and thriving church in New York, she also established a K–12 school.[26] Elder Lucy Smith (1874–1952), founder of All Nations Pentecostal Church in Chicago, Illinois,[27] in the 1920s, established a charitable outreach that provided food and clothing for black Chicagoans in need.[28] Similarly, Bishop Marzella Hall-Weed, founder of Holiness Community Temple in 1937 in Chicago, maintained a food program and clothing bank.[29] In 1939, Gertrude Morgan founded Everlasting Gospel Revelation Temple (Apostolic) in New Orleans, Louisiana, and oversaw the construction of a chapel and an orphanage, which was destroyed in 1965 by Hurricane Betsy and never reconstructed.[30] Under the leadership of founder Overseer Annie Mae Lee, the Holy Temple of Jesus Christ, founded in 1954 and incorporated in 1958, in Houston, Texas, established a food bank and grew to include twelve churches.[31]

More Recent Projects

Women leaders and members of the Evangelical Charismatic and Neo-Pentecostal groups that began thriving from the 1960s onwards embraced social ministry also. But most made their contributions as pastor's wives, who often held dual leadership responsibilities with their husbands in pastor/wife "teams" as did Sandra Montgomery, wife of Ed Montgomery, pastor of Abundant Life Cathedral in Houston, Texas. Sandra Montgomery founded and directed "Y-Win," an acronym for "You! Women in the Now," which encompassed 29 home fellowship

25. Ibid., 157, Entry 1223.

26. Ibid., 266, Entry 1760.

27. Ibid., 67, Entry 476.

28. Best, *Passionately Human, No Less Divine*, 149.

29. DuPree, *African–American Holiness Pentecostal Movement*, 513, Entry 2888.

30. Ibid., 257, Entry 1730.

31. Ibid., 261 Entry 1744.

groups for women. She also helped oversee the establishment of a daycare and kindergarten under the church's direction.[32] Similarly, Mia K. Wright, who co-labors with her husband, Remus E. Wright, Senior Pastor of Fountain of Praise in Houston, Texas, serves as Director of Ministries and oversees training and leadership development for the church's various outreaches. The church's vision includes a commitment to "[r]ebuilding [the] local and global community, economically and educationally, through faith-based projects that combine spiritual teachings with social reforms."[33] Wright demonstrates a personal commitment to the community at large by serving on the boards of My Place, Inc., a woman's resource center for breast cancer and awareness, and the Houston's Girls' Health & Wellness Project, a partnership between the Houston Institute for Women's Health of Texas Woman's University and the Houston Independent School District.[34]

Sandra Montgomery and Mia Wright's social involvement notwithstanding, their church leadership and that of the other women leaders treated thus far constitute auxiliary expressions of their respective churches or denominations. But their efforts provide important contrasts to the independent social organizations that African American Pentecostal women founded on an increasing scale from the late twentieth century onwards.

Building on the contributions of their predecessors, African American Pentecostal women leaders of the late twentieth century began to establish an increasing number of independent organizations that combined faith and service to the community. This development can be attributed to a number of factors, including but not limited to the continued contestation of the pulpit as off-limits to women in established African American Pentecostal denominations, the tax exemption status provided for nonprofit organizations, the tax breaks afforded donors to such organizations, the general growth and professionalization of the nonprofit sector, the increase in partnerships among charitable organizations offering complementary services, the establishment of federal agencies that encourage a broadly-defined communal approach

32. Ibid., 309–10, Entry 1966.

33. Fountain of Praise, Church information, http://www.tfop.org/church_info.html (last accessed 16 April 2007).

34. Bio, Mia K. Wright, Fountain of Praise, http://www.tfop.org/firstlady_bio_print. htm (last accessed 16 April 2007).

to solving the many problems plaguing American cities, the secure place such organizations have gained in the American economy over time, and most recently federal policies favoring the establishment of faith-based social organizations.[35] These independent social organizations do not replace traditional churches, but they have become perhaps a permanent thread in the fabric of American religious culture and create shared and meaningful, albeit contested, space where faith meets society.

Prototypes for independent, as opposed to auxiliary, social organizations among Pentecostals appeared as early as 1949, with Ida Murphy's Palatka Community Prayer Band in Palatka, Florida. While the Prayer Band's primary goal was to "spread the gospel with missionary zeal," members of the prayer band supported the community by rendering services to hospitals, homes, schools, nursing homes, and jails.[36] Over time an increasing number of extra-church organizations formed to address the needs of specific target populations. In 1972, Grace Lee Paige founded The Lorton Reformatory Prison Ministry, which she started by gathering neighborhood children at risk.[37] The same year, Reverend Mother Sidney Adams founded Youth Unlimited Community Christian Club, Inc., in Denver, Colorado, and organized programs that focused on teenage pregnancy prevention, workshops, retreats, bible studies, and initiatives for young black men.[38]

Husband and wife teams also established nonprofit Christian organizations with a social focus. In 1989, Jefferson and Debra Edwards, founders of Inner-City Christian Center, a nondenominational organization in Kansas City, Missouri, promoted spiritual freedom among young black men and women. The organization sponsored programs for the unemployed and senior citizens, and focused on child and health care.[39] Inner City Lights, founded in De Moines, Iowa, by Lewis and Cheryll Ray, aimed to reach youth and sponsored summer and winter camps. The organization sponsored myriad recreational activities including skiing, horseback riding, and bowlarama, as well as social

35. "Faith–Based and Community Initiatives," http://www.whitehouse.gov/government/fbci/ (last accessed 24 April 2007).

36. DuPree, African–American Holiness Pentecostal Movement, 521, Entry 5188.

37. Ibid., 525, Entry 2961.

38. Ibid., 528, Entry 2975.

39. Ibid., 524, Entry 2956.

outreach activities, including food and furniture distributions for the needy and tutoring services.[40]

In 1989, Dr. Patricia Miles and her husband founded Creative Neighbors Always Sharing (CNAS), in Los Angeles, California, a shelter that offers temporary living accommodations for battered and abused families, women, and children. Once clients reach a place of stability, productivity, and thriving, the organization helps them find transitional and permanent housing through First-time Homebuyers and other low-income housing programs available to California residents.[41] CNAS also collaborates with various local and state agencies to meet the needs of clients, including mental and physical health therapy programs, daycare programs, community coalitions, local and state government agencies, and social service agencies.

Different from most of the social service organizations whose establishment generally post-dated that of affiliated churches, CNAS was established before the church that Miles and her husband eventually founded. The vision for CNAS began while Miles was working at the Jamal Drug Rehabilitation Center, affiliated with the Charles Drew Medical Center in the Los Angeles area. At Jamal, she began learning about the different types of drugs and the various personality and mood disorders associated with drug use, including depression, schizophrenia, bi-polar disorder, and others. Because of the impressive work she was doing with clients, she was encouraged to apply for a contract with the State Department of Corrections but told that she would need to secure a building in order to qualify for the contract. She and her husband began seeking a place for the shelter, which they procured through means that Miles described as simply "miraculous."

CNAS eventually reached an annual operational budget of $2 million dollars per year. Miles had hoped to receive funding from private organizations, particularly churches, given her desire for a Christian-based approach. But over the organization's sixteen-year history, CNAS received only two one-time gifts of $400 and $500 dollars from two local COGIC churches. Other churches offered prayers of support or simply reassured Miles that God would provide if she had indeed been "called" to establish the shelter. With negligible support from local

40. Ibid., 524, Entry 2957.

41. Karen Kossie-Chernyshev, Interview with Dr. Patricia Miles, Houston, Texas, 3 September 2006.

churches, CNAS's operational funds came from local and state government agencies, which required a clear separation of church and state, as
government supported faith-based initiatives were nonexistent at the
time. The organization served clients' basic needs and offered optional
spiritual counseling. Miles also provided an opportunity for CNAS
clients to worship at her home church, but discovered that they were
not being treated impartially by others in the congregation. To ensure
that CNAS clients could worship with dignity, she and her husband
decided to found Living Hope Evangelistic Ministries, an independent
Charismatic church. Miles's example affirms why social ministries like
CNAS play an important role in the American religious landscape.

Given the limitations of most traditional churches whose primary
commitment is to their particular doctrinal stance and local church
programs, women founders and directors of community-based initiatives and corporations of the twenty-first century welcome the support of umbrella charitable organizations, particularly the United Way,
which offers management assistance and leadership development programs for nonprofit organizations.[42] Approximately 80 of the near 964
nonprofit organizations listed for the Houston Area and surrounding
counties maintain a Christian focus and are directed by women.[43] Those
clearly affiliated with African American Pentecostal traditions include
Evangelist Temple COGIC, where Louisa Kyles, the pastor's wife, directs
the food pantry; Greater Law COGIC, where Erma Henderson, the pastor's wife, directs the food pantry; Open Door COGIC, where Pastor
Margie Russell oversees selected social programs, as well as clothing
and food distribution; and Miracle Deliverance Holiness Church, where
Ezzie Mae Williams is pastor and Lugenia M. Spiller manages the social
ministries of the church.[44] Most social ministries headed by women are
generally best described as "Christian-based," as no particular theological bent is evident from the organization's profile.

42. United Way Houston, http://www.unitedwayhouston.org/nonprofits/workshops
.html (last accessed 24 April 2007).

43. *Community Resource Directory: Metropolitan Houston and Surrounding Counties*, 24th ed., 2005.

44. Ibid.; see pages 167 (Evangelist COGIC), 202 (Greater Law COGIC), 369 (Open
Door COGIC); and 328 (Miracle Deliverance Holiness Church).

Conclusion

The existence of such organizations can be interpreted in at least two ways. On the one hand, they reaffirm how complicated women's access to traditional sites of leadership has been since the advent of the modern Pentecostal movement. On the other hand, they demonstrate how committed African American Pentecostal and Charismatic women have been to social ministry, whether or not they were ordained to preach—a one-dimensional image of leadership often represented in authoritarian terms.

Perhaps the best way to appreciate the historical trajectory of African American Pentecostal-Charismatic women's social contributions is to embrace a broader definition of leadership—one that will ultimately welcome the full range of opportunities available to African American Pentecostal women beyond the pulpit, whether they unfold in established churches and denominations or independent ministries with a decided social focus. My quest for a broader definition of leadership does not aim to overlook relevant discussions about African American Pentecostal-Charismatic women and traditional expressions of leadership, but rather to ensure that the socially-engaged visions of these women are not categorized solely as "sublimated paths to ministry."[45] For their efforts merit appreciation as essential social expressions of the denominations and churches with which the women are affiliated and the independent social organizations they continue to establish.

45. See Lincoln and Mamiya, *The Black Church in the American Experience,* 281–85.

5

Sanctified Saints—Impure Prophetesses

A Cross-Cultural Reflection on Gender and Power in Two Afro-Christian Spirit-Privileging Churches

Deidre Helen Crumbley[1]

Introduction

> For emphasis, it is repeated here that female members during menstruation are not allowed to come within the precincts of the Church until after their sanctification after seven clear days (Lev. 15:19; Matt. 5:17–19) ... They are not allowed to perform any spiritual functions connected with conducting of services in the Church other than saying the prayers when asked and reading portions of the Bible quoted by the preacher ... [U]nder no circumstances shall women say the grace during devotional services or lead men in prayers ... in accordance with St. Paul's injunction. (1 Cor 14:34–35; Genesis 3–16)[2]

1. The ethnographic endeavor is one of delving deeply into the particular. In the study of religion, it immerses a researcher in the minutiae of faith as a lived experience and entails thickly describing the ritual and symbol of a specific faith. As enriching as such in-depth research is, at certain points, one longs for an intellectual moment to step back from phenomena, to engage, not so much in rigorous comparative analysis, as to reflect on wide ranging data in the same intellectual moment. Being invited to contribute to Regent's scholarly symposium on "women's ministry and leadership within global perspective" has created such a moment. For this, and the opportunity to bring ethnographic findings to bear on what the letter of invitation refers to as "issues central to [the] life and ministry" of the church, I thank the colloquium conveners Drs. Amos Yong and Estrelda Alexander and Regent University's Divinity School.

2. *Celestial Church of Christ Constitution 1980*, Published by The Board of Trustees

There is neither Jew nor Greek, there is neither bond nor free,
there is neither male nor female: for ye are all one in Christ
Jesus. (Galatians 3:28 KJV)

Central Question

This paper opens with two quotations. The first is from the constitution
of an African Instituted Church (AIC), which selectively weds Christian
and African religious traditions. The second is regularly quoted from
the pulpit of an inner city African American Sanctified Church. In the
first, women may not speak in church and are excluded from both ritual
space and high office; in the other, women have held both ritual and
political power as doctrinal arbiter and sole ultimate authority. Despite
virtually antithetical gender practices, in both churches Spirit shapes
worship and doctrine, biblical literalism grounds theological reflection,
and religious adepts serve as human conduits of divine revelation. How
might socio-cultural legacy, the gender of the founder, and institutional complexity inform the extremes of gender practices in these two
churches, and what strategies might this suggest for addressing women's
leadership in the global Pentecostal and Charismatic movement?

Methodological Concerns

To answer this two-part question, this investigation, using a case study
ethnographic approach, delineates the socio-cultural legacies, gendered
leadership, and organizational processes of each church, and then explores how differences in these areas might explain their differing gender practices. What follows, then, is an intellectual exercise of sifting
through rich ethnographic material for interpretive clues to address a
major issue for twenty-first century Pentecostal/charismatic churches—
namely, the role of women in church ministry and leadership opportunities which have gradually eroded.

The case study churches are the Celestial Church of Christ (CCC),
an Aladura ("ala" = owners of "duura" = prayer) church, founded
among the Yoruba of West Africa, and the Church of Prayer Seventh
Day (COPSD),[3] an African American inner city storefront Sanctified

---

for The Pastor-in-Council of the Celestial Church of Christ (Nigeria Diocese), 50; cited
hereafter as CCCC, followed by page number.

3. The author, at the request of the church members, has used pseudonyms for the
church and its leader.

Church founded in the northeastern United States. The Celestial data was collected during four consecutive years of field work in Nigeria, expanded upon by ongoing communications with the Celestial Church in America, where a half million Africans immigrated between 1992 and 2002; of these, 75,000 are Nigerians, who have helped establish Aladura Christianity within the American religious landscape.[4] Data about COPSD follows from a larger book project about the author's home church.[5] Complicating the distinctions between emic and etic, between the researcher and the researched, this approach reflects a perspective in the anthropology of religion, which considers the beliefs of the researcher to be integral to the ethnographic endeavor.[6]

The members of the two case study churches may not refer to their faiths as "Pentecostal" or "charismatic," yet they share with these a practice of privileging Spirit in ways that directly, and often dramatically, inform worship, doctrine, and authority structures. In this study, then, Spirit-privileging churches, such as those found in the Pentecostal, Charismatic, and Holiness movements are characterized by (1) experienced imminent Spirit often embodied within and expressed through believers, e.g., by glossolalia, religious dance, prophesying, or healing; (2) biblical literalism that shapes church doctrine, discipline, and theological reflection; and (3) divine will as revealed through human conduits whose spiritual adeptness lends them charismatic authority.

The extremes of gender practices represented by the case study churches mirror that of the Pentecostal, Charismatic, and Holiness movement, in that some churches prohibit female ordination, others have ordained women from their emergence, and still others ordain women but only to certain levels. For example, the Church of God,

---

4. See US Department of Homeland Security, 2003: 12–14, 17–18; cf. especially the essays by Jacob K. Olupona, Elias Bomba, Akinade Akintunde, Regina Gemignani, and Deidre Crumbley in Jacob Olupona and Regina Gemignani, eds., *African Immigrant Religion in America* (New York: New York University Press, 2007).

5. Deidre Helen Crumbley, *Divine Mother Holy Saints: Race, Gender and Migration in the Rise of a Storefront Sanctified Church* (Gainesville: University Press of Florida, forthcoming).

6. Walter Randolph Adams, "An Introduction to Explorations in Anthropology and Theology," in Frank Salamone and Walter R. Adams, eds., *Explorations in Anthropology and Theology* (Lanham, MD: University Press of America, 1997), xi–xii and 1–3; and Bennetta Jules-Rosette, *African Apostles: Ritual and Conversion in the Church of John Maranke* (Ithaca, NY: Cornell University Press, 1975), 15, 22, 207.

Anderson, Indiana (CHOG), a Holiness denomination, has "ordained" women in various ministries from early in its history, with Sarah Smith answering her call in 1882 and Jane Williams bringing her entire African American congregation in Charleston, South Carolina, into the CHOG fold in 1886. However, while "in 1925 women served as pastors of one third of all CHOG congregations," they comprised "only 2% of its senior pastors" in 2002, due to the fact that "pulpit committees refuse to consider women as pastoral candidates and . . . their ordinations [we]re delayed despite a valid call to ministry."[7]

The Assemblies of God (AG) has ordained women since its inception in 1914, and women may aspire to the office of General Superintendent as there is no injunction against a woman holding this highest church office. Still, women are outnumbered at the highest levels of the AG organization.[8]

In the history of the Church of God (Cleveland, Tennessee), founded in 1886, Etta Lamb and Lillian Thrasher (who later joined the AG), pioneered churches at home and abroad, but in 1909 the church banned women's ordination.[9] Today, the church website is clear about its commitment to developing the leadership of men and women. Now

7. Jeannette Flynn, *Go! Preach my Word* (Anderson, IN: Warner Press/Church of God Ministries Inc., 2004), 5, 10–11. The CHOG website states that "since its inception, women have been a vital part of the Church of God movement . . . God has used women and men alike to accomplish his work" (http://www.chog.org/MinistriesandPrograms/WomeninMinistry/tabid/413/Default.aspx, accessed 17 May 2007). Paula Walford, administrative assistant to Reverend Jeannette Flynn, explains Reverend Flynn's office as being one of CHOG's three team directors; the only position above this level is that of the general director, currently held by Dr. Ronald V. Duncan (telephone interview with Paula Walford, 21 May 2007).

8. Reverend Arlene Allen, National Director of the Women's Ministry Department, in her analysis of the status of women in the church, explained that Assemblies of God (AG) church policies provide access to leadership to women across the board, up to and including the highest levels of church governance (telephone interview with Arlene Allen, 17 May 2007). In her 17 May 2007 email, Joy Wootton, Administrative Coordinator to the National Director dates the origin of ordained women's ministry as 1914, adding that men and women hold the same kinds of ministry positions. She also directed me to the website www.WomenInMinistry.ag.org (accessed 17 May 2007), which, among other things, describes strategies to help credentialed women be successful on "dual–gender teams." For more on these topics the reader is directed to the article by Barbara Cavaness within this volume.

9. For more on the Church of God (Cleveland), see the article by David Roebuck in this collection.

women are ordained like men; as "exhorters" and "ministers" but not on the third level, as bishops.[10] The two churches in this study, then, are mined as sources of ethnographic clues to the extreme range of gender practices in these and other spirit-privileging churches.

The case study churches are also described as "Afro-Christian," a concept which is explored at greater length elsewhere.[11] Drawing on Hood's transcontinental and transnational conceptualization of "Black Religion "and "Afro-cultures,"[12] Afro-Christianity, in this study, refers to the way people of Africa and its Diaspora rework symbolic content and institutional forms of Christianity, often within situations of inequitable cultural contact, by wedding, to varying degrees, African and non-African symbolic and ritual content, in ways that reflect an internal logic of intersecting cultural legacy and social adaptation.

The remainder of this paper falls into three parts: The first is an introduction to the case-study churches—their institutional origins, beliefs, and practices. The next section explores how differences in their cultural, historical, and institutional dynamics might inform differences in their gender practices. The paper concludes with a discussion of findings and their implications for addressing women's leadership in spirit-privileging churches.

The Celestial Church of Christ (CCC)

Origin Narrative: The Bush, The Call, and The French

Abandoned and lost, Samuel Oshoffa found himself wandering in "the bush," which he had entered to pursue his trade in ebony wood. When he emerged three months later, he did so as an empowered West African prophet-healer. His visions and miracles attracted loyal followers, and when he returned to Porto Novo, capital of the Republic of Dahomey,

10. "*We commit ourselves to identifying and developing individuals whom God has called and . . . will demonstrate our commitment by:* Creating an environment in which men and women with ministry gifts are developed to serve as servant-leaders" (http://www.churchofgod.cc/about/mission_vision.cfm, accessed 17 May 2007).

11. See Deidre Helen Crumbley, "On Both Sides of the Atlantic: A Transatlantic Assessment of Afro-Christian Independent Church Movements," *Spirit, Structure, and Flesh: Gendered Experiences in African Instituted Churches among the Yoruba of Nigeria* (Madison: University of Wisconsin Press, 2008).

12. See Robert E. Hood, *Must God Remain Greek? Afro Cultures and God-Talk* (Minneapolis: Fortress, 1990), 10, 35–41, 76, 210, 204–5, 208–10.

now Republic of Benin, members of established mission churches, the Aladura, and Muslims congregated around him—some skeptical, some convinced.[13] In 1947, Dahomey was governed by French colonial rulers who were uncomfortable with the potentially destabilizing affect of proliferating indigenous churches. Additionally, established churches tended to be hostile toward Oshoffa, who eventually fled his homeland in 1951, resettling in Nigeria the native land of his mother, and a country where Aladura churches had been proliferating since 1918.[14]

The Celestial Church of Christ (CCC) that Papa Oshoffa introduced into the Nigerian religious landscape was revealed to him on September 29, 1947, in a visionary call to establish a church for "nominal" African Christians who, during crises, abandon Christianity for "pagan" traditional African religions. The gift of "miraculous works of Holy divine healing" and revelation were bestowed on Oshoffa to bring these lost Africans back to Christ.[15] With its skilled and readily available prophets and prophetesses, along with formalized and personalized rituals of purification, healing, and protection, CCC displaced traditional diviners and healers in the lives of Celestial believers. It has since spread from West Africa, into Britain, and throughout both Europe and North America, including the cities of Los Angeles, New York, Dallas, and the Research Triangle of central North Carolina.

Central Beliefs and Practices: Revealed Knowledge— Protecting Power

Celestial doctrine embraces the Christian Trinity of Father, Son, and Holy Ghost, in which Jesus Christ is the redeemer of souls and worker of miracles. God is Creator, who intervenes through the Holy Ghost in the daily life of believers. All aspects of the Celestial Church, including its tenets, are "revealed through the Holy Spirit as promised by our Lord Jesus Christ" (see John 14:25).[16] Each parish has its own local prophets and prophetesses, who undergo varying degrees of training and testing before qualifying for this office. The paramount prophet, however,

13. CCCC, 2–12.

14. A. U. Adogame, *Celestial Church of Christ* (Frankfurt: Lang, 1999), 26; cf. CCCC 4, 13.

15. CCCC, 2.

16. CCCC, 29.

was the pastor-founder Oshoffa, premier conduit of divine knowledge. Therefore, not to comply with Celestial "tenets" as revealed to the founder represents non-compliance with divine revelation, and those who presumed to question or advise the founder were readily asked, "Were you in the bush with me?"—i.e., Did God call you or me to found this church?

Evil is neither denied among Celestial Christians nor ignored. Evil is identified and aggressively resisted through prayer and ritual. The sacred text is literally interpreted, Old and New Testament alike. The menstrual rite in the opening quotation is supported by referencing Old Testament levitical purity rites and the New Testament gospel. Similarly, New Testament wonders performed by Jesus and his disciples are cited to legitimate the miracles of the pastor-founder Oshoffa.[17]

Celestial members are readily identifiable by their "white garments," or "sutana" and by not wearing shoes once they have donned these gowns. Celestial worship is highly formal when compared to the liturgy of other major Aladura churches, such as the Church of the Lord Aladura (CLA) or Christ Apostolic Church (CAC). Still, Spirit is embodied, for while clapping is forbidden, Spirit "shakes" members who may speak in unknown tongues. Spirit also works through the bodies of prophets and prophetesses to reveal future or hidden events in the life of believers. The Celestial compound is a place of holiness, protection, and power, where special prayers are made, for example, by women seeking deliverance from barrenness, and where the vulnerable, such as pregnant women, may repair for "abo" or protection.

Gender Practices: Proclaiming the Gospel—Excluded from the Pulpit

Celestial "tenets" consist of twelve "rules and regulations."[18] Three of the twelve directly address gender. They prohibit men sitting next to

17. CCCC, 31–33.

18. The first eleven tenets are prohibitions against: (1) traditional African religious practices, (2) the use of tobacco products, (3) alcoholic beverages, 4) pork, (5) red and black clothing, (6) wearing shoes within church premises, (7) men sitting next to women within church premises, (8) menstruating women within church premises, (9) women approaching the altar area and leading worship, (10) all colored candles except white, and (11) fornication and adultery. The twelfth is a general exhortation for all members "to be clean in body and in soul."

women in the church, women from the compound when menstruating, and women from the altar area, behind which ordained males sit, at all times.[19] Still, Celestial women are not excluded from all aspects of church life and governance.

Women sit on the parochial committees of their local parish, and the diocesan "General Committee" includes appointed lay members, "one male and one female."[20] Women's organizations and committees also have emerged, and at least one woman has earned the high status and epithet of "right arm" to the pastor, her opinion informing national and international discourse on succession and church unification.[21] Furthermore, while women may not preach within the church, they may do so "outside the sanctuary" and to a congregation of women. Thus, Celestial women members have been on the forefront of pioneering parishes in Africa and abroad.[22]

Furthermore, women may hold church offices or "anointments" and can ascend lay or prophetic hierarchies, rising from the level of "sister" to "superior senior" levels. Similarly, male members rise through either lay or prophetic hierarchies to superior senior levels. At this level, however, the power structures change radically for there are no higher anointments for female members. To rise above this level to that of "evangelist" requires ordination. Since ordination is prohibited to women, only men can become ordained "evangelists" and aspire to the highest office of "pastor" who heads the Celestial Church.

The Church of Prayer Seventh Day (COPSD)

Origins: The Stable, the Call, and the Great Migration

World War II was waging in Europe, as Mother Brown sat alone in the upper room praying for direction in the inner city of Philadelphia. She knew that she had been called to preach as a young woman in Virginia, even though members of her Baptist church told her, "God never called

19. CCCC, 29–30.

20. CCCC, 38–46.

21. See Deidre Helen Crumbley, "Patriarchs, Prophets, and Procreation: Sources of Gender Practices in Three African Churches," *Africa* 73.4 (2003): 584–605, esp. 584; and O. Obafemi, *Life and Times of Papa Oshoffa*, vol. 1 (Nigeria: n.p., 1985), 6.

22. Deidre Helen Crumbley, "Impurity and Power: Women in Aladura Churches," *Africa* 62.4 (1992): 505–22, esp. 509.

a woman to preach." Indomitable, she continued in prayer, alone, in the "little upper room" she had rented above a horse stable in North Philadelphia. One day, she had a vision in which she saw wild goats on the top of a mountain. When they suddenly ran down the mountain and lay at her feet, she knew what this vision meant: God would send her a church.

Shortly thereafter, people began to "come into the church" that grew along matrifocal extended families lines. Mother Brown would be central to the life of the church and the lives of founding members, for more than a teacher, preacher, and healer, she was the mouthpiece of God. As her teachings drew upon the Bible, and the Bible is considered the literal word of God, the authority of scripture conflated with her personal charisma, so that, on the rare occasion she was opposed, she did not hesitate to quote the injunction: "Touch not mine anointed, and do my prophets no harm" (1 Chr 16:22).

Recently arrived from the rural South, the vast majority of "saints," or members, were part of the Great Migration, which would relocate about five million other southern Blacks in industrialized cities like Philadelphia throughout America between 1915 and 1960.[23] With the Great Migration came the spread of the Sanctified Church, an institutionalized legacy of African-derived slave religion valorized by the American Holiness movement.[24] Most of the "saints" or members had been Baptists in the South, but were attracted to Mother Brown's upper room, because, she "taught the Word" and she laid hands on saints to "heal their conditions." The membership of The Church has stabilized at about a hundred adults and children. It remains an unaffiliated institu-

23. Alferdteen Harrison, *Black Exodus: The Great Migration from the American South* (Jackson: University Press of Mississippi, 1991), vii.

24. For details, see Albert J. Raboteau, *Slave Religion: The Invisible Institution in the Ante-bellum South* (New York: Oxford University Press, 1978), 149; Raboteau, "Introduction," in Clifton Johnson, ed., *God Struck Me Dead: Voices of Ex-Slaves* (Cleveland: Pilgrim, 1993), xxiii; Cheryl Sanders, *Saints in Exile: The Holiness-Pentecostal Experience in African American Religion and Culture* (New York: Oxford University Press, 1996), 3–5; Zora Neale Hurston, *The Sanctified Church* (Berkeley: Turtle Island, 1981), 101–5; and Cheryl Townsend Gilkes, "'Together and in Harness': Women's Tradition in the Sanctified Church," in Micheline R. Malson, et al., eds., *Black Women in America: Social Science Perspectives* (Chicago: University of Chicago Press, 1990), 223–44, esp. 228.

tion and has survived the death of the pastor founder who lived to be 105 years old.

Central Beliefs and Practices: The Holy Ghost, the Law, and the Millennium

The Holy Ghost is experienced-spirit. It "fills" the saints and is manifested bodily through shouting—the holy dance of the saints—healing, and tongues. The Old and New Testament are literally interpreted; Jesus is redeemer of a sinful world that is fast approaching the end of time and the coming of the millennium. God, as creator and intervening judge, bestows blessings on commandment-keepers, for although Jesus' self sacrifice is redemptive, "faith without works is dead" (Jas 2:20 KJV).

Worship consists of "pressing through" to receive the Holy Ghost, shouting, and glossolalia. In addition, serious attention is given to communal reading and studying "the Word." Ritual observances include the weekly twenty-four hour Sabbath and annual Passover/ Communion, with foot washing. Traditionally, women and girls wear white dresses with white mantles on their heads, while men and boys wear black suits.

Women at the Helm

Female leadership is both normative and divinely sanctioned in the COPSD. Biblical passages sanctioning women's subordination, e.g., 1 Corinthians 14:34–35, are not avoided, but the passage in Galatians cited above is regularly quoted. While gender is rarely addressed directly, the author grew up conversant with biblical narratives about Deborah the Judge of ancient Israel and New Testament references to Lydia, Priscilla, Eunice, and Lois.

While Mother Brown was advised by female "head saints," and male deacons handled financial matters, she had the final word in all matters. Prior to her death, she also put an organizational structure in place which replaced the pastorate with a "biblically based" dual-governance structure, consisting of an all male "deacon" board responsible for "business" matters and a body of male and female "Elders," responsible for spiritual direction:

> Then the twelve called the multitude of the disciples unto them and said, "It is not reason that we should leave the word of God, and serve tables. Wherefore, brethren, look out among you seven men of honest report full of the Holy Ghost and wisdom, which we may appoint over this business. But we will give ourselves to prayer, and to the ministry of the word." (Act 6:2–4 KJV)

Literalism is applied selectively here, for while the all-male deacon board complies with the "seven men of honest report," the "twelve" apostles, who are male in the biblical text, become a body of male and female "Elders," (who in most cases were spouses and founding church members). The outcome is a male-female power sharing arrangement, nuanced by seniority. Today, the Elders, who range from their seventies to their nineties, consist of more females than males, males having died earlier than their female spouses. Elders are the object of greater deference and status than are deacons. Furthermore, while they "lead" the church "spiritually," Elders also have informal veto power over the deacons' proposals. Thus, they directly affect administrative discourse and decision-making.[25]

Discussion

In addition to their gender practices, the two churches differ in sociocultural legacies, gender of the founder, and institutional scale. One is African, male founded, and global; the other is African American, female founded, and has remained an unaffiliated congregational church. How might these differences inform their differing gender practices?

Gender Legacies—The Aladura Case

For westerners unfamiliar with African gender practices and inundated by persistent images of Africa as dark, dangerous, and backwards, it would be easy to assume that the ritual and administrative constraints on Celestial churchwomen follows naturally from African gender practices. However, the gender practices of the Yoruba people, among whom Aladura churches emerged, have traditionally included women in leadership roles in social, political, and religious spheres. Yoruba women

25. Deidre Helen Crumbley, "Miraculous Mothers, Empowered Sons, and Dutiful Daughters: Gender, Race, and Power in an African American Sanctified Church," *Journal of Anthropology and Humanism* 32.1 (2007): 30–51.

were traditionally free to initiate divorce and to remarry.[26] Domestic and public arenas of mother-wife and entrepreneur overlapped, and women's control of the marketplace fostered financial autonomy.[27] Furthermore, while Yoruba society is virilocal and patrilineal, there is also a tendency among some Yoruba toward bilateral kinship, allowing children to inherit land through the mother.[28]

The term "oba," previously mistranslated "king," is the un-gendered Yoruba word for ruler, some of whom have been female in major Yoruba kingdoms. It should be noted, however, that Yoruba names are largely un-gendered, i.e., Bola can be the name of a male or female, which complicates the process of determining the gender of recorded oba. As *Iyalode*, women have headed the female-dominated marketplace, while directly affecting palace politics.[29] In the religious sphere, the Supreme Being Oludumare is genderless, despite earlier mistranslations of "Oludumare" as Father-God.[30] The *orisa*, or divinities, however, can be

26. Judith Hoch-Smith, "Radical Yoruba Female Sexuality: The Witch and the Prostitute," in Judith Hoch-Smith, et al., eds., *Women in Ritual and Symbolic Roles* (New York: Plenum, 1978), 265–66, and 295.

27. See Dorothy Remy, "Underdevelopment and the Experience of Women: A Nigerian Case Study," in Rayna R. Reiter, ed., *Toward an Anthropology of Women* (New York: Monthly Review Press, 1975), 358–71, esp. 370–71; Niara Sudarkasa, "The 'Status of Women' in Indigenous Africa Societies," in Rosalyn Terborg-Penn, Sharon Harley, and Andrea Benton Rushing, eds., *Women in Africa and the African Diaspora* (Washington, DC: Howard University Press, 1987), 25–39; and Sudarkasa, "Female Employment and family organization in West Africa," in Filomina Chioma Steady, ed., *The Black Women Cross-Culturally* (Cambridge: Schenkman, 1981), 49–63, esp. 49–55.

28. J. S. Eades, *The Yoruba Today* (Cambridge: Cambridge University Press, 1980), 37–38 and 49–50, and J. D. Y. Peel, *Ijeshas and Nigerians: Incorporation of a Yoruba Kingdom 1890's–1970s* (Cambridge: Cambridge Universe Press, 1983), 51–52.

29. On this point, see Oyèrónke Oyewùmí, *The Invention of Women* (Minneapolis: University of Minnesota Press, 1997), 84–91 and 107–12; Eades, *The Yoruba Today*, 99; and LaRay Denzer, "Yoruba Women: A Historiographical Study," *The International Journal of African Historical Studies* 27.1 (1994): 1–39, esp. 10.

30. Oyewùmí, *The Invention of Women*, 136–42; Ifi Amadiume, *Male Daughters, Female Husbands: Gender and Sex in an African Society* (London: Zed, 1987), 123; Mercy Amba Oduyoye, *Daughters of Anowa: African Women and Patriarchy* (Maryknoll, NY: Orbis, 1995), 173–80; J. D. Y. Peel, *Religious Encounter and the Making of the Yoruba* (Bloomington: Indiana University Press, 2000), 119; and Harold Turner, *History of an African Independent Church: The Church of the Lord (Aladura)*, 2 vols. (London: Oxford University Press, 1967), 2:42.

male or female, and they possess both men and women devotees.[31] Not only have Yoruba women been orisa priestesses but also *babalawo*, the priest who serves the paramount Yoruba oracle, *Ifa*.[32]

Such gender practices in West African societies have been described as a "dual-sex" system in which women operate within power arenas that are separate from, but not subordinated to, men's arenas.[33] Traditional Yoruba society, like most, but not all human societies,[34] is not without constraints on women's roles and bodies. Most pre-colonial obas appear to have been male, and female babalawo seem the exception to the rule.[35]

Moreover, traditional menstrual rites required women to avoid holy places and objects when menstruating. Such menstrual rites also have been associated with female subordination and the reassertion of male domination.[36] However, what is significant in the Yoruba case is that the state of "ritual impurity" for women is temporary. Thus, having a female body, with its natural reproductive processes, traditionally did not permanently disqualify Yoruba women from social, political, economic, or religious leadership. In contrast, in the Celestial Church, women are prohibited both from ordination and from the altar area, behind which ordained men are seated. The gender patterns of the Celestial Church, then, diverge sharply from Yoruba tradition rather than simply follow from them.

31. Diedre Badejo, *Osun Seegesi: The Elegant Deity of Wealth, Power, and Femininity* (Trenton, NJ: Africa World Press, 1996), 175–77, and M. T. Drewal, *Yoruba Ritual: Performers, Play, and Agency* (Bloomington: Indiana University Press, 1992), 172–77, 180–86, 190.

32. Karin Barber, *I Could Speak Until Tomorrow: Oriki, Women, and the Past in a Yoruba Town* (Washington, DC: Smithsonian Institution Press, 1991), 103, 288–89.

33. Nkiru Nzegwu, "Gender Equality in a Dual Sex System: The Case of Onitsha," *Canadian Journal of Law and Jurisprudence* 7 (1994): 73–95, esp. 84–95.

34. Shan Shan Du, "'Husband and Wife Do it Together': Sex/Gender Allocation of Labor among the Qhawqhat Lahu of Lancang, Southwestern China," *American Anthropologist* 102.3 (2000): 520–37, and Du, "*Chopsticks Only Work in Pairs": Gender Unity and Gender Equality among the Lahu of Southwest China* (New York: Columbia University Press, 2002), 1–12, 107–35, 185–96.

35. Crumbley, "Patriarchs, Prophets, and Procreation," 591–94.

36. Mary Douglas, *Purity and Danger: An Analysis of the Concepts of Pollution and Taboo* (London: Routledge & Kegan Paul, 1966), 3–4, 35, 113.

The Sanctified Case

The gender dynamics inherited by the saints of COPSD reflects what Gilkes describes as a "dual-sex" West African cultural legacy of normative female leadership, buttressed by the leveling affect of North American racial practices.[37] Chattel slavery in America shifted the control of Black bodies, male and female alike, along with their labor and offspring, to slave owners, thereby undermining Black male and female relationships and requiring Black women to assume leadership roles to maintain their offspring. In the South, after emancipation, the threat and actual rape of Black women reasserted White male dominance, and being female did not exempt them from the racial violence of lynching.[38] Black women entered the labor market to supplement their husband's salaries, diminished by racially-biased hiring and compensation practices. Often working as domestics, Black women dealt with sexual harassment by White men and labor exploitation by White women. Because they were less likely to be fired than their husbands, their steady but low wages were crucial to the economic stability of their families.[39]

Black women's leadership in the economic arena extended to the religious sphere as well. Sanctified Churches, in particular, tended to provide greater opportunities for female leadership than older Black Independent Churches, some of which resisted female ordination until the mid-twentieth century.[40] By the First World War, Sanctified

37. Cheryl Townsend Gilkes, "Together and in Harness"; and Gilkes, "The Politics of Silence: Dual-Sex Political Systems and Women's Traditions of Conflict in African-American Religion," in Paul E. Johnson, ed., *African-American Christianity* (Berkeley: University of California Press, 1994), 80–109.

38. Fifty of 2,522 Black people lynched between 1889 and 1918 were women. Pregnancy did not preclude lynching. See Donna L. Franklin, *What's Love Got to Do with It? Understanding and Healing the Rift between Black Men and Women* (New York: Simon & Schuster, 2000), 124–25 and 152–53, and Jewel L. Prestage, "Political Behavior of American Black Women: An Overview," in La Frances Rodgers-Rose, ed., *The Black Woman* (Beverly Hills, CA: Sage, 1980), 239.

39. Patricia Hill Collins, *Black Feminist Thought: Knowledge, Consciousness, and the Politics of Empowerment* (New York: Routledge, 1991), 49–54; Prestage, "Political Behavior of American Black Women," 238; Judith Rollins, *Between Women: Domestics and Their Employers* (Philadelphia: Temple University Press, 1985), 67–79, 131–55, 162, 186–88, 212–13; and Franklin, *What's Love Got to Do with It?* 152–56.

40. The African Methodist Episcopal Zion (AMEZ), began formally ordaining women as early as 1884, while the African Methodist Episcopal (AME) church did not do so until the 1940s, and the National Baptist Convention, not until 1953. See Jacquelyn

churchwomen like Ida B. Robinson and Bishop Mary Magdalena Lewis Tate were answering the "call" to preach the gospel by starting their own churches.[41] Mother Brown stands in this tradition, leaving her Baptist home church to start the COPSD.

Still, not all Sanctified churches have welcomed women into their ordained ministry, for The Church of God in Christ (COGIC), the largest and oldest institutionalized Sanctified church, has yet to ordain women. Thus, while Mother Brown's leadership follows logically from West African gender legacies reinforced by American racial practices, this does not appear to have happened across the board among Black churches, given the historical resistance to female ordination in Black church history even into the twenty-first century.

Gendered Leadership—The Aladura Case

The Celestial Church was founded by a Yoruba man, raised in a Yoruba area where women were especially successful in an active market region.[42] Female autonomy and a dual-sex gender system would have been normative for him, so why did the gender practices of the church he founded depart so dramatically from them? One explanation is that it reflects the impact of inequitable culture contact. Oshoffa came of age during French colonial rule. The Catholic Church was a strong missionary presence, and at the age of seven he was sent to a Methodist

Grant, "Black Women and the Church," in Johnnetta B. Cole, ed., *All American Women: Lines That Divide, Ties That Bind* (New York: Free Press, 1986), 359–69, esp. 362 and 368; Delores Carpenter, "Black Women in Religious Institutions: A Historical Summary from Slavery to the 1960s," *The Journal of Religious Thought* 46 (1989–90): 7–27, esp. 12 and 18; and William J. Walls, *The African Methodist Episcopal Zion Church: Reality of the Black Church* (Charlotte, NC: AME Zion Publishing, 1974), 48.

41. See Estrelda Alexander, "Gender and Leadership in the Theology and Practice of Three Pentecostal Women Pioneers (Mary Magdalena Lewis Tate, Aimee Semple McPherson, Ida Robinson)," (PhD dissertation, The Catholic University of America, 2003), 78–126; 176–224; Felton Best, "Breaking the Gender Barrier: African–American Women and Leadership in Black Holiness-Pentecostal Churches 1890–Present," in Felton O. Best, ed., *Flames of Fire: Black Religious Leadership From the Slave Community to the Million–Man March* (Lewiston, NY: Mellen, 1998), 153–68, esp. 158–65, 168; and Cheryl Townsend Gilkes, "Some Mother 's Son and Some Father's Daughter: Gender and Biblical Language in Afro–Christian Worship Tradition," in Clarissa W. Atkinson, Constance H. Buchanan, and Margaret R. Miles, eds., *Shaping New Vision: Gender and Values in American Culture* (Ann Arbor: UMI Research Press, 1987), 73–95, esp. 81.

42. Crumbley, "Impurity and Power," 515 and 518.

mission for several years.[43] Neither of these churches had embraced the ordination of women, and colonial educational and hiring practices tended to limit the social latitude of African women, leaving them more dependent on their husbands and outside the pulpit.[44]

Another explanation is that Celestial's gender practices are a consequence of an "unholy alliance" between African and European gender asymmetries intersecting and reinforcing each other.[45] But whether imposed or willingly adopted, constrained female leadership and the gender asymmetry do not necessarily follow from male leadership. For example, Josiah O. Ositelu founded the Church of the Lord—Aladura (CLA), self-described as "Pentecostal in Power," in 1930.[46] From its inception, women functioned in leadership roles, and by 1959 the founder established the ordination of women as "a divine injunction." Additionally, for each male office there is a female office with the same duties and responsibilities.[47] As in the Celestial Church, CLA members comply with menstrual rites. Thus, an ordained female minister on her period does not enter the sanctuary of the parish she heads but manages

43. CCCC, 5.

44. See Karen Armstrong, *Shifting Ground and Cultured Bodies: Postcolonial Gender Relations in Africa and India* (Lanham, MD: University Press of America, 1999), 9; Oyewùmí, *The Invention of Women*, 124–28, 130–35, 150–56; LaRay Denzer, "Domestic Science Training in Colonial Yorubaland, Nigeria," in Karen Tranberg Hansen, ed., *African Encounters with Domesticity* (New Brunswick, NJ: Rutgers University Press, 1992), 117–39, esp. 116–17 and 121, and Denzer, "Yoruba Women," 19–20 and 25–28; A. Mama, *Women's Studies and Studies of Women in Africa During the 1990s* (Senegal: Codesria, 1996), 4, 28, 37, 61–66; Amadiume, *Male Daughters, Female Husbands*, 134–35; R. I. J. Hackett, "Sacred Paradoxes: Women and Religious Plurality in Nigeria," in Y. Y. Haddad and E. B. Findley, eds., *Women, Religion and Social Change* (New York: State University of New York Press, 1985), 248–71, esp. 254–55, 260–63, and 268; Oduyoye, *Daughters of Anowa*, 104 and 172; Karen Sacks, "An Overview of Women and Power in Africa," in J. F. Barr, ed., *Perspectives on Power and Women in Africa, Asia and Latin America* (Durham, NC: Duke University Press, 1982), 1–10, esp. 5–7; and L. N. Predelli, "Marriage in Norwegian Missionary Practice and Discourse in Norway and Madagascar, 1880–1910," *Journal of Religion in Africa* 31.1 (2001): 36–37.

45. E. Schmidt, "Patriarchy, Capitalism, and the Colonial State in Zimbabwe," *Signs: Journal of Women in Culture and Society* 16 (1991): 733–56, esp. 734, 741, and 753–56.

46. Rufus Okikiolaolu Olubiyi Ositelu, *African Instituted Churches* (New Brunswick, NJ: Transaction, 2002), 201.

47. Turner, *History of an African Independent Church*, 2:46, 48; E. S. Sorinmade, *Lecture Delivered to Mark the 10th Anniversary of the Death of Dr. J. O. Oshitelu* (Ake: Abeokuta Nigeria, 1976), 12; and Church of the Lord (CLA) Constitution 2001 (Shagamu, Nigeria: Grace Enterprises, 2001), 10–18 and 60–61.

church affairs through her representative; however, when her period is over, so is the restriction. Compliance with menstrual rites, then, does not necessarily indicate low female status, and a male founder does not necessarily predict male-dominated church hierarchies.[48]

The Sanctified Case

Common sense suggests that a female-founded church sets precedence for and fosters women's leadership. However, a female founder guarantees neither gender egalitarian structures nor a female successor. Ellen White is described as the co-founder of the Seventh Day Adventist (SDA) Church along with James White and Joseph Bates. Nevertheless, her prolific prophetic writings, not theirs, are readily cited during SDA sermons as biblical commentary. After her death in 1915, women's leadership dropped dramatically, and today, while both men and women complete four-year seminary training, women are "commissioned" while males are ordained, and only an "ordained" minister can aspire to be President of the worldwide SDA church.[49]

In the Sanctified tradition, Bishop Tate, mentioned above, founded a very successful Church of the Living God, Pillar and Ground of the Truth, which incorporated women into leadership on every level of the church along with men.[50] Several branches or "dominions" of her

48. Deidre Helen Crumbley, "Power in the Blood: Menstrual Taboos and Female Power in an African Instituted Church," in Marie Griffith and Barbara Savage, eds., *Women and Religion in the African Diaspora* (Baltimore: Johns Hopkins University Press, 2006), 81–97.

49 See Bert Havoliak, "A Place at the Table: Women and the Early Years" (2007), http://www.sdanet.org/atissue/wo/haloviakchapter.htm, and Kit Watts, "Moving Away From the Table: A Survey of Historical Factors Affecting Women Leaders," http://www.sdanet.org/atissue/wo/welcome2.htm (both accessed 8 March 2007).

Heidi Ford, who directs the Women's Resource Center at La Sierra University, a Seventh Day Adventist (SDA) institution, noted that the subject of women's ordination has been raised at the worldwide meeting of church "divisions" from around the world, held every five years. In 1995, the North American Division proposed that female ordination be decided on the division level. It is noteworthy that this was voted down, in large part because those supporting the proposal were outnumbered by delegates from the developing world, where SDA, like many Christian denominations, is growing exponentially and which tends to be socially and theologically conservative (telephone interview, 8 March 2007, with Heidi Ford, Director of the Women's Resource Center, La Sierra University; also see http://www.adventistwomenscenter.org/, accessed 11 May 2007).

50. Alexander, "Gender and Leadership in the Theology and Practice of Three

churches survived her demise, and the largest of these was pioneered by Archibald White, who disapproved of women bishops, the number of which has decreased dramatically over time.[51] While women still are at the helm in the COPSD, the power structure that Mother Brown put in place before her death ended the centralization of power in a sole female leader. Without a formal constitution delineating the process of Elder formation as part of a permanent organizational structure, might another power structure emerge which goes the way of many new religious movements as they become more stable institutions?

Scale, Complexity, and Structuration

Often, as new religious movements become more established, egalitarian tendencies, such as gender equity, are displaced by "structuration"—a return to institutionalized hierarchy.[52] The Celestial Church, within the lifetime of the founder, spread abroad into developed nations. As one church leader observed, such rapid growth made it necessary to "get organized." A written constitution was published in 1980, formalizing the exclusion of women from high office and sacred spaces. However, women are recalled, from its emergence, as falling primarily into two categories—devoted believers and adepts or ritually careless practitioners digressing from protocols of purity and propriety.[53]

Although these representations eventually became institutionalized roles as the church became more organized, it is important to note that structuration is not inevitable. In the Church of the Lord Aladura (CLA) women's leadership roles actually expanded with organizational formalization, menstrual rites not withstanding. Resurgent hierarchy, then, is not inescapable. Regardless of dominant ideologies, social constraints, and cultural legacies, people can and do make choices that favor gender equity. Another example of this is the creative dual govern-

Pentecostal Women Pioneers," 106–13.

51. Ibid., 80, 98, 114–15; and Best, "Breaking the Gender Barrier," 164–65.

52. Victor Turner, *The Ritual Process: Structure and Anti-Structure* (Chicago: Aldine, 1969), 133–35, 139, 153.

53. For example, his elder sister Elizabeth Ekundayo became one of his earliest followers after he raised her son from the dead, and his wife Yaman not only accompanied Oshoffa on his evangelical outreach, but received a divine visitation. However, in contrast to these images of devotion, there are narratives of women castigated for being on their periods in the sanctuary and for not donning the white sutana (see Crumbley, "Impurity and Power," 505; and CCCC 2, 7, 14, 18, 22).

ing structure that Mother Brown put in place before her death, in which men and women share power, and age is venerated.

Conclusion: Interpretation and Implications

This essay poses a two-part question: How might socio-cultural legacy, leadership, and institutional complexity inform the antithetical gender practices of the case study churches, and what strategies might this suggest for addressing women's leadership in other spirit-privileging churches? First, it is clear that socio-cultural legacies, leadership style, and organizational scale inform gender practices, but in very complicated and sometimes surprising ways. A cultural legacy of women-inclusive leadership, whether integral to traditional culture in the case of the Yoruba, or buttressed by structural racism in the United States, fails to predict or preclude female leadership. Secondly, a female founder guarantees neither gender equity nor female succession, and a male founder does not predict male dominated structures. Finally, while structuration may tend toward re-engendered hierarchies, these can be preempted by the imponderables of human agency. These findings preclude simplistic conclusions and make a strong case for careful ethnographic attention to detail, especially of unfamiliar gender practices, such as those that certainly will inform the twenty-first century Pentecostal and charismatic movement as it rapidly expands among developing people of the global South and among those living as minoritized groups within developed nations.

In addition to providing a heuristic for assessing gender practices in a globalizing church, and beyond a caveat against overgeneralizations, the ethnographic clues provided above also point to a thematic relationship that has consequences for policy formation. This relationship derives not from an exploration of differences between the churches but rather of what they have in common. I refer here to the tendency of spirit-privileging churches toward biblical literalism and the valuing of divine revelation. Both Mother Brown and Papa Oshoffa were highly venerated for their charismatic gifts. To their church members, they were divine mouthpieces, speaking for God through literally interpreted Holy Scripture revealed to them through the Holy Spirit.

Thus, their gender practices, though extremely different, are legitimated by the authority of their charismatic leaders' holy pronouncements from the same literally interpreted Bible. Biblical literalism, however, is selective, if only because biblical content reflects over two millennia of Judeo-Christian sacred text production and translation, filtered through diverse cultural lenses. In spirit-privileging churches, selective literalism has the potential to liberate or constrain women's leadership—or both, depending on the exercise of human imagination and agency. When the tongues have quieted and the shouting has died down, when the heady days of revival gives way to church-building, the saints are faced with the same challenges that face all human beings—namely, how to regularize relationships, divide work, and apportion resources in day-to-day life. There is a tendency for new movements to reintroduce hierarchy as they become more formalized, but institution-alized inequity is not inevitable.

Spirit-privileging churches offer at least two gifts to World Christianity. One is the democratization of mysticism, which transforms all believers into "saints" and makes intense experiences of divine intimacy normative rather than the exception to the rule. Another is the pre-eminence of on-going divine revelation over fixed canons, church disciplines, and by-laws. The element of revitalization, usually limited to the early stages of a religious movement, is incorporated into the core of Pentecostalism by its spirit-driven critique of mere religiosity. While formal structures are essential to institutional sustainability, in churches where the Spirit is the ultimate authority, rules—including gender rules—are subject to inspired reformulation.

To embrace intimate experience of Spirit is to claim the power to challenge dominant ideologies. This is what Holiness and Pentecostal Christians did when they first broke with established churches in late nineteenth century America. In the intervening century that counter-culture vitality has waned, but it need not disappear, and with it the brightest and the best churchwomen. The challenge to sprit-privileging churches in the twenty-first century is to reclaim the Spirit of resistance to social injustice. As Jeannette Flynn, one of the three directors of the Church of God (Anderson) writes:

> If the wind of the Spirit blew the church to commitment and practices that disregarded the cultural norms of society that was fine with those early pioneers. Conformity to the dominant culture was no match for conformity to Christ and his leadership of a church that indeed imagined a new way of being the people

of God . . . Will we have the imagination, courage and grace to
follow where they led?[54]

54. Flynn, *Go! Preach my Word*, 12.

6

"Third Class Soldiers"

A History of Hispanic Pentecostal Clergywomen in the Assemblies of God

Gastón Espinosa[1]

Introduction

> Rev. J. Roswell Flower: I am appealing to the Executive
> Presbytery of the Assemblies of God, because of the rejection of
> my application for ordination with the Spanish Eastern District
> [Council of the Assemblies of God]. The rejection was a com-
> plete violation of the constitution of the Assemblies of God,
> Article VI, section 4, part B. I met all the requirements of our
> Credential Committee and had the full backing and blessing
> of every Official of my District, but because of pure prejudice
> against the ministry of women, I was rejected . . .

AIMEE GARCÍA CORTESE PROTESTED HER SHODDY TREATMENT IN
July 1958. After a long and drawn out struggle, she was finally ordained
to the ministry by the Spanish Eastern District in 1962, but only after
Anglo-American leaders put pressure on the District to do so.[2] In spite
of a long history of ordaining women to the ministry in the Assemblies

1. The author wishes to acknowledge and thank The Pew Charitable Trusts, Virginia
Brereton, and Margaret Bendroth, and the Steering Committee members of the Women
and Twentieth Century Protestantism Project for their generous support in the research
and writing of this article.
2. Aimee García Cortese, letter to Rev. J. Roswell Flower, 11 July 1958, in possession
of the author.

of God, Rev. Cortese was rejected for no other reason than that she was a woman. Cortese's struggle captures the dilemma that many Latinas have faced in the eight Latin District Councils of the Assemblies of God.

While there is a small but growing body of literature on the important roles of Anglo and Black Pentecostal women, we know virtually nothing about the history and contributions that women like Aimee García Cortese made to Latino Pentecostalism. Furthermore, the little that has been written on Latina women in religion has tended to focus on Catholicism or Mainline Protestantism.[3] Women did play an important role in the origins and development of the Latino Pentecostal movement, which is the largest segment of Latino Protestantism today. The Hispanic Churches in American Public Life National Survey found that 23 percent of all U.S. Latinos self-identified as Protestant or other Christian and that 64 percent of all Latino Protestants are Pentecostal or Charismatic.[4]

3. See for example, Ada María Isasi-Díaz and Yolanda Tarango, *Hispanic Women: Prophetic Voice in the Church* (Minneapolis: Fortress, 1992); Ada María Isasi-Díaz, *En La Lucha, In the Struggle: A Women's Liberation Theology* (Minneapolis: Fortress, 1993); Jeanette Rodríguez, *Our Lady of Guadalupe: Faith and Empowerment among Mexican–American Women* (Austin: University of Texas Press, 1994); Ada María Isasi-Díaz, "The Cultural Identity of the Latina Woman: The Cross–Disciplinary Perspective of Mujerista Theology," in Anthony M. Stevens-Arroyo and Gilbert R. Cadena, eds., *Old Masks, New Faces: Religion and Latino Identities* (New York: Bildner Center for Western Hemisphere Studies, 1995), 93–116; Ada María Isasi-Díaz, "'Apuntes' for a Hispanic Women's Theology of Liberation," *Apuntes: Reflexiones Teológicas desde el Margen Hispano* 6.3 (1986): 61–71; and Minerva Garza Carcaño, "Una perspectiva bíblico-teológica sobre la mujer en el ministerio ordenado," in Justo L. González, ed., *Voces: Voices from the Hispanic Church* (Nashville: Abingdon, 1992), 24–31 and 112–21. For articles on Latina Protestantism see, Minerva N. Garza, "The Influence of Methodism on Hispanic Women Through Women's Societies," *Methodist History* (January 1996): 78–89; Jill Martínez, "Worship and the Search for Community in the Presbyterian Church (U.S.A.): The Hispanic Experience," *Church and Society* (March/April 1986): 42–46; and Denis Lynn Daly Heyck, *Barrios and Borderlands: Cultures of Latinos and Latinas in the United States* (New York: Routledge, 1994). See my biographical articles on Nellie Bazán, Francisca Blaisdell, Aimee Cortese, Juana García Peraza (a.k.a. Mita), Leoncia Rosado (a.k.a. Mama Leo), Chonita Morgan Howard, and Romanita Carbajal Valenzuela in Stanley Burgess, ed., *The New International Dictionary of Pentecostal and Charismatic Movements* (Grand Rapids: Zondervan, 2002)—hereafter *NIDPCM*.

4. I use the term "Latino(a)" as an inclusive umbrella term that includes, unless otherwise noted, any person of Mexican, Puerto Rican, and Latin American descent living in the United States. Gastón Espinosa, Virgilio Elizondo, and Jesse Miranda, *Hispanic Churches in American Public Life: Summary of Findings* (Notre Dame, IN: Institute for Latino Studies, University of Notre Dame, 2003), 14–16.

This article examines the uphill struggle women in ministry in the U.S. Latino Pentecostal movement. More specifically, it examines the history and contributions of women in the ordained and lay ministry in the Latino Assemblies of God. This study suggests that although the Latin District Council was founded in the U.S. Southwest in 1915, only one year after the General Council of the Assemblies of God was founded in Hot Springs, Arkansas, in 1914, it took a very different trajectory concerning the role of women in the ordained ministry in the twentieth-century than did its parent organization. While the Assemblies of God has licensed or ordained Latinas to serve as evangelists, missionaries, and pastors since at least 1916, it never witnessed the kind of Golden Age of women in ministry that Charles Barfoot and Gerald Sheppard describe in their germinal article, "Prophetic vs. Priestly Religion: The Changing Role of Women Clergy in Classical Pentecostal Churches."[5]

5. Charles H. Barfoot and Gerald T. Sheppard, "Prophetic vs. Priestly Religion: The Changing Role of Women Clergy in Pentecostal Churches," *Review of Religious Research* 22 (1980): 2–17. The dichotomy between the prophetic and priestly should not be overdrawn. Clearly within most Pentecostal traditions there are elements of both. Furthermore, even in those denominations which allow women a prophetic voice, Edith Blumhofer has correctly pointed out that this voice is often muzzled or relegated to the margins. While I do not agree with all that Barfoot and Sheppard suggest, I do believe that their terminology and distinction between the prophetic and priestly is helpful in comparing and contrasting women's roles in the Apostolic Assembly of the Faith in Christ Jesus and the Latin American District Council of the Assemblies of God. For discussions of Anglo and Black women in Pentecostalism see Edith Blumhofer, "The Role of Women in the Assemblies of God," *A/G Heritage* (Winter 1987–88): 13–17; Edith Blumhofer, *Restoring the Faith: The Assemblies of God, Pentecostalism, and American Culture* (Urbana: University of Illinois Press, 1993), 174–75; Elaine J. Lawless, *Handmaidens of the Lord: Pentecostal Women Preachers and Traditional Religion* (Philadelphia: University of Pennsylvania Press, 1988); Elaine J. Lawless, *God's Peculiar People: Women's Voices & Folk Tradition in a Pentecostal Church* (Lexington: University of Kentucky Press, 1988); R. Marie Griffiths, *God's Daughters: Evangelical Women and the Power of Submission* (Berkeley: University of California Press, 1997); Edith L. Blumhofer, *Aimee Semple McPherson: Everybody's Sister* (Grand Rapids: Eerdmans, 1996); Peter Goldsmith, "A Woman's Place is in the Church: Black Pentecostalism on the Georgia Coast," *Journal of Religious Thought* 46 (Winter–Spring 1989–90): 53–69; Cheryl Sanders, *Saints in Exile: The Holiness-Pentecostal Experience in African American Religion and Culture* (New York: Oxford University Press, 1996); Cheryl Gilkes, "'Together and in Harness': Women's Traditions in the Sanctified Church," *Signs: Journal of Women in Culture and Society* 10 (Summer 1985): 678–99; Cheryl Gilkes, "The Role of Women in the Sanctified Church," *Journal of Religious Thought* 43 (Spring–Summer 1986): 24–41; Susie Stanley, "The Promise of the Father: Women Called to Minister," *Evangelical Journal* 12 (Spring 1994): 35–40; Pearl Williams-Jones, "A

There was no great reversal in the accumulation of power or right to ordination for Latinas in the early twentieth-century such as there was in Anglo-American Pentecostalism. Instead, the history of Latinas in ministry is long but checkered. Latinas have faced an uphill struggle against gender discrimination and the right to full ordination. Pentecostal women have practiced a kind of paradoxical domesticity whereby they are exhorted to be end-times prophetesses in the public sphere and devoted mothers and good wives in the private sphere. Despite the seemingly paradoxical lives they live, Pentecostal women are, by their own accounts, "liberated." In general, the Trinitarian Latino Pentecostal movement has adopted a more prophetic attitude (openness to women preachers and leadership over men) toward women in ministry that has been shaped by the degree of institutional acculturation, education, and cultural orientation to U.S. values and gender roles. As the cultural orientation of Latino Pentecostalism has changed, so too has its attitude towards women. This study is based on original primary and secondary research in Spanish and English sources and a dozen interviews. Most of the names of the informants have been changed to protect their anonymity.

The practice of ordaining women in the Latin District Council of the Assemblies of God is an outgrowth of the larger Anglo Assemblies of God's position on the role of women in ministry. The Anglo Assemblies of God technically takes a prophetic view of women in ministry and allows women to be ordained to the ministry.[6] The founder of the Latin District Councils, Henry C. Ball, adopted this prophetic view of women in ministry when he began his work in south Texas. On July 4, 1915, he introduced nine Mexicans to the baptism in the Holy Spirit in Ricardo,

Minority Report: Black Pentecostal Women," *Spirit: A Journal of Issues Incident to Black Pentecostalism* 1 (1977): 31–44; James Shopshire, "A Socio–historical Characterization of the Black Pentecostal Movement in America" (PhD dissertation, Northwestern University, 1975); and Melvin Williams, *Community in a Black Pentecostal Church: An Anthropological Study* (Pittsburgh: University of Pittsburgh Press, 1974).

6. Although this has not always been the case. There is considerable evidence that indicates that many men wanted women's roles restricted in the Assemblies of God. See, for example, "A Timely Word," *The Pentecostal Evangel* (15 September 1923): 9, and Minutes of the Fifteenth Annual Session of the Arkansas-Louisiana District Council of the Assemblies of God, 1927, 12. For a discussion of the origins of the Assemblies of God in the U.S. see Edith Blumhofer, *The Assemblies of God: A Chapter in the Story of American Pentecostalism, Volume 1—To 1941* (Springfield, MO: Gospel Publishing, 1989).

Texas.[7] This event reportedly gave birth to the Latin District Council of the Assemblies of God in the U.S.

The first Assemblies of God women to effectively minister among Latinos in the United States were Anglo-American. Alice E. Luce, Sunshine Marshall, Florence Murcutt, Carrie Judd Montgomery, and many others ministered to Latinos in the U.S. Southwest, Mexico, and Puerto Rico from 1912 to the 1940s. The most important Anglo-American woman to pioneer the work among Latinos in the U.S. was Alice E. Luce. A former British Episcopalian missionary to India, Luce was converted to Pentecostalism in India and later felt called to minister to the Spanish-speaking in Mexico and the United States. In 1915, Luce and her friend Sunshine Marshall met Henry C. Ball in south Texas and were ordained to the ministry. They, like Ball, were interested in ministering to Mexicans and had planned to set up a Pentecostal work in Monterrey, Mexico. After the bloody Mexican Revolution (1911–17) thwarted their stay in Monterrey, they began to help Ball with his evangelistic work among the Mexicans living in Texas.[8]

Luce pioneered the Latin District Council work in Los Angeles in 1918 by renting a hall in the Mexican Plaza District in Los Angeles, where Rosa and Abundio López of Azusa Street Revival fame had preached 12 years earlier. She began conducting evangelistic services along with a Jewish convert named Rev. Florence Murcutt. Their work was difficult, not only because Mexicans followed the seasonal harvests, but also because the Oneness Apostolic Assembly of the Faith in Christ Jesus, Inc., had already established itself in southern California and was reportedly undermining their work.[9] Despite the difficulties she faced as a pioneer Anglo woman ministering in Mexican Los Angeles, she conducted open-air evangelistic services, Bible studies, organized testimonials, taught Sunday School, and led door-to-door evangelism, prayer for the sick, and tract ministry.[10] Luce represents one of the clearest examples of a prophetic woman's life in early Pentecostalism.

---

7. Victor De León, *The Silent Pentecostals* (Taylors, SC: Faith Publishing, 1979), 42.

8. De León, *Silent Pentecostals*, 21, 46–47.

9. Alice E. Luce, Missionary File (1920).

10. De León, *Silent Pentecostals*, 19–23, 47.

Latina Assemblies of God Women in the Prophetic Ministry

Alice Luce, Sunshine Marshall Ball, and other Anglo-American women like Aimee Semple McPherson (who was ordained in the Assemblies of God) served as role models for Latina Pentecostal women in ministry. Although they laid the foundation for women's prophetic ministry, the number of Latinas that have followed their example has been, until recently, relatively small. Despite their small numbers and in contrast to the Barfoot/Shepherd thesis of a Golden Age of women in the early Pentecostal ministry, the documentary evidence indicates that there have always been licensed and/or ordained Hispanic women actively ministering in the Assemblies of God. In fact, the numbers and percentages are growing and at an all-time high.[11]

The first Latina we know for certain that was ordained by the Assemblies of God was Dionicia Feliciano. She and her husband Solomon were ordained in California in July 1916. She went on to help pioneer the Assemblies of God work in California, Puerto Rico, and the Dominican Republic. She was joined in her evangelistic work in Puerto Rico by Isabel Lugo, who herself was ordained in 1920. They were soon joined in the larger Puerto Rican work by other women like María Teresa Sapia and Julia and Matilde Vargas. The Vargas' patterned their evangelistic healing services after the famous faith-healing evangelist Francisco Olazábal and dressed like Aimee Semple McPherson, with her characteristic cape and upheld hand—symbolic of calling on sinners to come to the altar and repent.[12]

As Isabel and Juan Lugo and Solomon and Dionicia Feliciano pioneered the Assemblies of God work in Puerto Rico in 1916, Ball, Marshall and Luce's work with Rodolfo Orozco in the American Southwest and northern Mexico in 1915 resulted in the ordination of a number of Mexican American women such as Nellie Bazán, Francisca Blaisdell, Chonita Morgan Howard, Natividad Nevarez, and others.

11. In addition to the women mentioned in this section, we know that the following Latinas were credentialed by the Assemblies of God: Isabel Lugo (1920), Mary J. Inostroza (1930), Francisca Blaisdell (1937), Elvira Perales (1956), Josephine López (1956), Rachel Ortíz (1955), Bertha García (1956), and Rebecca Ortíz (1955). This is by no means a comprehensive list.

12. David Ramos Torres, *Historia De La Iglesia De Dios Pentecostal, M.I.* (Río Piedras, Puerto Rico: Editorial Pentecostal, 1992), 46.

Most of these women worked alongside of their husbands and served as co-pastors.[13]

Rev. Manuelita (Nellie) Treviño Bazán (1895–1995) was one of the first Mexican American women to be ordained to the Pentecostal ministry in the United States. Like many other husband-wife teams, both she and her husband were ordained together in 1920. She ministered along with her husband Demetrio in Texas, New Mexico, and Colorado, where she regularly preached from the pulpit at least 30 times a year and conducted door-to-door evangelistic work. She also wrote her own autobiography, *Enviados de Dios*, wrote regular articles for *La Luz Apostólica* (the Latin District Assemblies of God monthly periodical), composed poetry, and raised ten children. She herself planted three churches in Texas and New Mexico during her 75-year ministry. While she was allowed to exercise her prophetic ministry on a regular basis, she was also expected to submit to her husband's spiritual authority at home. As at the Azusa Street Revival itself, women's roles in the Latino Assemblies were somewhat paradoxical—women were exhorted to exercise their prophetic gifts in the public sphere but submit to their husband's authority in the private sphere of the home. Early Latino Pentecostals did not believe the point of the prophetic gifts was to erase gender distinctions, but rather to empower men and women for Christian service in the end-time drama in which they found themselves actors. This kind of paradoxical domesticity has remained the norm for Latina Pentecostal women throughout much of the twentieth-century.[14]

Rev. Nellie Bazán was soon joined by another pioneer evangelist that worked in Arizona and northern Mexico named Francisca

13. I have been unable to locate Francisca Blaisdell's maiden name. But see Lillian Valdez and Berta Garcia, "Historia," *La Luz Apostolica* (August 1967): 3; C. Morgan Howard, "Historia De Los Primeros 50 Años De Las Asambleas De Dios," *La Luz Apostolica* (September 1967): 7; Nellie T. Bazán, "Historia: 50 Años De Cristiana y De Ministerio Cristiano," *La Luz Apostolica* (December 1967): 7–8.

14. Gastón Espinosa, "Bazán, Nellie," in *NIDPCM*, 368; Nellie Bazán with Elizabeth B. and Don Martínez, Jr., *Enviados De Dios: Demetrio and Nellie Bazan* (Miami: Editorial Vida, 1987). The material for this section draws from this autobiography and an interview I conducted with her son and daughter-in-law, Alex and Anita Bazan, Vista, California, November 1996. See also Nellie T. Bazán, "Historia: 50 Años De Cristiana y De Ministerio Cristiano," *La Luz Apostolica* (December 1967): 7–8; Nellie T. Bazán, "Historia de Los Primeros 50 Años De Dios: Segunda Parte De Mi Testimonio," *La Luz Apostolica* (November 1967): 7–8; Nellie T. Bazán, "Historia de Los Primeros 50 Años De Dios: Conclusion," *La Luz Apostolica* (January 1968): 8–9.

D. Blaisdell (ca. 1885–1941). The Mexican American Blaisdell began preaching the Pentecostal message in Mexico in 1915 and was later ordained an Assemblies of God missionary-evangelist by Ball and Juan Lugo in 1923. She, along with her Anglo husband, Rev. George Blaisdell, pioneered evangelistic work along the Arizona-Mexican border in Douglas, Arizona, and Nacozari, Sonora, Mexico. Around 1922, Francisca helped organize the first women's group in Agua Prieta, Sonora, Mexico. She is important not only because she was one of the first evangelists to pioneer the Pentecostal work in the U.S. and Mexico, but also because she pastored churches in Douglas, Arizona, Agua Prieta, Sonora, Mexico (1932–33, 1938–39), and El Paso, Texas (1933–35). In these churches, she preached to 40–80 Mexican parishioners every Sunday morning and evening and two or three times a week. Along with her regular work in Arizona and Mexico, she conducted evangelistic tours, often by horseback, throughout northern Mexico and the U.S. Southwest.[15]

Like Francisca Blaisdell, Concepción (Chonita) Morgan Howard (1898–1983) was a Mexican American whose father was an Anglo, and mother a Mexican.[16] Chonita was converted to Pentecostalism in 1913 in the small mining town of San José de las Playitas, Sonora, Mexico. She was a pioneer Latina Pentecostal evangelist, pastor, and women's leader in the U.S. and Mexico. Not long after her conversion and baptism with the Holy Spirit in 1913, she felt called to the ministry and traveled the dusty evangelistic trail on horseback in northern Mexico and Arizona preaching the Pentecostal message. She eventually traveled to California where she came under the influence of George and Carrie Judd Montgomery, who had attended the Azusa Street Revival in 1907 and were responsible for bringing the Pentecostal work to Sonora. Under their influence, she began evangelistic work in the U.S. around 1915. In 1919, she met and married a young Anglo Pentecostal preacher named Lloyd Howard, who was pastoring a small group of Mexicans in the border town of Pirtleville, Arizona. In 1928, the Assemblies of God

15. Gastón Espinosa, "Blaisdell, Francisca," in *NIDPCM*, 432; De León, 146–47; Annual Questionnaire for Ordained Preachers in the Assemblies of God (1930s); Sunshine L. Ball, "Historia: Yo Me Acuerdo," *La Luz Apostolica* (October 1968): 9.

16. The information on Chonita Morgan comes from De Leon, 146–48, Espinosa, "Morgan Howard, Concepcion (Chonita)," in *NIDPCM*, 907–8, her ordination application form, and additional information contained in her minister's file.

recognized her evangelistic work and ordained her as an evangelist to the Mexicans living along the Arizona-Mexican border. In addition to her pastoral and evangelistic work, she served as the second president (after Sunshine Marshall Ball) of the Women's Missionary Council (*Concilio Misionero Femenil*) from 1941 to 1962. Chonita conducted pioneer evangelistic work in California, Arizona, New Mexico, and Sonora, Mexico, from 1915 to 1968. From 1966 to 1968, she pastored Betel Asamblea de Dios in Douglas, Arizona. Her fifty-three year pioneer ministry touched the lives of thousands of Latinas and helped establish the AG work on both sides of the U.S.-Mexican border.

Although most of the women credentialed during the early period, were licensed as evangelists, there were cases of Latinas actually ordained as pastors. Natividad Nevarez, for example, was ordained a "pastor" in 1937 in Los Angeles, where she served as co-pastor of the famous Aposento Alto church. María Inostroza was ordained in the early 1930s and pastored churches in the 1940s and 1950s.[17]

The pioneer evangelistic work of Mexican American and Anglo women in the U.S. served as a source of inspiration to Pentecostal women in Mexico. Ana Sanders was one of the first women to pioneer the Assemblies of God work in Mexico City in 1921.[18] She dedicated the rest of her life pioneering the work in Mexico. By 1928, her prophetic work along with that of Chonita Howard, Francisca Blaisdell, and others inspired Mexicans to go into the ministry.[19] Together, these women helped pioneer the AG work in Mexico.

Despite the fact that Latinas have been ordained in the AG since at least 1916, prior to World War II it was uncommon for a single woman to pastor her own church or even be ordained to the pastoral ministry. More often than not, women were licensed rather than ordained and served alongside their husbands, as interim pastors, or as pastors of small congregations. While other Latinas were ordained from 1916 to the 1970s in low numbers, there was a sharp increase in the number of ordained women in the Latino Assemblies of God beginning in the

17. Ministerial files for Natividad Nevarez and Maria Inostroza (in possession of the author).

18. Luisa Jeter de Walker, *Siembra y Cosecha: Reseña histórica de las Asambleas de Dios de México y Centroamérica, Tomo 1* (Deerfield, FL: Vida, 1990), 19–20.

19. Minutes of the District Council of the Assemblies of God of Texas and New Mexico, June 1928, 34–36.

early 1980s.[20] The exact reason for this shift is unclear. There is little doubt, however, that the progressive tendency of a new generation of leaders like Rev. Jesse Miranda has much to do with this trend.

The problems that Latinas have historically faced in ministry in the Latin District Council in the latter half of the twentieth-century are illustrated by the story of Rev. Aimee García Cortese. Born to Puerto Rican parents in New York in 1929, Rev. Cortese was converted, along with her parents, in a small Spanish-speaking Pentecostal storefront church in the early 1940s. Reacting against the legalism she saw in this church, she got involved with a Lutheran and then a Methodist church, before returning to the Latin District Council. She was given an exhorter's certificate in 1947 and licensed to preach in 1951. She later attended the A.G. sponsored Instituto Biblico Hispano in New York City and Central Bible College of the Assemblies of God in Springfield, Missouri. A year after her graduation in 1957, she sought ordination from the Spanish Eastern District in New York. As noted earlier, her request for ordination was denied for no other reason than that she was a woman. Only after Anglo–American leaders in Springfield intervened and put pressure on the District did it finally ordain Cortese in 1962, making her the first woman ordained by the Spanish Eastern District.

It was precisely her cultural orientation towards Springfield and contact with Anglo-American leaders that provided her with the leverage and denominational clout that enabled her to scale some of the barriers of sexism in the late 1950s and early 1960s. Her active ministry has touched the lives of thousands, yet the gender bias still rampant in the Latin District Council initially made it difficult for her to find a job as pastor.

Because "no one's looking for a female pastor," Cortese founded her own church, Crossroads Tabernacle, in 1982 in the Bronx. "If you want to get a church you have to start your own," Rev. Cortese stated. Yet, rather than remain bitter against the Spanish District, in my interview with her in the 1990s she said she held no grudges against the A.G. or the District. Her ministry in the south Bronx met with phenomenal

20. It is virtually impossible to know exactly how many Latinas have been credentialed by the Assemblies of God because they could have been credentialed through a numbers of means including Latin Districts, Anglo Districts, as a home missionary, and as a foreign missionary. Furthermore, many of the files at these places and offices are incomplete.

success and has grown from 37 people in 1982, to 1,500 every week, making it one of the largest Latino churches in New York. The gender bias and discrimination she has faced in the Spanish District is slowly abating, she stated.[21] Today there are a growing number of women like Rev. Cortese, Rev. Julie Ramírez, and Rev. Julia Hernández pastoring very large Latin District Council churches in the U.S.[22]

The attitudes that Pentecostal women faced was perhaps best summed up by Leoncia Rosado Rousseau, or "Mama Leo" as she is better known, when she stated: "we women were treated as third class soldiers by some of our male counterparts."[23] This prompted some women to create their own female-led denominations. Despite a guarded openness to prophetic women's voices in the Assemblies of God, Latinas who really wanted to preach and have true autonomy and freedom prior to 1960 had to leave the AG. No one better illustrates this than "Mama Leo" herself. She co-found the Damascus Christian Church denomination in New York City in the late 1930s. In 1957, she pioneered one of the first church-sponsored drug-rehabilitation programs in the United States through the Damascus Youth Crusade. Other Puerto Rican women like Juana García Peraza left the AG work on the island of Puerto Rico in 1942 to found her own denomination, Mita Congregation. This denomination, like Mama Leo's work, sponsored a wide range of social programs and targeted at-risk youth and economically impoverished families.[24] Still other Latinas like Rev. Aurora Chavez in the Southwest helped found Spanish-speaking Pentecostal denominations like Concilio La Peña de Horeb, which granted greater autonomy to women. Rev. Chavez conducted "marvelous" evangelistic healing crusades in Los Angeles and throughout the Southwest in the

21. Rev. Aimee Cortese, telephone interview by Gastón Espinosa, South Bronx, NY, March 1998. Virginia Sánchez Korrol, "In Search of Unconventional Women Histories of Puerto Rican Women in Religious Vocations Before Mid–century," in Denis Lynn Daly Heyck, ed., *Barrios and Borderlands: Cultures of Latinos and Latinas in the United States* (New York: Routledge, 1994), 141–51.

22. Julie Ramírez, "He Who Does Not Work Shall Not Eat" (July 1978): 21.

23. Gastón Espinosa, telephone interview with Leoncia Rosado Rousseau, Santa Barbara, CA, fall 1996.

24. For a further discussion of Juana García Peraza and Mita Congregation see my articles on her and the denomination she founded in Puerto Rico in *NIDPCM*, 659, 901. Also see Torres, *Historia De La Iglesia De Dios Pentecostal*, 126–31.

1950s. Reflecting the influence of Aimee Semple McPherson, she wore a cape and held evangelistic healing services throughout the U.S.[25]

Congruent with Edith Blumhofer's findings, while the Latin District Council has officially ordained women for most of the twentieth-century, they have discretely kept women out of key pastoral and administrative positions until just recently.[26] Women who did pastor churches often did so in small churches or missions where men were unwilling to go.[27] While these moves can be interpreted as genuine gestures of gender and racial inclusivity, they can also be interpreted as a safe way to theoretically include women that would never be a real threat to the male leadership of the AG because they could never garner the nation-wide support needed to be elected or make any serious structural changes.

Despite the difficulties that women like Cortese and others have faced, the Latin District Council has turned a new leaf, at least in the area of credentialing women. By the 1990's, the Spanish Eastern District, which once gave Cortese so many problems, had one of the highest percentages of credentialed and ordained women in the Assemblies of God. Overall denominational statistics indicate that the number of Latinas credentialed to the prophetic ministry was significantly higher than the average for Anglo women nation-wide. The total number of Latina clergy (ordained, licensed, and certified) in the AG increased from 624 in 1990 to 741 in 1997. The number of Latinas fully ordained in the AG almost doubled, going from 8 in 1990 to 141 in 1997. While women made up 15.8 percent of all credentialed ministers in Anglo Assemblies of God in 1995, they made up 24.8 percent of all credentialed ministers in the eight Latin Districts.[28] The AG now claims more Latina clergy than any other denomination in the U.S., including the United Methodist Church—which had around 100 in 1998.

25. Rev. Aurora Chávez, "Gran Campaña De Salvación y Sanidad Divina," flier with picture (August 1957); flier in possession of the author.

26. In the 1980s Latinas began to be elected presbyters to the Latin District Councils. Edith Blumhofer, "The Role of Women in the Assemblies of God," *A/G Heritage* (Winter 1987–88): 13–17, and Blumhofer, *Restoring the Faith*, 174–75.

27. This is also true for Anglo Pentecostal women ministers; see Lawless, *Handmaidens of the Lord*, 11.

28. Sherri L. Doty, Office of Statistician of the General Council of the Assemblies of God, Ministers' Marital Status/Gender Summary, 1–2.

However, these figures are deceptively high because if you examine the number of women actually ordained as pastors or serving as co-pastors and senior pastors, the numbers drop significantly. However, they do indicate that women in the Latin District Council are moving into greater prophetic roles as officially recognized clergy, even if the percentage and raw number of female senior pastors is significantly lower than their male counterparts.

Women, Theological Education, and Spanish-language Bible Institutes

Women in the Assemblies of God have not only been allowed to exercise their prophetic role in the credentialed ministry, they have also been able to receive ministerial theological training traditionally closed to them in Catholic and in many Protestant denominations in the U.S. prior to the 1950s.[29] The theological and ministerial training that women received at the Bible institutes has opened many otherwise closed doors to the ministry with opportunities to teach at these same institutes and to write for Spanish-language periodicals such as *La Luz Apostólica* and *The Word.*[30]

The AG Bible Institutes have provided Latinas an alternative professional route to the normal option of mothering by giving them the opportunity to acquire theological training and to nurture and eventually exercise their prophetic gifts alongside of men. While the career options after graduation were limited, they nonetheless exercised a certain level of agency that would have been otherwise unavailable to them in the Apostolic Assembly or in most other Protestant denominations prior to the 1950s.[31] While some used their training at Latin American Bible Institute (LABI) to exercise their prophetic gifts of evangelism and pastoring, the majority of women who attended LABI became co-pastors, Christian educators, and lay leaders in the church. Regardless of whether or not they used their Bible training, the fact that women

29. Interestingly enough, this is not the case with their sister denomination in Mexico, the Apostolic Church, which does allow women to attend their Bible schools.

30. For example, Nellie Bazán and Mary Ruth Prado wrote regular articles for both periodicals.

31. "Reaching Latin Americans in the U.S.A.," *The Pentecostal Evangel* (14 April 1957).

could and did receive the same training for the prophetic ministry as men allowed women to nurture their prophetic gifts despite the sexism they encountered in the Latin Districts.

Conflict between Prophetic and Priestly Voices in the Latin Districts

Emphasis on male headship in the home has caused friction between ordained couples. Rev. Gloria Garza stated, for example, that there was conflict in some homes when the woman was the better preacher in a husband-wife pastoral or evangelistic team. Some Latin District Council wives complained privately that their husbands were jealous of their preaching and even put them down. In some extreme cases, husbands would not let their wives preach even though they were called to preach. This jealously was hard for some Latinas to accept and led to friction in the home. Garza's advice to women in this situation was to be patient, wait, and pray. In spite of the small number of men who are jealous of their wives' preaching ability, Garza stated that the vast majority of men are openly supportive and actually encouraged their wives to preach from the pulpit and in evangelistic crusades. However, because of paradoxical and often contradictory messages and experiences, most of the Latinas that have and currently do pastor Latin District churches tend to be older and married to pastors. While women are allowed and even encouraged to preach, they are also expected to bear the brunt of the work in tending to the children. This was not only the case in the past with Rev. Natividad Nevarez and Rev. Nellie Bazán, who each raised 10 children, but also with women today such as Aimee Cortese, who raised 4 children of her own, one of which followed her into the ministry.

"We've Got a Voice, but We Know Our Place": Feminism, Chicanismo, Evangelicalism, and the Construction of Latina Ethnic Identity

Latina Pentecostal women in the Assemblies of God construct their identity by drawing on the images of women in the Bible, denominational standards and doctrine, and, contrary to statements otherwise, on larger trends in society. Assemblies of God women stated that they rejected the militant aspects of the feminist movement because of its

ties to the larger gay-rights movement, and because the images it projects seem to conflict with the images of women in the Bible, or at least
the images they have been taught. The feminist movement's open affirmation of gay rights is the most difficult hurdle for Latina Pentecostal
women to overcome. They see homosexuality as directly challenging
the divinely ordained biblical notion of the family, affirming premarital
and adulterous relationships (i.e., gays and lesbians cannot be married
and thus engage in sexual relations either in premarital or extramarital
contexts), and because it disrupts community and goes against their
Latin American cultural orientation and values. One strong-willed
woman stated that many women had not embraced the feminist movement because "when ladies think of the feminist movement they think
of the gay community . . . [and] the stereo-type I don't need a man."[32]
Aware of the critique that Latina Pentecostal women are simply doormats controlled by men, she further stated: "I tell my husband [who
is a bishop in the Apostolic Assembly] that a woman's place is in the
house *and* the Senate." She went on to conclude: "We've got a voice, but
we also know our place." This seemingly paradoxical and simultaneous
rejection of feminism and assertion of women's agency resonated in all
of my interviews with Latina Pentecostal women.

Many Latina Pentecostals reacted negatively to the somewhat pa-
tronizing perception that they were in need of liberation. Patty Galaviz
stated that the "women's lib movement has not taken [root in] any part
in our church."[33] The elderly stateswoman in the Apostolic Assembly,
Egla Montero, brazenly stated:

> We have always been liberated. First of all we have been liber-
> ated from sin. People feel that because we talk about subjection
> and being subject to our husbands and to the ministry, they feel
> we are stepped on and are doormats, but it's totally the opposite
> . . . I feel that if any organization has given women liberty it is the

32. This sentiment was shared by Aimee Cortese who stated that the feminist
movement didn't have an impact on the Latin District Council because the "movement
was tied with homosexuality." In her estimation, this connection between the feminist
movement and gay movement was "too close to the danger mark."

33. This sentiment is common not only among Latina Pentecostals but also in Anglo
Pentecostalism; see Lawless, *Handmaidens of the Lord*, 69. Lawless states, "Sister Anna
staunchly denies any 'feminist' leanings. To acknowledge any desire to be considered a
'liberated' woman would be to castigate herself in her own community. She does not
have to fight for liberation; she is in many ways liberated . . ." (xix).

Apostolic Assembly because they recognize our place, because they recognize the liberty we have in Christ, they recognize our work, the ministry we have, the place we have in God's plan of salvation and the way God can use us in the church.

This re-imagining of what it means to be truly liberated was a common theme that ran through all of my interviews. Rev. Gloria Garza, Rev. Rose Nodal, and Rev. Cortese agreed that the feminist movement had little impact on the Latin District Council because "there is freedom in the Lord" and because the feminist movement is "too pushy."

While many Latina Pentecostal women distanced themselves from the feminist movement, they openly embraced the broader Anglo Pentecostal and Evangelical sub-culture. For example, both Apostolic and Latin District women listened to Pentecostal preachers like Oral Roberts, John Hagee, Kathryn Kuhlman, and Benny Hinn. Egla Montero claimed, for example, that she attended an Oral Roberts healing crusade in Bakersfield and received divine healing. Next to denominational literature and books, James Dobson, his books on child-raising, marriage, and self-esteem, and the *Focus on the Family* radio show were the most popular Christian influences on both Latin District Council and Apostolic women.

Conclusion

This investigation into the rich and complex role of women in the Latino Pentecostal movement has only scratched the surface of a hitherto untold story. The struggle between the prophetic and priestly is not simply a story played out between two denominations but also within each denomination. While there have always been strong prophetic female voices within the Latino Pentecostal movement, they have faced gender bias and discrimination and an uphill calling. Despite this fact, Latinas have generally stayed the course and continue to quietly and skillfully negotiate their own space by practicing a kind of a paradoxical domesticity. It would be inaccurate to equate the struggles of García Cortese, and others with Latina feminism. In fact, strong and articulate clergywomen such as Leoncia Rosado Rousseau, Gloria Garza, Aimee García Cortese, and many others reject secular feminism because of what they perceive as its rejection of the traditional biblical and Latin American gender roles and notion of family. From a feminist perspective, Latina

Pentecostals might seem to live paradoxical lives. Yet they believe they have real power to transform people and communities. For them, the message of repentance, forgiveness, and a born-again, Spirit-filled relationship with Jesus Christ constitute true liberation. Far from being "doormats" suffering from a false consciousness, Pentecostal women believe they have found real freedom despite the problems they face. If we take seriously how most Latina Pentecostal women perceive themselves, then they are by their own account "liberated" and "empowered." Although there are clear limitations to their "freedom in Christ," their stories nonetheless challenge conventional interpretations of women and religion, historical agency, and what it means to be a truly liberated woman. If the leaders of the Latino Pentecostal denominations in the U.S. cannot find a way to accommodate women's voices in a more meaningful way in the near future, they may find themselves in conflict with the prophetic voices of their daughters—women not unlike Aimee García Cortese.

7

Leadership Attitudes and the Ministry of Single Women in Assemblies of God Missions

Barbara L. Cavaness

Introduction

PHILOSOPHERS ARGUE OVER "IS" VERSUS "OUGHT." DOES WHAT ACTU-
ally happens provide a model for, or in any way predict, what ought to
happen? Historians, on the other hand, are focused on what happened,
whether or not it ought to happen, or predicts a trend. A broad shift
in historiography has occurred recently, from telling the story of great
men, and sometimes women, to digging out the smallest details of a
time or place—history from the bottom up, in addition to history from
the top down. Fernand Braudel[1] and others have been our teachers in
this new approach to history, which gives us encouragement as we look
more closely at the subject of early ministry among Pentecostal men
and women.

Pentecostals treasure their spiritual experiences. They tell and re-
tell the story, through oral history, from fathers and mothers to sons and
daughters. Some of this oral tradition has come to be written; however,
the oral history of our "foremothers"—women with leadership roles in
the church—has often failed to find its place on the printed page. It
is nonetheless true that early Pentecostal women had great effect on

---

1. Fernand Braudel, *Civilisation Materielle, Economie et Capitalisme, XVe-XVIIIe
Siecle*, 3 vols. (Paris: Collin, 1979; reprint, 1997); also in English as *Civilization &
Capitalism, 15th–18th Centuries*, 3 vols. (Berkeley: University of California Press,
1992).

their times. Many "called and anointed" women served as pastors, missionaries, evangelists, church planters, administrators, and founders of denominations. It is also true that many of their male associates in ministry treated them as "co-laborers" and sought their counsel.

Historians and theologians looking at the Holiness and Pentecostal stirrings of the late nineteenth century connect emphasis on Spirit baptism to the ministry of women. "Pentecostals, who take the authority of the Bible very seriously but also believe in direct revelation through visions, have opened a wider space for women than most other Christian denominations."[2]

In answer to how the Pentecostal message was carried so far so fast, Harvey Cox advances two crucial factors, the first of which is women in ministry leadership:

> One [factor] is the extraordinary part that *women* have played in the spread of the movement. . . . Pentecostalism is unthinkable without women. Seymour was touched in his youth by a woman with a gift, then recommended by a second woman to a third who actually provided him with a place to exercise his call. From Sister Hutchins and Aimee Semple McPherson to Kathryn Kuhlman . . . women have continued to play a disproportionately prominent place in the Pentecostal movement.[3]

Many doubt that a "golden age" of women ministering in leadership roles ever existed in the early days of the movement.[4] While varying degrees of openness to women ministers cannot be denied, one must acknowledge an earlier general acceptance of "God's anointing and call" on them to lead, which was greater than exists now.

The openness women did find, while it may not have been fully egalitarian according to early twenty-first century standards, was due partly to an increased understanding of the role of the prophet in the Bible. Pentecostal theology emphasized an individual's calling and the

2. Harvey Cox, *Fire from Heaven: The Rise of Pentecostal Spirituality and the Reshaping of Religion in the Twenty-first Century* (New York: Addison-Wesley, 1995), 131. See also Barbara Cavaness, "God Calling: Women in Pentecostal Missions," in L. Grant McClung, Jr., ed., *Azusa Street and Beyond: Pentecostal/Charismatic Essays on the Global Movement of the Holy Spirit* (Gainesville, FL: Bridge-Logos, 2006), 53–66.

3. Cox, *Fire from Heaven*, 121 (the second being the "centrality of music" to carry the message.)

4. Ibid., 137. Cox notes that many early Pentecostals came from other denominations and brought with them established biases against women teaching or preaching.

group's recognition of the Spirit's anointing on the called one in keeping with their view of the latter-day fulfillment of Joel's prophecy.[5] An often-quoted article on "prophetic versus priestly religion" agrees that the "uniqueness of the Pentecostal experience and theological importance of 'a calling' were most responsible for the multiplicity of female roles in early Pentecostal expression."[6] Thus one observes not only female evangelists and "faith" missionaries, but women filling virtually every role filled by men in the early Pentecostal churches.

So what has happened to move the church from biblical patterns and women's involvement in the early Pentecostal movement? No simple answer is possible. By introducing a number of women who were integrally involved in the ministries of major leaders of the early movement, and thus setting a baseline for judging women's participation and acceptance in one later movement, we may draw some conclusions about the multiple complex factors influencing the decline. Looking at the factors brings new insights to the commonly-held "institutionalization" rationale and suggests ways to reverse the trends exemplified by the case study and to recapture the original vision of Acts 2 and Azusa Street.

Two First-Generation Leaders

Many commentators on Pentecostal history have told the stories of Charles Parham and William Seymour, but few have cited the roles ministering women played in their successes. These first-generation Pentecostal leaders believed that God was calling and anointing women to preach. Their generally positive attitudes—respecting and affirming women—empowered them as they launched out to be used by God in the new movement.

---

5. Letha D. Scanzoni and Susan Setta, "Women in Evangelical, Holiness, and Pentecostal Traditions," in Rosemary Ruether and Rosemary Keller, eds., *Women and Religion in America*, vol. 3 (San Francisco: Harper & Row, 1986), 226.

6. Charles Barfoot and Gerald Sheppard, "Prophetic vs. Priestly Religion: The Role of Women Clergy in Classical Pentecostal Churches," *Review of Religious Research* 22 (1980): 2. The biblical basis for women in ministry is further discussed in Deborah Gill and Barbara Cavaness, *God's Women—Then and Now* (Springfield, MO: Grace & Truth, 2004).

Charles Parham

Every student of the Pentecostal movement knows the name Charles Parham. Many have written about his role in formulating the foundational tenets of classical Pentecostal theology. His missionary fervor, leading to his teaching on *xenolalia*[7] and on the restored manifestations of signs and wonders for evangelism, is well documented. Few, however, have traced Parham's openness to women ministers or the intersections between his ministry and theirs. At a time when mostly men entered the ministry, the stated purpose of his Bible school was "to fit men and women to go to the ends of the earth to preach."[8] It is significant that in Pentecostalism one finds such an early use of inclusive language.

One of the first revival meetings Parham held was near Tonganoxie, Kansas. One of the last to rededicate their lives in the revival was Sarah Thistlethwaite. Four years later they were married.[9] Even on their honeymoon, they held evangelistic services where she joined with him in the preaching.[10]

Parham began preaching the message of divine healing and opened Bethel Healing Home in Topeka in 1898. His ministry touched another member of Sarah's family, her sister Lilian Thistlethwaite. She was one of the people in the upper room of Bethel Bible School who were speaking in tongues when Parham came back on January 3, 1901, and received the experience himself.[11] During the demise of the Topeka school and other hard times, Parham came to value Thistlethwaite as a minister in her own right.

The spring of 1903 brought a turning point in Parham's ministry. At the request of a woman minister who had come to faith in his 1901 meeting in Lawrence, Parham held a meeting in her Nevada, Missouri,

7. Defined as speaking an existing foreign language without having prior knowledge of that language (also *xenoglossa*). Parham and others believed that the tongues they were receiving were enablement for missionary service.

8. Charles F. Parham, *A Voice Crying in the Wilderness*, 2nd ed. (Baxter Springs, KS: Apostolic Faith Bible College, 1910), 75.

9. Sarah E. Parham, *The Life of Charles F. Parham* (Baxter Springs, KS: Mrs. Charles F. Parham, 1930), 15–29.

10. See Sarah's sermons in Robert Parham's compilation, where he credits her as "co-founder of the original Apostolic Faith Movement"; Robert Parham, comp., *Selected Sermons of the late Charles F. Parham and Sarah E. Parham* (Baxter Springs, KS: Apostolic Faith Bible College, 1941), Preface.

11. S. Parham, *The Life of Charles F. Parham*, 57–65.

mission. From that revival on, acceptance for his preaching grew.[12] In 1904, Parham held meetings in Melrose, Kansas. Thistlethwaite followed up with services there later in the year and many conversions and testimonies of healing followed. As a result of her ministry there, "the first Apostolic, Pentecostal or Full Gospel Chapel of all modern movements" was erected at the Keelville crossroads nearby.[13]

Following successful July meetings with the team in Texas, Parham returned to Kansas for other commitments. In September he received an urgent telegraph request from Texas for evangelists to continue the outreach there. God supplied the money for train fare and Parham asked Thistlethwaite and Sarah Bradbury to go to Houston for meetings until he and other workers were able to come.[14]

In Parham's first organization, the Apostolic Faith Movement (1906), he ordained elders and appointed three State Directors for Texas, Kansas, and Missouri. The Director for Kansas was Miss Rilda Cole, a Keelville convert. One of the Directors' duties was to sign credentials of evangelists and fulltime Christian workers in their respective states. In addition, Parham named a General Secretary of the Apostolic Faith Movement (second in charge) in the person of his sister-in-law and respected co-worker, Lilian Thistlethwaite.[15] Parham left the extension of the Toledo, Ohio, work in her hands in 1907.[16]

One woman to have a strong impact on Parham was someone he only read about in a holiness periodical. Jennie Glassey believed she had seen the Lord in a vision, calling her to Africa, and giving her a language to use there that she had not learned.[17] Details of her ministry reached Parham and he recounted Glassey's story in his *Apostolic Faith* publication from Topeka.[18] Glassey's testimony may have brought Parham to his initial awareness that the Holy Spirit would confer "missionary tongues" in the end time. He came to believe they were a key to reaching

12. Klaude Kendrick, *The Promise Fulfilled: A History of the Modern Pentecostal Movement* (Springfield, MO: Gospel Publishing, 1961), 57.

13. S. Parham, *The Life of Charles F. Parham*, 100, 110.

14. Ibid., 128.

15. James R. Goff, Jr., *Fields White Unto Harvest: Charles F. Parham and the Missionary Origins of Pentecostalism* (Fayetteville: University of Arkansas, 1988), 118.

16. S. Parham, *The Life of Charles F. Parham*, 192.

17. "Going on Still," *Tongues of Fire* (1 Apr 1897): 54–55.

18. "The Gift of Tongues," *Apostolic Faith* (Topeka) (3 May 1899): 5.

the world in the last days and necessary to the equipping of missionaries in his school.[19]

A devout Christian worker, thirty-year-old Agnes Ozman, first heard Parham preach in Kansas City in the fall of 1900. After hearing of the Bethel Bible College Parham was opening in Topeka, Ozman enrolled. According to her account,[20] it was after Parham laid hands on her on the evening of 1 January 1901, that she was the first to begin to speak fluently in another language, by the power of God's Spirit.[21]

Among those who came for healing to the Parham home in El Dorado Springs, Missouri, in 1903, Mary Arthur stands out. Suffering from numerous illnesses, she testified to receiving complete healing after prayer. Arthur and her husband invited Parham to hold meetings in their Galena, Kansas home that fall, and revival followed. The meetings soon became overcrowded, so twice-a-day services were moved first to a big tent, then a store building in the center of town seating from one to two thousand.[22] It was reported that hundreds of people received salvation, healing, and the Spirit's infilling during the three-month revival.[23] Parham left Mary Arthur and Fannie Dobson in charge of the Galena church.[24] Arthur later affiliated with the Assemblies of God (AG).

Walter Oyler and his wife, from Orchard, Texas, had been filled with the Spirit in Galena and received healing in Parham's Joplin meeting. There they had met Anna Hall, one of Parham's workers, and asked

19. C. Parham, *A Voice Crying in the Wilderness*, 28; Goff, *Fields White Unto Harvest*, 72–78.

20. Though Parham's account of these events differs in some respects, accounts agree that Parham and at least a dozen others, including his wife and sister-in-law, spoke in tongues on January 3. Ozman had the distinction of being the first. See Agnes Ozman, "The First One to Speak in Tongues," *Latter Rain Evangel* (Jan 1909): 2.

21. Agnes N. O. LaBerge, *What God Hath Wrought: Life and Work of Mrs. Agnes N. O. LaBerge* (Chicago: Herald, n.d.), 28–29. Ozman later served with the Gospel Tabernacle in Lincoln, Nebraska. In 1911 she married another Pentecostal preacher, Philemon LaBerge, and they traveled in evangelistic meetings (ibid., 39, 54). Agnes received credentials with the AG in 1917 and ministered twenty more years. See Edith L. Blumhofer, "Ozman, Agnes N.," in Stanley Burgess and Gary McGee, eds., *Dictionary of Pentecostal and Charismatic Movements* (Grand Rapids: Zondervan, 1988), 657.

22. S. Parham, *The Life of Charles F. Parham*, 88-89.

23. Goff, *Fields White Unto Harvest*, 92.

24. Ethel E. Goss, *The Winds of God: The Story of the Early Pentecostal Movement (1901–14) in the Life of Howard A. Goss*, rev. ed. (Hazelwood, MO: Word Aflame, 1977), 59.

her to return home with them to spread the Pentecostal message. She conducted meetings in Orchard until Parham could come. Whole families converted to Christianity as Hall and Parham ministered together. In May, 1905, Parham headed home to recruit workers and Hall continued to evangelize in the area.[25] In August of the next year, Hall reported that God was leading her to go to California. Subsequently she got a call to come and help in William Seymour's meetings. Parham helped to raise her train fare. When Hall arrived, evening crowds at the Azusa Mission ran up to 1,200, and morning and afternoon groups were growing.[26] She preached in area churches and assisted at the mission.

Mabel Smith and Jessie Brown had worked with Parham in Kansas. In October 1906, when the nightly seekers in Zion, Illinois, increased to 200, Parham sent for these two of his co-workers to help him. After they came, the group grew even faster. Within the month, Marie Burgess, together with Fred Bosworth and Jean Campbell, received their Pentecost after Brown admonished the group to start praising God for what they were about to receive. Not long afterward, a group of twenty-five young people were baptized, reportedly bursting forth in tongues at the same time. Toward the end of October, Parham left the Zion group in the care of Smith and Brown and headed to Los Angeles.[27] Stanley Frodsham related that Smith preached every night to great crowds in Chicago that fall.[28] Howard Goss noted that Smith had also preached mightily in Texas and was the first to bring the Pentecostal message to Chicago. By the power of God, Smith had "spoken and been understood by foreigners" in eighteen languages.[29]

William Seymour

Almost all existing Pentecostal denominations "can trace their lineage to the Azusa Street Mission."[30] Various women figured prominently in

25. S. Parham, *The Life of Charles F. Parham*, 107–9.

26. Ibid., 148; Goff, *Fields White Unto Harvest*, 113.

27. Gordon P. Gardiner, *Out of Zion into All the World* (Shippensburg, PA: Companion, 1990), 5, 8, 35.

28. Stanley Frodsham, *With Signs Following* (Springfield, MO: Gospel Publishing, 1946), 43.

29. B. F. Lawrence, *The Apostolic Faith Restored* (St. Louis, MO: Gospel Publishing, 1916), 66–67.

30. Vinson Synan, *The Holiness-Pentecostal Movement in the United States* (Grand Rapids: Eerdmans, 1971), 114.

William Seymour's coming to Los Angeles and to his success. Cox notes that "both black and white deacons and both black and white women . . . were exhorters and healers"; Seymour "believed that the breaking of the color line and the exercise of spiritual gifts by women were among the signs that a new descent of the Holy Spirit was taking place."[31]

Women played vital roles of preaching and leadership at Azusa Street as well as receiving the blessing of the group as they carried the message across the continent and overseas. When the Azusa Street group organized as the Apostolic Faith Mission, among its first eleven elders were six women: Jennie Evans Moore, Sister Prince, May (Mrs. G. W.) Evans, Clara Lum, Florence Crawford, and Phoebe Sargent.[32] The elders examined those who wanted to be licensed as missionaries or evangelists, and commissioned the ones who were approved by prayer and the laying on of hands.[33]

Though Seymour stressed that "God is no respecter of persons," where women in ministry were concerned he may have espoused a "blend of admission and restriction."[34] Blumhofer, however, ascribes an unsigned article in *The Apostolic Faith* to Seymour. In it he says that since women were anointed at Pentecost "to preach the same as the men. . . . We have no right to lay a straw in her way."[35]

Lucy Farrow is an important link between Parham's teachings and the Azusa Street Revival. Pastor of a Black Holiness church near Houston, Texas, she left her church in the care of her friend, William Seymour, to travel to Kansas with the Parhams. There she heard more of Parham's teachings about the Holy Spirit baptism, and received the experience.[36] During this time Mrs. Neely Terry came from Los Angeles to visit relatives in Houston, where she heard Seymour preach. She took back a favorable report of his pastoral skills to her Holiness group in

31. Cox, *Fire from Heaven*, 58, 79.

32. Richard M. Riss, *A Survey of 20th Century Revival Movements in North America* (Peabody, MA: Hendrickson, 1988), 59.

33. Rachel A. Sizelove, "A Sparkling Fountain," *Word and Work* 57.3 (Mar 1935): 2, 12.

34. Edith L. Blumhofer, *Restoring the Faith: The Assemblies of God, Pentecostalism, and American Culture* (Chicago: University of Illinois Press, 1993), 172.

35. "Who May Prophesy?" *Apostolic Faith* (Los Angeles) 1.12 (1908): 2

36. Douglas J. Nelson, "For Such a Time as This: The Story of Bishop William J. Seymour and the Azusa Street Revival: A Search for Pentecostal/Charismatic Roots" (PhD dissertation, University of Birmingham, England, 1981), 166–67.

California, led by Julia W. Hutchins. When Farrow returned to Houston in October, she testified to Seymour about her experience of speaking in other tongues and introduced him to Parham. He then studied under Parham that December.[37]

Before long, Hutchins sent an invitation and train fare for Seymour to come and assist in pastoring her Holiness mission. Parham helped with expenses and sent him on his way.[38] He arrived in Los Angeles by way of Denver on 22 February 1906.[39] Because Seymour began preaching Parham's position—that the ability to speak in tongues evidenced a true Spirit baptism—Hutchins prevented him from continuing his services in her mission. Cousins of Neely Terry, Richard and Ruth Asberry, soon opened their home on North Bonnie Brae Street for nightly prayer meetings. As attendance was growing, Seymour requested help and sent train fare so Lucy Farrow and Mr. J. A. Warren could come from Houston immediately.[40]

The great outpouring began on 9 April 1906, with the baptism of Edward Lee at his home when Farrow laid hands on him.[41] Seymour first spoke in tongues on April 12.[42] Julia Hutchins and her Holiness associates soon accepted the Pentecostal message, and many experienced Spirit baptism. Both Hutchins and Farrow eventually had ministry on the East coast and in Liberia, West Africa.[43] Jennie Moore, the first woman to speak in tongues on April 9, traveled as an evangelist and two years later became Seymour's wife and associate pastor.[44] She worked

---

37. Parham, *A Voice Crying in the Wilderness*, 137.

38. Ibid., 142; Nelson, "For Such a Time as This," 91.

39. Cecil M. Robeck, Jr., "William J. Seymour," in Gary B. McGee, ed., *Initial Evidence: Historical and Biblical Perspectives on the Pentecostal Doctrine of Spirit Baptism* (Peabody, MA: Hendrickson, 1991), 72.

40. Cecil M. Robeck, Jr., *The Liberian Connection*, unpublished manuscript, author's files.

41. Frank J. Ewart, *The Phenomenon of Pentecost* (Houston, TX: Herald Publishing, 1947), 70.

42. (Untitled), *Apostolic Faith* (Los Angeles) 1.4 (1906): 1.

43. Julia W. Hutchins, "Speeding to Foreign Lands." *Apostolic Faith* (Los Angeles) 1.5 (1907): 3; see also "Pentecostal Missionary Reports," *Apostolic Faith* (Los Angeles) 1.11 (1908): 1.

44. Jennie Moore, "Music from Heaven," *Apostolic Faith* (Los Angeles) 1.8 (1907): 3; Nelson, "For Such a Time as This," 263.

alongside him in the leadership of the Mission and preached and managed the affairs of the Mission when he traveled.

Seymour and Azusa Street impacted the lives of many other women ministers—too many stories for this brief paper.[45] Florence Crawford, one of the founding elders, was sent out as an evangelist and eventually started her own denomination in Portland, Oregon. Clara Lum, mission secretary and likely editor of the *Apostolic Faith*, used her gifts to spread the revival message. Rachel Sizelove brought the Pentecostal message from Azusa to Springfield, Missouri. Evangelist Ivey Campbell took it to Ohio with great power, influencing such church leaders as Claude McKinney, Levi Lupton, and W. A. Cramer.[46]

Many first-generation Pentecostal leaders affirmed and supported women in ministry. Along with the tongues, miracles of healing, and other manifestations of the Spirit's power, they received the calling and anointing of women for ministry as part of God's work in the last days. Female ministers opened doors for male leaders and vice versa. Women influenced men's theology, served as team members and administrators in their organizations, and ministered as co-evangelists and pastors of churches that resulted from revival. The "ministry role for women became a characteristic of early Pentecostalism and its missionary enterprises."[47] Within two years the Azusa Street Mission claimed to have missionaries in over 50 countries and many of them were single women.[48]

Estrelda Alexander, however, discusses some of the restrictions for women that soon found their way into the Azusa Street Mission. Seymour, in his 1915 doctrinal statement, specifically excluded women from holding positions of authority, baptizing, or participating in the prayer and laying-on of hands in ordination services. She says, "The freedom available to women in the earliest days of the revival quickly

45. See Barbara Cavaness, "Factors Influencing the Decrease in the Number of Single Women in Assemblies of God World Missions" (PhD dissertation, Fuller Theological Seminary, 2002), ch. 3.

46. Frodsham, *With Signs Following*, 45; Ivey Campbell, "Report from Ohio and Pennsylvania," *Apostolic Faith* (Los Angeles) 1.6 (1907): 5.

47. Gary B. McGee, *"This Gospel Shall Be Preached": A History and Theology of Assemblies of God Foreign Missions to 1959* (Springfield, MO: Gospel Publishing, 1986), 46.

48. Nelson, "For Such a Time as This," 61–62.

gave way to limitations on their leadership that were encoded into the very fabric of the movement and increased as the work took on more structure."[49]

Case Study: One Denomination—The Assemblies of God

Out of the rapidly growing Pentecostal movement spreading from Azusa Street, with its many "flavors," proof texts, and doctrinal positions, a new fellowship formed in 1914 around the goal of world evangelization. They called themselves the General Council of the Assemblies of God (AG). From the beginning men took the leadership, but many Spirit-filled women joined their ranks. By 1918, when only 21% of AG credentialed ministers were women, 53% of their foreign missionaries and 64% of their home missionaries were women; by 1928, women—single and married—constituted 68% of the foreign missionary force.[50] This alarmed some of the men.[51]

Elsewhere I have discussed factors influencing the decrease in number and the diminishing role of single women appointed as AG missionaries.[52] The percentage of single women in the total of fully appointed missionaries has declined from over 40% (in the 1920s) to less than 5% (in the 1990s), despite the fact that perhaps the most significant

49. Estrelda Alexander, "The Role of Women in the Azusa Street Revival," in Harold Hunter and Cecil Robeck Jr., eds., *The Azusa Street Revival and Its Legacy* (Cleveland, TN: Pathway, 2006), 67–68.

50. Cavaness, "Factors Influencing," 382, and Barfoot and Sheppard, "Prophetic vs. Priestly Religion," 10.

51. Ralph Riggs, "The Place of Men in the Work of the Church," *Pentecostal Evangel* (5 Feb 1938): 24; J. Roswell Flower, "Men Wanted," *Pentecostal Evangel* 7 (Apr 1923): 12.

52. In Cavaness, "Factors Influencing," I divided the church's historical events and documents into three time periods: Formation—from the first meeting to the adoption of the AG Constitution (1914–1927); Growth—from the Constitution to the Council resolution reaffirming the ordination of women (1928–1977); and Maturity—from the distribution of the unofficial position paper affirming women to the writing of my dissertation (1978–2000). Chapter 8 displays tables paralleling for each year historical events in the denomination, published writings significant to women, and the changes in the number/percentage of single female missionaries. Analyses and summaries of the variables are included. Appendices A–G show the quantitative data, the totals, categories, and gain or loss in the number of single (including widowed and divorced) women missionaries for the years 1914 to 2000.

role of women in the denomination has been in the area of world missions. Analysis of archival data yields three major factors influencing the decrease, including "limiting" historical events/documents, mixed theological messages in publications, and restrictive leadership attitudes. Two of the lesser factors include conservative evangelical pressures, and the effects of the women's movement in increasing male bias against female ministers. All of these are directly or indirectly connected. The decrease is seen less as a result of institutionalization than a reflection of the values of some of the male leaders of the denomination, who from its inception sought to circumscribe the ministries of women while at the same time granting them credentials to minister.

The "ideal" AG theology concerning women in ministry was initially stated in the April 1914 *Minutes*. In passing the "Rights and Offices of Women" Resolution, the brethren agreed that: "the hand of God is mightily upon many women to proclaim and publish the 'good tidings of great joy' in a wonderful way."[53] Most of the Scriptures in the four statements that followed, however, were given interpretations which largely limited rather than liberated the "actual practices" relating to women ministers. Galatians 3:28 was restricted to apply "in the matter of salvation," not to ministry roles. The passage from 1 Timothy 2:11–15 was said to mean that "women are commanded to be in subjection and not to usurp authority over the man." Another point relegated women to being "helpers in the Gospel" according to Romans 16:3. Only one point acknowledged that women "are called to prophesy and preach the Gospel" and that a woman who "prophesieth speaketh unto men to edification, to exhortation and to comfort," citing Acts 2:17 and 1 Corinthians 14:3.

From the outset, the AG wanted to be seen as holding the ideal of supporting women in ministry. The actual practice recommended to the churches was stated after the scriptural considerations of the resolution: that women could be ordained as evangelists and missionaries, but not as elders. Other publications explained that women were thus excluded from serving as pastors and from administering the ordinances of the church.[54]

53. *Minutes* (General Council of the Assemblies of God) (Springfield, MO: Gospel Publishing, 1914), 7.

54. See citations in Grant Wacker, *Heaven Below: Early Pentecostals and American Culture* (Cambridge: Harvard University Press, 2001), 166. He concludes that "the

Women, however, continued to pastor congregations and actively engage in evangelism, church planting, and missionary work. In Council meetings they were received as "advisory members" and in 1920 were given voting rights.[55] New ordination papers issued to AG women in 1922 for purposes of obtaining railroad passes had an attached letter of explanation. It said the credentials were not intended "to encourage the women to do these things [to be pastors, to marry people, or to administer Baptism and the Lord's Supper] in the future any more than in the past."[56] In the area of missions more women than men continued to volunteer, prompting the treasurer to call for men to take over the stations where women had done the hard pioneering work.[57]

Attitudes against women in leadership impacted the fledgling movement from such non-Pentecostals as C. I. Scofield, whose reference Bible was frequently advertised in the *Pentecostal Evangel*. This influence increased when AG Bible schools looked to graduates from Dallas Theological Seminary (and other institutions not supportive of women ministers) to fill faculty posts.[58]

It became more difficult for women to gain credentials after the AG adopted its constitution in 1927. The Council passed a stringent resolution in 1931, allowing women to be ordained only as evangelists

overall intent was to encourage women in some forms of public ministry but to exclude them from the most powerfully symbolic and publicly authoritative forms."

55. Wacker, *Heaven Below*, 167: "According to one eyewitness, Chairman J. W. Welch disapproved of Aimee McPherson speaking to the denomination's 1920 convention because he disliked the idea of a woman preaching."

56. "Credential Committee Letter" (Springfield, MO, 1922); unpublished document in author's files.

57. Flower, "Men Wanted," 12.

58. Edith L. Blumhofer, *The Assemblies of God: A Chapter in the Story of American Pentecostalism, Vol. 1—To 1941* (Springfield, MO: Gospel Publishing, 1989), 370. See also Blumhofer, *Restoring*, 159. Denominational leaders also came from various conservative backgrounds (mostly southern). Noel Perkin, missionary secretary (1926–59) was taught by the Christian & Missionary Alliance (CMA). See the founder's views in Leslie Andrews, "Restricted Freedom: A. B. Simpson's View of Women," in David Hartzfeld and Charles Nienkirchen, eds., *The Birth of a Vision* (Beaverlodge, Alberta: Buena Book, 1986), 219–40. Simpson approved female missionaries and preachers, but not women holding the offices of pastor, elder, or bishop. Women could anoint the sick only if a "proper elder" were not available. Anecdotal evidence shows the number of single women missionaries in the CMA has declined steadily over their history as well.

and forbidding them to perform church ordinances.[59] While the resolution was reversed in 1935, some scholars believe that because of it
women will "never have the freedom they once had during the earlier
years of the movement."[60] This public action merely masked private
feelings of uncertainty of individual leaders about women in ministry
and impacted the AG for years afterward.[61] In spite of the reversal, tolerance and pragmatism continued to give way to tighter restrictions and
centralized authority. Individual districts refused women ordination.

Assemblies of God membership in the newly-formed National
Association of Evangelicals, the changing "ideal woman" role following
WWII, and the "Latter Rain" controversy around Pastor Myrtle Beall resulted in a further move of AG leadership away from support for ministering women and toward support for "traditional" roles.[62] Women
missionaries could still preach in AG churches, but as men came home
from the war to take over jobs and pulpits, even tolerant partnership
attitudes toward women in leadership deteriorated.[63]

The AG officials largely ignored the secular women's movement
and civil rights movement of the 1960s. My survey of missions leaders, however, revealed that even in 1997 the backlash against perceived
excesses of radical feminists was still influencing these men to be suspi-
cious of women, especially single women who were espousing egalitarian treatment.[64] Cheryl Bridges Johns writes, "The difference in the

59. *Minutes* (General Council of the Assemblies of God) (Springfield, MO: Gospel
Publishing, 1931), 17–18.

60. Barfoot and Sheppard, "Prophetic vs. Priestly Religion," 14–16.

61. Howard Kenyon, "An Analysis of Ethical Issues in the History of the Assemblies
of God" (PhD dissertation, Baylor University, 1988), 230; and legalistic regulation of
women's dress in *Minutes* (General Council of the Assemblies of God) (Springfield,
MO: Gospel Publishing, 1939), 61–62.

62. Cecil M. Robeck, Jr., "National Association of Evangelicals" in Stanley Burgess
and Gary McGee, eds., *Dictionary of Pentecostal and Charismatic Movements* (Grand
Rapids: Eerdmans, 1988), 635.

63. Roberta Hestenes, "Women in Leadership: Finding Ways to Serve the Church,"
Christianity Today (3 Oct 1986): 4–10; and Cavaness, "Factors Influencing," 159–80,
322–23.

64. Cavaness, "Factors Influencing," 262, 317–27. See also Grant Wacker, "Searching
for Norman Rockwell: Popular Evangelicalism in Contemporary America," in Leonard
Sweet, ed., *The Evangelical Tradition in America* (Macon, GA: Mercer University Press,
1984), 308–9. He quotes two historians who have argued that much of the fear of
feminism "grows from distrust of the deregulated adult male. In its heart of hearts, they

'place' for women in Pentecostalism, when we were the 'orphan daughter' of the religious world, and women's 'place' as we are becoming a 'mighty man' can be seen in the relegation of women to auxiliary ministries. . . . Moves toward integrating women into the mainstream of church life have been met with accusations of radical, secular feminism."[65]

Though General Secretary Joseph R. Flower published an unofficial position paper affirming women in ministry in 1978, he admitted prejudice against them still existed.[66] The official AG stance on women's ministry, formulated in 1990, strongly advocates for women in positions of spiritual leadership, but contradictions are apparent between the public stance and local church policies and rhetoric. An examination of published writings of AG pastors and leaders reveals that they have sent mixed theological messages (often using a fundamentalist hermeneutic) and shows that the issue of restricting women's place in ministry was present at the birth of the movement and remains part of the on-going AG organizational culture. A few negative voices have outweighed the positive ones because those who wrote limiting rhetoric and interpreted the scriptures restrictively were men of high office and were considered to have spiritual authority.[67]

Pamela Holmes points out the similarities in the situation of the Canadian Pentecostal movement which beginnings are connected with Ellen Hebden's 1906 mission in Toronto and the ministry of other anointed female evangelists. Holmes asserts that history was "rewritten" and describes women's participation in Pentecostal Assemblies of Canada (PAOC) ministry as:

> accepted but limited, affirmed but restricted . . . . The PAOC was
> to be an organization controlled and led by male elders and

---

note, the Evangelical Right believes that feminism will liberate men rather than women from conventional expectations."

65. Cheryl Bridges Johns, "Pentecostal Spirituality and the Conscientization of Women," in Harold Hunter and Peter Hocken, eds., *All Together in One Place: Theological Papers from the Brighton Conference on World Evangelization* (Sheffield: Sheffield Academic, 1993), 165.

66. Kenyon, "An Analysis of Ethical Issues," 269; Cavaness, "Factors Influencing," 179–82.

67. Cavaness, "Factors Influencing," 191–256. For further discussion of Pentecostal use of a Fundamentalist hermeneutic, see Janet Everts Powers, "Recovering a Woman's Head with Prophetic Authority: A Pentecostal Interpretation of 1 Corinthians 11:3–16," *Journal of Pentecostal Theology* 10.1 (October 2001): 11-37.

male pastors. . . . Once the PAOC institutionalized, the necessity for order, limited finances . . . , a professional understanding of ordination along with formal requirements for education and ministry experience, the availability of more men, and the re-emphasizing of a "separate sphere" ideology for men and women restricted women's options.[68]

The PAOC did not allow the ordination of women until 1984, nor women's holding of district or national leadership positions until 1998.

Conclusion

Factors contributing to the present lack of consensus in the AG, as well as the larger Pentecostal-Charismatic world, on the questions of women in ministry leadership could fill several dissertations. Several factors that have influenced the decline in single women missionaries in the AG do have relevance to many similar situations.[69]

We live in a changing world, so even the influences apparent in one denomination's history are modified by new issues of religious pluralism, social and economic shifts, and increasing secular opportunities for women in what some call our post-modern, post-Christian country. For some, opposing women in leadership is an issue of pride or holding on to power. For others, it may be an honest questioning of the scriptural passages, or for still others, a close-minded certainty about the same scriptural passages. Some may just be comfortable with the status quo or afraid to rock the boat.

Positive AG leadership attitudes nearly a century ago included: 1) respect for God's call and anointing equally on women as on men;

---

68. Pamela Holmes, "The 'Place' of Women in Pentecostal/Charismatic Ministry Since the Azusa Street Revival," in Harold Hunter and Cecil M. Robeck Jr., eds., *The Azusa Street Revival and Its Theology* (Cleveland, Tenn.: Pathway, 2006), 301–4. See also Kenyon, "An Analysis of Ethical Issues," 251. He observes that the constitution of the Pentecostal Church of God (Joplin, MO) also bars women from holding leadership positions. What they have legislated the AG has unofficially practiced. Also David Roebuck, "Pentecostal Women in Ministry: A Review of Selected Documents," *Perspectives in Religious Studies* 16 (Spring 1989): 40, says of the Church of God (Cleveland), "Emphasis on the organization and administration of the church . . . brought about increased exclusion of women."

69. The nineteen specific recommendations in my dissertation to solve the contradiction between words and actions in the AG included changes to the organization itself and to its ministerial formation and placement.

2) belief that the church was in the "last days;" and needed every willing hand for evangelism; 3) recognition of ministries by the acceptance and ordination of women as evangelists, church planters, missionaries, and many other leadership roles; 4) reciprocity in sharing of pulpits; 5) appointment of women to leadership positions; and 6) recognizing the influence of women in many fellowships. In reverse order, the "top six" negative leadership attitudes that increasingly restricted ministering women are: 6) attempting to legislate (through resolutions and publications) the extent of God's call upon women; 5) believing that the "weak shoulders" of women cannot carry the responsibilities of institutions they have started, so strong men should take over; 4) devaluing the efforts of women and using fear of "feminization of the church" in attempts to encourage more men to assume leadership (read power); 3) desiring acceptance among "older and wiser" denominations that restrict women in leadership, 2) believing that letting women lead means bringing abortion and all the evils of secular feminism into the church; and 1) acknowledging that while "God may choose to use women, we prefer not to, and we really think the Bible says we shouldn't."

What *was*—the acceptance of women in Pentecostal ministry and leadership—is a wonderful part of what we *ought* now to revive and pass on. Telling history from the bottom up reminds us that only as leaders yield to the Holy Spirit, finding personal spiritual renewal and bringing revival to the group, are trends reversed and status quo attitudes changed. When true Pentecostal revival awakens a church, more of its women answer the call to minister and more of its men are humbly inclined to bless them. History shows, however, that social and attitudinal changes during revivals don't necessarily translate into renewed institutional structures. Neither do the examples, however numerous, of powerful and effective ministering women—evidenced by the fact that the Church of the Open Bible (with roots in Florence Crawford's Apostolic Faith Mission) and the Foursquare Church (founded by Aimee Semple McPherson) have been led by men for most of their histories. Since hermeneutical consensus on the New Testament passages is weak, social conditioning takes over and co-opts the group.

In a recent interview with former U.S. Department of Health and Human Services Secretary Donna Shalala, news anchor Brian Williams asked about ongoing gender bias documented in the fields of math, science, and engineering. Commenting on Shalala's data Williams said,

"I suppose, Madam Secretary, that becomes the big question—societal change—coming out of this report. Isn't it like turning a battleship around? How do you go about that?" Shalala responded, "Well, you get a tugboat probably. And that's called leadership. We need to make some institutional changes. . . ." She told a briefing, "It is not a lack of talent, but an unintended bias . . . that is locking women out."[70] While the details differ, the larger picture has similarities. Should the people who believe Joel 2:28 be simply a reflection of the unbelieving world? The AG denomination and Pentecostal/Charismatic movement are large and the people at the top have to be committed to "turning the ship." Change is thus unlikely to take place quickly from an organizational perspective.

The steps Shalala suggested to institutions included "giving women more support, changing institutional power structures, and looking at our own biases in hiring." My suggestions are similar, addressing the denomination's need to affirm women in leadership, communicating the relevance of the gospel to today's single women, and working toward consensus on the scriptural issues. Proactive efforts to open more leadership roles to women and correct inequalities and restrictive attitudes were recommended to the AG World Missions division.[71] Missions leaders have since made attempts to "turn the ship" in the areas of boosting financial support, placing a woman on the executive committee, and slightly increasing the number of single women being commissioned—from an average of 5.8% of the total in the 1990s to 6.7% since 2000. The attitudes of female and male leaders are not the only factor. But in the end, these attitudes form a *significant* factor influencing the extent to which ministering women are stifled or empowered on local and regional levels.

The Spirit is moving in the Body of Christ and many are beginning to again acknowledge the individual gifts, callings, and anointing of women. As that continues in the church as a whole, issues are being addressed. Hundreds of books, articles, and other media on women and egalitarianism are being published.[72] Prophets hear the sound of women marching—women God is raising up. This move of the Spirit

70. "Gender Bias in Scientific Fields," http://www.nightlynews.msnbc.com (accessed 19 Sept 2006).

71. Cavaness, "Factors Influencing," 375–80.

72. See catalog of resources from Christians for Biblical Equality (CBE) at http://www.equalitydepot.com and www.cbeinternational.org.

will either being accepted or rejected one group at a time, one pastor at a time, one man or woman at a time.

PART II

Biblical/Theological Perspectives

8

Pentecostalism 101

Your Daughters Shall Prophesy

Janet Everts Powers

Introduction

THIS YEAR MARKS THE BEGINNING OF THE SECOND CENTURY OF THE Pentecostal movement. Pentecostals got their name from their insistence that the Spirit-baptism of Pentecost, which empowered the early church for the ministry of the gospel, is still available today, and that all who receive it are empowered by the Spirit to minister in Christ's name. For Pentecostals, the church is seen as a Spirit-baptized community of prophets, called to prophetic vocation as witnesses to the Gospel. This distinctive view of Spirit-empowered ministry, which Roger Stronstad has dubbed "the prophethood of all believers,"[1] has been one of Pentecostalism's major contributions to the twentieth century church.

But most Pentecostals and those who study them seem to have forgotten where they got this distinctive doctrine of ministry, and why this doctrine was originally developed. This view of Spirit-baptism was developed by Phoebe Palmer, one of the more influential Holiness teachers of the nineteenth century, as part of her argument for the ministry of women. It was adopted almost without modification by the leading teachers of the fledging Pentecostal movement. What Charles Fox Parham added to Palmer's doctrine of Spirit-baptism was the idea that

---

1. Roger Stronstad, *The Prophethood of All Believers: A Study in Luke's Charismatic Theology* (Sheffield: Sheffield Academic, 1999).

the evidence of this experience of the Spirit was speaking in tongues. It was this doctrine of Spirit-baptism that was spread around the world by William Seymour and the Azusa Street revival.

But in all of the excitement surrounding the Azusa Street centennial, Phoebe Palmer's theological contribution to the history of Pentecostalism was ignored. Everyone seemed to have forgotten that the doctrine of Spirit-baptism as empowering for ministry was a doctrine developed by a woman in support of the ministries of women. This collective amnesia cannot be explained by an appeal to the usual Pentecostal lack of historical and theological consciousness. The centennial celebration was full of historical awareness, ethnic inclusiveness, and theological sensitivity. But where was the celebration of the contributions of women, especially the absolutely crucial theological contribution of Phoebe Palmer? Why has her argument for the ministry of women lost credibility in the very tradition which was birthed from that argument?

Phoebe Palmer's prophetic defense of the ministries of women was extremely influential in the Holiness movement when it was first published, since she was one of the great Holiness teachers of her day and the editor of a major Holiness periodical.[2] Because the view of Spirit-baptism adopted by the Pentecostal movement half a century later owed much of its distinctive character to Palmer's work, her argument for women in ministry has been used by generations of Pentecostals to support the right of women to minister the gospel. This understanding of women and ministry led to an unprecedented number of women being licensed or ordained in Pentecostal churches. In the early days of Pentecostalism, women assisted in every aspect of the ministry of this rapidly growing movement.[3] Even today, over fifty percent of all women who have ever been ordained come from the Holiness-Pentecostal tradition.[4]

However, during the last half of the twentieth century, the number of women ordained by Pentecostal denominations has been steadily

2. David Roebuck, "Limiting Liberty: The Church of God and Women Ministers 1886–1996" (Ph.D. dissertation, Vanderbilt University, 1997), 9.

3. Ibid., 2.

4. Barbara Brown Zikmund, "Women and Ordination," in Rosemary Radford Reuther and Rosemary Skinner Keller, eds., *Our Own Voices: Four Centuries of American Women's Religious Writings* (San Francisco: Harper & Row, 1995), 299.

decreasing. Those who remain are often found in ministries that are peripheral to the central work of the gospel; few are senior pastors and many are nearing retirement age.[5] Just as mainline Protestant denominations are beginning to encourage the ministries of women, Pentecostals appear to be losing the theological passion that once made them leaders in affirming a woman's right to minister. Several reasons have been advanced to explain this decline. One popular account thinks the influence of Reformed theology, which came into Pentecostalism through the charismatic movement, is responsible.[6] Others blame the hermeneutics of fundamentalism, which has attacked many of the traditional Pentecostal arguments for the ministry of women.[7] But in Pentecostal circles the almost universal explanation given for this decline is that as revival wanes, the church institutionalizes and has more of a tendency to accommodate to the culture that surrounds it. This leads to less openness to Spirit empowered ministries and makes it more difficult for women to break out of traditional societal roles.[8] All these explanations allow Pentecostals to avoid taking responsibility for the disempowering of women in ministry that has occurred within the movement in the late twentieth century. What has happened to the ministries of women in the Pentecostal movement is really the fault of other Christian traditions or an inevitable pattern in revivalist expressions of Christianity that can only be corrected by the actions of the sovereign Spirit of God.

But before Pentecostals blame the Spirit, Reformed theology, or the fundamentalists for the decline in the ranks of Pentecostal women ministers, they must examine their own defense of the ministries of women. They still defend the doctrine of Spirit-baptism when it is attacked by those outside the movement. Most Pentecostals champion the idea of the prophethood of all believers against those who question the

5. Deborah M. Gill, "The Contemporary State of Women in Ministry in the Assemblies of God," *Pneuma* 17 (Spring 1995): 34–36.

6. Susan Hyatt, "Your Sons and Your Daughters: A Case for Pentecostal-Charismatic Egalitarianism with Special Emphasis on *Kephale* in the Pauline Literature" (M.A. thesis, Oral Roberts University, 1993), 57–65.

7. Lucille S. Dayton and Donald W. Dayton, "Your Daughters Shall Prophesy: Feminism in the Holiness Movement," *Methodist History* 14.2 (1976): 92.

8. Ibid., 92; Hyatt, "Your Sons and Your Daughters," 46–57; and Roebuck, "Limiting Liberty," 31.

centrality of Spirit-empowered ministry. Why aren't they defending the prophetic Spirit-empowered ministries of women?

Pentecostals need to be reminded of Palmer's contributions and her arguments for the ministries of women. They also need to be reminded that arguments against the ministries of women are seldom confined to criticisms of women in ministry. They are usually attacks on the prophetic, Spirit-empowered view of ministry that the Pentecostal movement inherited from Palmer and adopted as its own. This paper will trace the rise and triumph of Phoebe Palmer's prophetic argument for women in ministry in the Pentecostal church. It will also examine some of the factors that led to the undermining of this argument and its eventual eclipse in the very tradition which had originally used it to champion the ministries of women. In doing this, it will seek to remind Pentecostals that when they do not defend the ministries of women, they are not defending their own distinctive view of Spirit-empowered ministry and are in danger of losing the very doctrine that gave them their Pentecostal identity.

Phoebe Palmer's Prophetic Argument for the Ministry of Women

Phoebe Palmer published her impassioned defense of the ministry of woman, *The Promise of the Father: A Neglected Specialty of the Last Days*, in 1859. At one level her argument is deceptively simple. She bases it on the account of Pentecost in Acts 2 and maintains that because women as well as men received the mighty baptism of the Holy Spirit, women as well as men are empowered to preach and prophesy in the Christian dispensation. But at another level she is engaging in some rather thoughtful and creative theological construction. She is taking two of the distinctive doctrines of the Wesleyan tradition and reinterpreting them in rather unique ways.

The first doctrine is Wesley's idea of extraordinary call.[9] Although Wesley was initially opposed to the preaching of women and never approved the formal ordination of women, he came to understand that women of extraordinary character could receive an extraordinary call from God to preach and minister the gospel. As long as their

---

9. Phoebe Palmer, *The Promise of the Father: A Neglected Specialty of the Last Days* (Boston: Degen, 1859), 57.

ministry bore good fruit, especially in the conversion of sinners, he allowed women to serve as local lay preachers, itinerant evangelists, and local class leaders.[10] In nineteenth-century Holiness circles, this doctrine was often supported biblically by an appeal to the example of women prophets and the spirit of prophecy being poured out on women as well as men in Acts 2.[11]

As part of the Wesleyan tradition, Palmer was also a firm believer in a second experience of grace and reminds her readers that the full baptism of the Spirit is a grace to be experienced in the present.[12] In fact, Palmer was rather famous for having developed a "shorter way" to achieve this second experience of grace. This "shorter way" consisted of three steps to holiness: 1) entire consecration, 2) faith, and 3) testimony.[13] She believed that this consecration could be achieved instantaneously at the altar. Even more importantly, she equated holiness with power and understood that this power was given for service.[14] Both the idea of an instantaneous second experience of grace and equating this experience of grace with empowering for service were Phoebe Palmer's own theological contributions.

Phoebe Palmer's genius lay in the way she combined these two ideas to support the ministries of women. For Palmer, the baptism of the Holy Spirit is not just about sanctification, it is also about empowering for ministry. This experience is available to anyone who asks for it, and is willing to consecrate everything to God and accept the blessing from God's hand.[15] This baptism of the Holy Spirit can, therefore, be an experience of extraordinary call in the life of any woman who seeks it.[16] "It is the ordination which Christ gives his disciples, by the redemption

10. Nancy Hardesty, Lucille Sider Dayton, and Donald W. Dayton, "Women in the Holiness Movement: Feminism in the Evangelical Tradition," in Rosemary Reuther and Eleanor McLaughlin, eds., *Women of Spirit: Female Leadership in the Jewish and Christian Traditions* (New York: Simon & Schuster, 1979), 228–29.

11. Luther Lee, "Women's Right to Preach the Gospel," in Donald W. Dayton, ed., *Holiness Tracts Defending the Ministry of Women* (New York: Garland, 1985), 8–11.

12. Palmer, *Promise of the Father*, 55.

13. Kimberly Ervin Alexander, *Pentecostal Healing: Models in Theology and Practice* (Blandford Forum, UK: Deo, 2006), 12.

14. Ibid., 29.

15. Palmer, *Promise of the Father*, 348–56.

16. Ibid., 353.

of which they are empowered to go forth and bear much fruit."[17] She gives numerous examples throughout her book of women who received an extraordinary call to ministry as a result of this experience and supports her view with clear references to scripture.

The Pentecost account of Acts 2 is the passage of scripture that forms the basis of Palmer's argument that both sons and daughters of the church are now empowered to prophesy.[18] The prophesying mentioned in the quote from Joel 2:28 is the same as preaching and covers all edifying, exhorting, and encouraging words. Discourse is not preaching because it is delivered by a minister, but because it explains the teachings or enforces the commandments of Christ and the apostles.[19] Because this Pentecostal experience ushered in the last days and was given as a promise to "your children and all those who are far off," it is still in effect because the church is still in the "last days."[20] In fact the increased ministry of women is a sign of the "latter rain," a special outpouring of the Spirit before the Second Coming of Christ.[21] She also uses Jesus' commissioning of women to bear witness to the resurrection and the numerous biblical examples of women who ministered as prophetesses and labored alongside men in the apostolic church to support the present day ministries of women.[22] In Galatians 3:28, Paul proclaims the great truth that in Christ there is "neither Jew not Greek, there is neither slave or free, there is neither male nor female; for you are all one in Christ Jesus." She claims that where this truth is acknowledged, the preaching of women as a special gift from Christ is also acknowledged, since Christ alone has the power to appoint and qualify ministers.[23]

To those who insist that the Bible opposes the ministry of women and say they are to be subordinate to men, Palmer replies that scripture is meant to be interpreted by scripture and serious errors in faith and practice result when isolated passages are used to sustain a pet theory.[24]

17. Ibid., 178.
18. Ibid., 14–23.
19. Ibid., 26–27.
20. Ibid., 127.
21. Hardesty, Dayton, and Dayton, "Women in the Holiness Movement," 246.
22. Palmer, *Promise of the Father*, 9–10.
23. Ibid., 10.
24. Ibid., 49–50.

She deals with the Pauline passages most often used to argue against women in ministry and instead uses them to support her point of view. She points out that in I Corinthians 11:3–16, Paul assumes women will prophesy in church and only wishes them to behave with propriety. In I Corinthians 14:34, Paul cannot be saying that woman cannot prophesy; after all, he just told them how to do it in I Corinthians 11:3–16. Instead he is squelching the practice of women who asked disruptive questions during the service.[25]

But Palmer does not deal quite so authoritatively with 1 Timothy 2:8–15. She argues that the only restriction placed on a woman's ministry in this passage is that she not usurp the authority of the man.[26] Because Adam was formed first and then Eve, for all time woman must acknowledge the man as first and not usurp his authority. Here she clearly rejects the argument that the subordination of women is a result of the curse and instead sees it as a principle of creation. This doesn't mean that she thinks this creation principle in any way limits the ministries of women. She is absolutely convinced that any ministry a woman undertakes under the authority of the Spirit honors this principle. In the order of God and as the result of an extraordinary call, women can speak and act for God, since women who speak under the influence of the Spirit assume no personal authority over others—they are merely instruments of the divine.[27] But she also recognizes that this argument depends completely upon the Spirit and that when the church loses its spiritual fervor, the ministries of women go into decline.[28]

Arguments for (and against) the Ministry of Women in the Early Years of Pentecostalism

The early Pentecostals essentially adopted Phoebe Palmer's Spirit-baptism theology and used it to champion the ministries of women as well as their own understanding of Spirit-baptism as empowering for ministry. They believed that whoever received this empowering baptism of the Holy Spirit had an extraordinary call to minister. So Spirit-baptized women were fully qualified as ministers of the gospel. In

25. Ibid., 47.
26. Ibid., 48.
27. Ibid., 1–2, 8–9.
28. Ibid., 34.

this they were in complete agreement with Phoebe Palmer. But this Pentecostal argument that Spirit-baptism is the sole factor in qualifying a woman for ministry is not without its problems.

One of these problems can be clearly seen in Palmer's insistence that the Spirit-baptized woman who ministers is merely an instrument of the divine; she assumes no personal authority over others in her ministry. As David Roebuck has pointed out, in the doctrine of Spirit-baptism, the authority for ministry resides in the manifestation of the Spirit rather than in the human vessel. So, although this doctrine gives women the right to preach, it says nothing about the nature of a woman's authority.[29] In fact, the view espoused by Palmer and the early Pentecostals severely limits a woman's authority: "The gospel does not alter the relation of woman in view of priority. For Adam was first formed and then Eve. And though the condition of woman is improved, and her privileges enlarged, she is not raised to a position of superiority, where she may usurp authority and teach dictatorially, for the law still remains as at the beginning. It is an unalterable law of nature. Adam was first formed, then Eve, and all the daughters of Adam must acknowledge man first in creation, as long as time endures."[30]

As this quote from Palmer clearly shows, another problem is created by her insistence that, based on 1 Timothy 2:8–15, the subordination of woman is a creation principle. This creation principle was then accepted without question by many of the early Pentecostals as part of their argument for women in ministry and led to restrictions on the leadership roles of women in the early Pentecostal movement. Women were empowered by the Spirit as ministers, but they were not empowered as women. This principle also became the "loophole" that eventually allowed those who opposed the ministry of women to undermine the scriptural basis of the Pentecostal argument for the ministry of women.

So on the one hand, early Pentecostals clearly affirmed a woman's right to preach and often credentialed them so that they could hold formal ministry positions, but on the other hand they limited the leadership roles of these women ministers within congregations and

29. Roebuck, "Limiting Liberty," 4.
30. Palmer, *Promise of the Father*, 8.

denominations based on the principles set forth in 1 Timothy 2.[31] But even as they limited the roles of women, early Pentecostals almost never undermined the strong arguments from scripture for the ministries of women based on prophetic models of ministry or a prophetic understanding of Spirit-baptism. In fact, they used Palmer's strategy of developing a prophetic understanding of ministry to reinterpret texts traditionally used to argue against women in ministry. Employing this strategy, they were able to expand on her arguments and deal with new challenges to the ministry of women.

One rather humorous example of this strategy is found in some early issues of *The Christian Evangel*. In the 15 August 1914 issue, E. N. Bell, a staunch Pentecostal opponent of women's ordination, wrote a long article that argued against the ordination of women as elders. In it he says that here is no example in scripture of any women being appointed to a position where ruling with authority is inferred. Then in the 9 January 1915 issue, Mrs. A. R. Flower writes her "Pentecostal Notes on International Sunday School Lesson" on the story of Deborah and Barak. She points out that Deborah was "inspired and instructed by the Holy Ghost to deal justice to the people, redressing wrongs, and correcting abuses, particularly in matters pertaining to the worship of God. She was respected in her God-appointed capacity for 'the children of God came to her for judgment.'" Flower clearly presents Deborah as a woman given authoritative rule in the congregation of Israel. Flower continues her presentation of Deborah as a woman with authoritative rule with the comment: "The directing of the army still devolved upon her. God chose her as the head, to give the word; Barak as the hand to do the work." One wonders if E. N. Bell realized how effectively Flower undermined his previous argument against the ordination of women as elders.

If early Pentecostals dealt decisively with arguments against the prophetic ministries of women from within their ranks, they dealt even more decisively with attacks on their women preachers from those outside, especially when such attacks involved criticisms of the Pentecostal idea of prophetic ministry as well. The most virulent of these attacks came in a book entitled *Bobbed Hair, Bossy Wives and Women Preachers*. It was written by John R. Rice, a Fundamentalist preacher famous for

31. Roebuck, "Limiting Liberty," 4–5.

his contentious, reactionary spirit, and is considered a "classic piece of fundamentalist misogyny."[32] This book is quite clearly directed against the women preachers of Pentecostal and Holiness groups who had been strongly influenced by Palmer's Spirit-baptism argument:

> The followers of Aimee Semple McPherson, the large Pentecostal and Holiness groups, the Volunteers of America who have been led so long by Maud Ballington Booth, the Salvation Army where women preachers have always been welcomed, though in actual practice they usually did not have the leadership—all these and many others would insist on the right of women to preach, to do the work of an evangelist or pastor, or Bible teacher, the same as a man of like attainments.[33]

Rice then goes on to use the usual scriptural arguments based on the subordination of woman to man in creation against the ministry of women and says that because the Word of God is clear on this issue any woman who claims that God has called her is clearly being led by a false spirit and is teaching false doctrine.

But Rice's argument gets really interesting when he gets to the subject of prophecy. Rice recognizes the power of the prophetic argument for women's ministries, so he proceeds to undermine the importance of prophetic ministry. He first points out that prophetesses were not preachers. He claims that it is never stated that a biblical prophetess preached, although biblical prophets (masculine) sometimes preached. Instead Rice thinks a prophetess is a woman who receives divine revelation about the future; for Rice this is the usual definition of prophecy, a divine revelation about the future. "Prophecy does not mean preaching; it means divine revelation under the anointing of the Spirit."[34] Rice is even willing to take on Scofield and most of the Protestant tradition in order to make his point:

> There are . . . misleading notes in the Scofield Bible on the question of prophecy. Concerning 1 Corinthians 12:10 Dr. Scofield comments, "The NT prophet is not ordinarily a foreteller, but

32. Joel Carpenter, *Revive Us Again: The Reawakening of American Fundamentalism* (New York: Oxford University Press, 1997), 67.

33. John R. Rice, *Bobbed Hair, Bossy Wives and Women Preachers: Significant Questions for Honest Christian Women Settled by the Word of God* (Murfreesboro, TN: Sword of the Lord, [1941]), 38.

34. Ibid., 48–49.

rather a forth-teller, one whose gift enabled him to speak 'to edification, and exhortation, and comfort' (1 Cor 14:3)." . . . But prophecy is not preaching; it is an entirely new revelation from God referring usually, as far as we know, to the future, and certainly being a direct, immediate revelation, not an exposition of Scripture, not Bible teaching not evangelism not preaching. Prophecy is not preaching. Prophetesses in the Bible never preached.[35]

Pentecostals were not about to let Rice's attack on the ministry of women or the Pentecostal view of prophetic ministry go unchallenged. In 1948, W. L. Myers published an answer to Rice's argument, "Does God Call Women to Preach? Evangelist John R. Rice Says NO, Pastor W. L. Myers Says YES." He points out right away that, in 1 Corinthians 11, the Bible assumes women will prophesy and that in 1 Corinthians 14:3, prophecy is defined as speaking for edification, exhortation, and comfort. As far as he is concerned that pretty much settles the issue. Preaching and prophecy are the same thing and women are doing it in the New Testament church. In fact he accuses Rice of limiting the generally accepted definition of prophecy just because he wants to limit the ministry of women.[36] Although he goes on to answer Rice point by point, the basis of his argument is Palmer's understanding of Scripture and Spirit-baptism. Forty years after Azusa Street, Pentecostals still understood the importance of defending the prophetic ministry of Spirit-baptized women.

Arguments (for and) against the Ministry of Women in the Late Twentieth Century

But thirty years later things had shifted dramatically. With the advent of the charismatic movement, both baptism in the Holy Spirit and prophecy began to be thoroughly redefined. Charismatics had received the mighty Pentecostal experience of Spirit-baptism with the evidence of speaking in tongues, but most charismatics were from mainline Protestant denominations that did not believe in a second and subsequent experience of the Spirit. So they could not accept the Pentecostal

35. Ibid., 51–52.

36. W. L. Myers, "Does God Call Women To Preach? Evangelist John R. Rice Says 'NO' Pastor W. L. Myers Says 'YES'" (Rockmart, GA: Privately Published Pamphlet, 1948), 5–7.

understanding that this experience was an experience of empowering for service. Although they came up with many different understandings of what this experience might mean, these understandings centered on the basic idea of a deeper experience of the Spirit and a renewed relationship with God. So for charismatics, Spirit-baptism was usually more about their own relationship with God than it was about empowering for service. The explanation of "the baptism in the Holy Spirit" found in Dennis and Rita Bennett's *The Holy Spirit and You* is one of the most typical and influential of these charismatic redefinitions of Spirit-baptism:

> This "something" that needs to happen is that the Holy Spirit Who is living in your spirit needs to *flow out* to fill your soul and body . . . This is called in the Scripture, "the baptism in the Holy Spirit," because it *is* a baptism, a drenching, an overflowing, a saturating of your soul and body with the Holy Spirit . . . When we receive Jesus as Savior, the Holy Spirit *comes in*, but as we continue to trust and believe Jesus, the Indwelling Spirit can *pour out* to inundate, or baptize our soul and body, and refresh the world around.[37]

This also affected the charismatic understanding of prophetic ministry. For Palmer and the early Pentecostals, prophetic ministry involved all forms of Spirit-empowered ministry of the Word. Preaching, teaching, testimony, supernaturally-inspired messages, words of exhortation, and encouragement all qualified as prophetic ministry. But for most charismatics, prophecy was defined as a form of the gift of prophecy, as a directly Spirit-inspired, supernatural utterance. In fact, the Bennetts take a stance very typical of the charismatics and explicitly state that inspired preaching and witnessing is not prophecy.[38]

The way these new charismatic understandings worked together to redefine prophetic ministry can be seen in two articles found in the January 1977 issue of *New Wine* magazine. One is an excerpt from a book on *Prophecy* by Bruce Yokum, which explains New Testament prophecy:

37. Dennis and Rita Bennett, *The Holy Spirit and You* (Gainesville: Bridge-Logos, 1971), 11–12.

38. Ibid., 101–12.

Under the New Covenant God throws open the gates of the palace and all of his people can themselves enter (Heb 10:19). Thus, each of God's subjects can hear God's word from his own lips. Under this new arrangement, there still remains a role for the prophet. When a king chooses a messenger from among his people, he provides him with both a message *and with the authority to proclaim the message publicly.* The many subjects who can now enter the palace can hear a message directly from God, but he does not confer upon them the authority to publicly proclaim the message. The prophet then retains a unique function in declaring publicly the word of the Lord.[39]

Notice that for Yokum, and presumably the editors of *New Wine* magazine, the "prophethood of all believers" gives believers access to God and the right to hear from God, but not the right to proclaim a message from God publicly. In other words, their relationship with God is deepened, but they are not empowered for ministry or given the authority to proclaim God's word.

How this applies specifically to the ministry of women is made clear in another article in the same issue by Bob Mumford on "Levels of Prophecy." Mumford defines prophecy as "more than just inspired preaching or the mere foretelling of events; it is a supernatural speaking forth of the word of God in the language of the speaker and his hearers."[40] He goes on to say that everyone is able to prophesy in the sense of giving words of comfort and exhortation or revealing the secrets of a person's heart. Those with the gift of prophecy do this more regularly than others. But *"the office or ministry of the prophet . . .* in the New Testament . . . is held only by men, not women."[41] He doesn't really explain why, but the examples he gives make it clear that he regards this as an authoritative office and the reader is left with the impression that this is why women cannot exercise prophetic ministry.

At the same time, the fundamentalists had not given up arguing against the ministry of women. The basic premise of John R. Rice's contention against the prophetic argument for women in ministry was resurrected in a much more sophisticated and academic form by Wayne Grudem in his 1978 doctoral dissertation, *The Gift of Prophecy*

39. Bruce Yokum, "What is a Prophet?" *New Wine* 9.1 (1977): 6.

40. Bob Mumford, "Levels of Prophecy," *New Wine* 9.1 (1977): 10.

41. Ibid., 12.

in 1 Corinthians. This book has been through two revisions; the latest (and according to Grudem the last) in 2000. Grudem argues that in the New Testament, prophecy is not the authoritative ministry of the Word that prophecy was in the Old Testament. Prophecy is merely a public report of a spontaneous revelation of the Holy Spirit.[42] Of course, in making this argument, Grudem, like Rice, must ignore the definition of prophecy as words given for "edification, exhortation and encouragement" in 1 Corinthians 14:3. For Grudem, teaching is the authoritative ministry of the Word in the New Testament and is closely connected to the exercise of leadership—one of the qualifications for elders listed in 1 Timothy 3:3 and Titus 1:9 is that they are to be "apt teachers." Once he has devalued prophetic ministry and established teaching as the truly authoritative ministry of the Word in the New Testament, Grudem proceeds to identify preaching with the ministry of teaching. He claims that in modern usuage, preaching is much closer to what the New Testament means by teaching than to what the New Testament calls prophecy.[43] This means that the women prophets of 1 Corinthians 11 are not exercising an authoritative ministry of the Word or occupying an authoritative position in the church when they prophecy. So the New Testament encourages women to prophecy and to participate in church worship by using the gift of prophecy but does not permit them to engage in any type of authoritative ministry of the word or government of the church, including the judging of prophecy, teaching, preaching, serving as an elder, etc. These activities are reserved for men because of eternal created differences between men and women. Therefore, the fact that women prophesy in the New Testament cannot be used as an argument for women exercising an authoritative ministry in the church today.[44]

But the redefinition of prophecy put forth by both Grudem and Rice hardly does justice to the New Testament view of prophecy. It ignores the strong prophetic tradition of Luke-Acts, the basis of the Pentecostal understanding of prophecy, and never examines the prophetic ministry of Jesus as one who is anointed by the Spirit and mighty in words and deeds. Devaluing prophecy ends up devaluing the entire

42. Wayne Grudem, *The Gift of Prophecy in the New Testament and Today* (Wheaton: Crossway, 2000), 113–15.

43. Ibid., 118–20.

44. Ibid., 183–92.

New Testament message. It is also quite dangerous to separate prophetic ministry from the larger context of the ministry of the Word in the church. In the Old Testament, prophecy was not supposed to contradict the Law of God or lead God's people into rebellion (Deuteronomy 4:2; 12:32; 13:1–5). New Testament prophets are just as responsible for the content of their prophecies for "the spirits of the prophets are subject to the prophets" (1 Corinthians 14:32) and need to know how to "rightly divide the Word of truth" (1 Timothy 2:15). Throughout the New Testament, prophecy is considered a ministry of the Word and is usually listed ahead of teaching (Romans 12:6-8; 1 Corinthians 12:29; Ephesians 4:11). Grudem's and Rice's attempt to attack the ministries of women by devaluing prophecy is really only convincing to those who have already decided that women shouldn't be ministers and don't really think much of prophetic ministry either.

Like Rice, Grudem also appeals to woman's subordination as an eternal principle of creation. Although he mentions this argument in his book on prophecy, it is made exceptionally clear in the book he edited with John Piper, *Recovering Biblical Manhood and Womanhood: A Response to Biblical Feminism.* In this book, there is not even one article on the prophetic argument for women in ministry, nor any acknowledgement of the Evangelical feminist arguments of the nineteenth-century Holiness movement. Instead, the entire book is written from the perspective that the subordination of women to men is a creation principle that must be acknowledged by anyone who acknowledges the authority of the Bible.[45]

These same glaring omissions are evident in Grudem's most recent attack on women in ministry, *Evangelical Feminism: A New Path to Liberalism.*[46] He starts the book with an historical overview of the connection between liberalism and the ordination of women in the last half of the twentieth century. He deliberately ignores the readily available statistics which show that more women have been ordained in Holiness and Pentecostal traditions (which certainly qualify as Evangelical) than liberal traditions. Although he does admit that some denominations ordain women because of their historical tradition and a strong

45. John Piper and Wayne Grudem, eds., *Recovering Biblical Manhood and Womanhood: A Response to Evangelical Feminism* (Wheaton, IL: Crossway, 1991).

46. Wayne Grudem, *Evangelical Feminism: A New Path to Liberalism* (Wheaton, IL: Crossway, 2006).

emphasis on the gifting of the Spirit, he never once mentions the Evangelical feminists of the nineteenth century.[47] This is hardly an honest historical overview. He then deals with several peripheral arguments used by *some* (and Grudem clearly admits that only *some* use these arguments) Evangelical feminists to support their views. But he never deals with some of the core arguments of Evangelical feminists, arguments that have been seen as biblically sound for over 150 years. Specifically, he does not deal with the prophetic argument for women in ministry.

It is clear that, from Grudem's perspective, Phoebe Palmer's argument for the Spirit-empowered ministries of women isn't worth acknowledging or considering as a valid biblical argument for the ministries of women. In fact, he is not really interested in considering any solidly biblical argument which might allow women to have any type of authoritative ministry. He has already decided what the Bible says and believes that any argument for the ordination of women or any type of authoritative ministry for women undermines the authority of the Bible. In this, he is very much in agreement with John R. Rice. Grudem's argument might have been an interesting footnote in this debate had he not become one of the more influential theologians in the Vineyard churches and therefore an influential voice in the Pentecostal-charismatic movement as it moves into the twenty-first century. At the end of his book on *Evangelical Feminism*, Grudem mentions the denominations that he thinks are being influenced by liberal egalitarian positions and includes both the Association of Vineyard Churches and independent charismatic churches.[48] But it is far more likely that in these churches, where strong emphases on the gifts of the Spirit are found, the traditional Pentecostal arguments for the ministry of women based on prophetic empowering have not been completely lost and Grudem's arguments are not seen as totally convincing.

But in the face of Grudem's attack on the Spirit-empowered prophetic ministries of women, the almost complete silence from Pentecostal churches is deafening. Sixty years ago, W. L. Myers was eager to answer John R. Rice and defend the ministry of women. But today Pentecostals and charismatics seem to have accepted arguments like Grudem's and

47. Ibid., 23–29.
48. Ibid., 259.

are no longer aggressively championing the ministries of women. In fact some Pentecostal denominations are less open to the ministries of women than they were a hundred years ago. In interviews David Roebuck conducted with women ministers in the Church of God,[49] a very disturbing pattern emerged. Two of these women had daughters who have gone into ministry. Those who sought credentialing after the mid-1970s, when the charismatic movement and its theology began influencing the traditional Pentecostal churches, have encountered tremendous obstacles in their Pentecostal denomination. Lucille Walker's daughter wanted to be a missionary, but the Church of God refused to send her. When she was approved by the Assemblies of God (another Pentecostal denomination), her father pleaded with her denomination to reconsider their decision and the Church of God eventually decided to send her as an intern rather than a missionary. She now has a thriving ministry in Taiwan. Lucille Walker's other daughter is now seeking ministerial certification in another denomination.[50] Mary Graves was very disappointed that her daughter decided to be a Methodist, but understood why she made this decision. After a General Assembly where the issue of women in ministry was debated and the decision not to ordain women was upheld, her daughter said, "I am not going to put my ministry in the hands of men that feel like they do about women ministers."[51] The Spirit may be empowering women to preach, but the theology and denominational structures of Pentecostals are aborting the ministries of prophetically called women.

Is There a Future for the Prophetic Ministry of Women in Pentecostalism?

Phoebe Palmer would scarcely recognize the movement her theology of Spirit-baptism gave birth to at the beginning of the twentieth century. The Spirit-empowered ministries of women within that movement are seldom acknowledged, much less affirmed. The idea of Spirit-baptism as

49. David Roebuck conducted these interviews as part of an oral history project exploring possible reasons for the decline in the number of women ministers in the Church of God. See his article on "'Cause He's My Chief Employer': Hearing Women's Voices in a Classical Pentecostal Denomination," in this volume.

50. Janet Everts Powers, "Interview with Lucille Walker," 4 June 2005, and David Roebuck, "Interview with Lucille Walker," 21 June 1990.

51. David Roebuck, "Interview with Mary Graves," 26 June 1990.

an experience that empowers all who receive it for a prophetic ministry of the Word has too often been lost or reduced to a personal experience that has little to do with ministry. Prophecy is no longer seen as a ministry of the Word that includes preaching, explaining the words of scripture and all edifying, encouraging, and exhorting words. Instead it is reduced to non-authoritative and spontaneous Spirit-inspired words that have little connection to the ministry of the Word. These shifts have not just undermined the theological basis for the ministries of women in the Pentecostal movement, they have also undermined the original theological distinctives which gave the Pentecostal movement its power.

The early Pentecostals not only accepted Phoebe Palmer's understanding of Spirit-baptism as empowering for ministry, they also believed that the evidence of this experience of empowering was speaking in tongues. So when a second experience of the Spirit became less important in the charismatic movement, the evidence of speaking in tongues assumed new theological significance as an ecstatic experience of the Spirit. This kind of ecstatic experience of the Spirit is a form of prophetic experience, but as it assumed greater importance the understanding of the purpose of this experience shifted away from the ministry of the Word to the immediate personal experience of the Spirit. Those who received the gift of tongues were less empowered for ministry than they were renewed in their personal spiritual lives and their relationship with God. Unfortunately, those inside and outside Pentecostalism too often see this as the major contribution of Pentecostalism to the history of the Church.

Those who claim to be the heirs of Azusa Street no longer seem to be able to communicate the important connection between their experience of a deep encounter with the Spirit of God and the call to a prophetic ministry of the Word which that encounter brings. They seem to be content to enjoy their experience with God and their wonderful worship and prayer life. They appear to have forgotten that the purpose of their divine encounter and the baptism of the Holy Spirit is to empower all who receive it for a powerful and effective ministry of the Word. Perhaps this is related to the fact that they have forgotten to champion the right of women to engage in a prophetic Spirit-empowered ministry of the Word. Either Pentecostals believe in the prophethood of *all* believers who have received the baptism of the

Holy Spirit, and they champion the ministries of *all* believers who are empowered by the Spirit to bear witness to the gospel, or the doctrine of the baptism of the Holy Spirit empowering believers for ministry is worthless.

Roger Stronstad captures the essence of the theological crisis that faces the Pentecostal church as it enters its second century at the end of his book on *The Prophethood of All Believers*:

> Luke's doctrine of the people of God is that beginning in Jerusalem and co-extensive with the spread of the gospel they become the eschatological community of prophets—the prophethood of all believers. Luke's doctrine is not merely a matter of historical fact of inquiry. It is an urgent matter of con-temporary relevance and reality . . .
>
> As a prophetic community God's people are to be ac-tive in service. But all too often the Pentecostal, charismatic movements focus on the experience, the emotion and the blessing more than they do on Spirit-filled, Spirit-led and Spirit-empowered service. This shift in focus from vocation to per-sonal experience, from being world-centered to self-centered . . . is like selling one's birthright of Spirit-empowered service for the pottage of self-seeking experience and blessing . . .
>
> The antidote to this malaise in which the Spirit of prophecy is either quenched or misused is for the contemporary Church to recapture, both doctrinally and vocationally, the first-century reality which Luke reports. The reality is one in which all of God's people are prophets because the Lord has put his Spirit on them. It is a reality where once again 'speaking with other tongues' is the physical symbol of a Spirit-empowered, world-wide witness. It is also a reality where Spirit-baptized believers are prophets powerful in works and word, both within the com-munity and in the world.[52]

When this reality is restored to the twenty-first century Pentecostal church, Spirit-empowered women will again have an environment in which their ministries can begin to flourish. But the lessons of the last century are clear. It is important to empower women as women, not just as vessels of the Holy Spirit. Restoring Phoebe Palmer's great insight that Spirit-baptism empowers the one who receives it for ministry is just the beginning. Learning to honor all who minister in Christ's name and in the power of the Spirit as equals is the next necessary step.

52. Stronstad, *Prophethood of All Believers*, 123–24.

9

"You've Got a Right to the Tree of Life"

The Biblical Foundations of an Empowered Attitude among Black Women in the Sanctified Church

Cheryl Townsend Gilkes

Introduction

> Run, Mary, run!
> Run, Martha, run!
> Run, Mary, run, I say!
> You've got a right to the tree of life.

PENTECOSTALISM IS THE MOST WIDESPREAD EXPRESSION OF THE Christian emphasis on the person of the Spirit. On the other hand, the focus on christology is so established among Christian theologians that they sometimes question whether or not Pentecostal emphases on the Spirit are actually Christian. Yet Pentecostalism cannot be adequately understood apart from either this motif or its roots in the African American religious experience. In his now classic history of Pentecostalism, European scholar Walter Hollenweger pointed to the origins of twentieth century Pentecostalism in "a revival among the Negroes of North America."[1] This revival was embedded in a particular historical moment—a moment when African Americans were building new communities and religious institutions during the post-Reconstruction era—the historical moment starting around 1878 character-

---

1. Walter Hollenweger, *The Pentecostals,* trans. R. A. Wilson (Minneapolis: Augsburg, 1972).

ized by violent black-white confrontation, severe racial oppression, and black urban migration.[2] At that moment, organized African American religion was in its second century and a biblical defense of its emphasis on the Spirit was not only a part of the emerging Holiness and Pentecostal churches but also an important discourse among Baptists and Methodists. For the vast majority of African American Christians, the Bible was central.

Embedded in the history of African Americans and Pentecostalism is a history of emboldened, Bible-believing women. Women were central to the discourses and practices created and sustained among enslaved and free communities and churches. Their roles in the growth and development of Pentecostalism have not been fully described and appreciated. This essay focuses on the integral role of women in the shaping of "the Sanctified Church"—predominantly black Holiness, Pentecostal, and Apostolic congregations and denominations—and the biblical foundations of these churches and their distinctive constellations of women's roles. Lincoln and Mamiya identified a series of dialectical tensions that "the Black Church" negotiates,[3] one of which is the tension between the charismatic and bureaucratic. This tension was deeply and specifically implicated in the growth and development of the Sanctified Church. Partisans within the churches appealed to the Bible to assert the primary importance of the charismatic with its emphasis on the Spirit. For churches that emphasize the Spirit, women are often able to carve out more prominent leadership roles than in churches where the bureaucratic is given primacy. Furthermore, the bureaucratic/charismatic tension was complicated for women by what Evelyn Brooks Higginbotham called a "politics of respectability" with its emphasis on women's leadership aimed at uplifting the community.[4] This emphasis on respectability and uplift deeply affected the ways that women acted upon their callings within these settings. In the face of patriarchal opposition, women carved out roles that actually fostered

2. It is important to remember that the Pentecostal movement grew out of the Holiness movement, a movement where both black and white Christians interacted in churches and camp meetings.

3. C. Eric Lincoln and Lawrence H. Mamiya, *The Black Church in the African American Experience* (Durham, NC: Duke University Press, 1990).

4. Evelyn Brooks Higginbotham, *Righteous Discontent: The Women's Movement in the Black Baptist Church, 1880–1920* (Cambridge: Harvard University Press, 1993).

the growth of churches and the advancement of a movement. They exercised a spiritual agency that contradicted the use of biblical admonitions for women to be silent and invisible. At the same time they utilized the Bible to defend their participation in church leadership.

This essay seeks to tell a "thick story" about the ways that women in the Sanctified Church contributed to asserting the humanity of African Americans through their religious practices. Furthermore these practices are built into the foundations of Pentecostalism in the modern world. According to Cornel West and Eddie Glaude, telling a "thick story" is a crucial way "to describe and demystify cultural and social practices."[5] Telling the "thick story" of the African American experience with reference to American religion counters the cultural erasure that characterizes American racism. Although American Pentecostalism began in a black congregation and grew with a radical interracialism, white people retreated from that interracialism in the face of rising Jim Crow. The fissure was so deep and so complete that many contemporary white Pentecostals do not know or acknowledge their debt to African American religion. Not only does this essay seek to place what Toni Morrison calls the "Africanist" presence in the foreground,[6] but to examine the ways that African American Christians whose faith was deeply rooted in slave religion shaped the discourses and practices we often take for granted today.

Slave Religion and the Talking Book

The centrality of the Bible in African American Christianity runs deep. Biblical scholar Allen Callahan offered the most concrete assessment when he wrote, "African Americans are the children of slavery. And the Bible, as no other book, is the book of slavery's children."[7] Henry Louis Gates argues that one of the central questions guiding consciousness in the slave community was a question about whether the Bible could

5. Cornel West and Eddie S. Glaude, Jr., "Introduction: Towards New Visions and New Approaches in African American Religious Studies," in Cornel West and Eddie S. Glaude, Jr., eds., *African American Religious Thought: An Anthology* (Louisville: Westminster John Knox, 2003), xi–xxvi; quotation from xxiii.

6. Toni Morrison, *Playing in the Dark: Whiteness and the Literary Imagination* (Cambridge: Harvard University Press, 1992).

7. Allen Callahan, *The Talking Book: African Americans and the Bible* (New Haven: Yale University Press, 2006), xi.

speak to them.[8] As a result, the Bible became a speakerly text—a Talking Book. Slave religion was a biblical religion and slaves' engagement with the Bible shaped a definition of the situation that permitted widespread debate about the authenticity of the faith of the slave owners and offered sharp critiques of the religious contradictions that enslaved women and men observed.[9] Webber points out that Christians in the slave community made a distinction between what they viewed as slaveholding priestcraft and true Christianity. Biblical arguments undergirded major slave revolts led by Denmark Vesey and Nat Turner and those arguments opposed the biblical arguments that justified slavery. Over time, African Americans developed a specialized reading of the Bible that emphasized those prophetic and apocalyptic texts that bolstered their liberationist perspectives on slavery.

Many observers note the emphasis on the Exodus in spirituals such as "Go Down Moses" and in the use of the term "Moses" to describe Harriet Tubman. Indeed, political scientist Michael Walzer insists that the biblical Exodus is at the center of the idea of revolution in the West, himself being inspired to review the Exodus narrative after hearing a sermon on the Exodus in a southern black church during the civil rights movement.[10] However, Callahan argues that there are a number of major, logically-connected themes in the African American appropriation and interpretation of the Bible. Before the Exodus there was the experience of Exile that confronted the violent dislocation of capture and the Middle Passage—a reality grasped in the prophetic visions of Ezekiel. Only after the destructive tragedy of mass deportation and dismemberment were grasped in terms of the violence of exile did the Exodus become a theme that could be embraced. In the Bible, liberation came to a holy nation; the Exodus story was not only about the direct intervention of God in removing people from slavery, but also about God's intervention to shape and forge a community and nation out of a mixed multitude. For enslaved African Americans, an element of their identification as community and as God's people was facilitated by the biblical idea of Ethiopia, an idea that allowed enslaved women

8. Henry Louis Gates, *The Signifying Monkey: A Theory of Afro-American Literary Criticism* (New York: Oxford University Press, 1988).

9. Thomas L. Webber, *Deep Like the Rivers: Education in the Slave Quarter Community, 1831–65* (New York: Norton, 1978).

10. Michael Walzer, *Exodus and Revolution* (New York: Basic Books, 1985).

and men to locate themselves in the biblical text. Callahan points out that as early as the late eighteenth century, African American activists pointed to the African/Ethiopian presence in the Bible and the African/ Ethiopian role in the history of ancient Israel.[11] The slave community, however, reached beyond the Hebrew Bible to embrace Emmanuel, the suffering and resurrected Christ who is to be imitated and emulated. "More than the Lord and God of slavery's children, Jesus is their peer; he is as they are, for he has suffered as they have suffered."[12] Jesus places the entire biblical corpus before the enslaved as a source of encourage- ment to challenge the oppressive world around them and as a resource with Jesus as the principal but not only role model.

The record of African American biblical consciousness in the slave community is quite clear and rich. Almost every Negro spiritual contains within it a direct reference to the Bible. Folklore and interview testimony also depict a deep consciousness of the Bible and the details of stories significant for liberation. There is an emphasis on the gospels and a very clear hermeneutics of suspicion where Paul is concerned. Additionally, African American Christianity does not maintain the wall of separation between the Old Testament/Hebrew Bible and the New Testament that white Christians seem to do. As a result, Old Testament/Hebrew Bible preaching does not usually take a supercessionist approach. Instead the "law and the prophets" are an important tool to criticize and oppose racial oppression. Furthermore, ancient Israelites are important role models, positive and negative, for approaching problems in living and for shaping roles within the church and community.

In spite of their limited literacy during slavery, African Americans implanted the Bible into their oral traditions and used the Bible as a measuring rod to evaluate the larger world and their oppressive situa- tion. Although this assertion requires more research, African Americans probably utilized the Bible as a tool for mediating their negotiations among the diverse religious perspectives they inherited from their African forbears. Again Callahan is helpful:

> American slaves did not read the Bible through, or even over
> and against, the traditions they brought with them from West
> Africa: they read the Bible as a text into which these traditions

11. Callahan, *Talking Book*, 142.
12. Ibid., 238–39.

were woven. The characters and events of the Bible became the functional equivalent of the ancestors and heroes long celebrated in West Africa. The many ancestral and natural spirits were subsumed by the Holy Spirit, and the mighty acts of God supplanted ancient tales of martial valor. Biblical patriarchs and heroes now sat on the stools of the esteemed ancestors of ages past.[13]

Slave Religion and the Road to Azusa Street

The Christianity that African Americans forged during slavery was a Christianity that emphasized the workings of the Spirit. In an essay on the sorrow songs that concluded *The Souls of Black Folk* (1903), W. E. B. Du Bois asked the question, "Your country how came it yours?"[14] In framing a preliminary answer to that question, Du Bois identified three gifts of the African presence in America: the gift of labor, the gift of song, and the gift of the Spirit. Du Bois understood that American history and American institutions, including and especially religion, were tied intimately to the history of the African presence in the New World. Without a detailed discussion, Du Bois asserted that the United States was distinctive in its spiritual fertility, nurturing a variety of Christian denominations that emphasized the person of the Holy Spirit. Three years before the 1906 Azusa Street Revival, Du Bois underscored the importance of the Spirit and the Africanist factor in that emphasis. By 1924, and at a time when the Pentecostal movement was well underway, Du Bois provided a more definitive answer to his question in a book titled *The Gift of Black Folk: The Negroes in the Making of America*.[15] In that book Du Bois emphasized not only the gift of the Spirit but also the critical role women played through their religious and community networks. As the source of organizational integrity in black communities and churches, women's networks fostered the survival of communities and advanced the educational and political goals of African Americans.

13. Ibid., xii.

14. W. E. B. Du Bois, *The Souls of Black Folk*, reprinted in Henry Louis Gates, Jr. and Terri Hume Oliver, eds., *The Souls of Black Folk: Authoritative Text, Contexts, and Criticism* (New York: Norton, 1999), 1–164.

15. W. E. B. Du Bois, *The Gift of Black Folk: The Negroes in the Making of America* (1924; reprint, Millwood, NY: Kraus-Thomson, 1975).

Both individual piety and communal practice incorporated the workings of the Holy Spirit. The earliest denominations shaped in the free black communities of the North were Methodist: African Methodist Episcopal (A.M.E.) and African Methodist Episcopal Zion (A.M.E.Z.). Additionally, the African Methodist Union was formed in the Delaware area during slavery and Colored (later Christian) Methodist Episcopal was formed in 1870 by black Methodist congregations in the South after slavery. This Methodist root contained a well articulated emphasis on conversion and sanctification. Wesleyan perspectives on the Holy Spirit were well integrated in the early stages of the Black Church.

Alongside these Methodist bodies, enslaved African Americans embraced the Baptist faith. The distinctive aspect of this embrace has been called "an Afro Baptist" faith, a way of being Christian that built upon the African background to foster a visionary ethos that required an encounter with Jesus by way of the Holy Spirit.[16] Both free and enslaved churches, visible and invisible churches, affirmed the importance of the Spirit in guiding individual practice ("every time I feel the Spirit moving in my heart") and facilitating ecstatic worship and community ("walk together, children, and don't you get weary"; "let us praise God together"), particularly in the form of shouting. Indeed, shouting emerged as an all encompassing term for expressions of the Spirit during worship. Additionally, the folk wisdom argued that "the Spirit" arrived on "the wings of a song," cementing a relationship between music and the experience of the Holy Spirit.[17]

Women were central to the development of African American religion. During slavery, and this was particularly true for the "invisible church," women were active participants in the life of churches. The life of the church, even in the most repressive of circumstances, depended upon people who could pray and raise a song. Women prayed and raised songs and sometimes emerged as the most important prayer

16. Mechal Sobel, *Trabelin' On: The Slave Journey to an Afro-Baptist Faith* (Westport, CN: Greenwood, 1979).

17. In an essay in *The Souls of Black Folks* titled "Of the Faith of the Fathers," Du Bois points to three major dimensions of African American religion: the preacher, the music, and the frenzy. In contemporary terms, the fundamental elements of African American Christianity can be viewed in terms of the interrelationship of leadership, music (improvisation and creativity), and ecstatic/Spirit led worship. The rest of African American religious tradition and its intercalation with the organizations and institutions of the larger black community rest on this tri-partite foundation.

warriors. Preaching occurred less often and when it occurred was most often presented by males, but not exclusively. Women were also preachers and exhorters.[18] Not only were women licensed in the A.M.E. and A.M.E. Zion churches, but black women evangelists conducted revivals in the South as well as the North.

Spirit-filled, visionary women and men emerged as leaders during slavery. Women in the slave community developed autonomous and independent spiritual practices.[19] They held their own prayer meetings and developed their own leaders, leaders so powerful that they could bring plantation routine to a halt. Not only did women raise their voices in song but they left behind pieces of material culture, such as quilts, that evidenced their biblical consciousness. Their perspectives, like that of the larger slave community, evinced a prophetic-apocalyptic reading of the Bible that spoke against injustice and posited a new, just world shaped by God's ultimate judgment.

The biblical consciousness of slave religion generated a paradigm that took seriously the roles of women in salvation history. In contrast to the English hymn tradition that was silent on the roles of women, Negro spirituals directly named the women who brought the news of the resurrection to the Twelve. The spirituals speak of Jesus' mother Mary, who "rocked Him in a weary land." One song describes the agony of her travels: "Mary's on the road / Most done traveling." Other songs talk about Mary and Martha and the resurrection. One song in particular asserts that Mary has "a right to the tree of life." The song, one of several such songs, points to the biblical story where women came to the tomb and went *running* to tell the disciples. The songs recognize that it was *mourners* who came early to the tomb ("the graveyard"). This pivotal role of women as the first to give voice to the resurrection placed *mourning* as a critical experiential dimension of life in the Spirit in African American churches, hence the development of the Mourners' Bench. Furthermore, when opponents of women's preaching attempted to silence women and to elide their role in carrying the good news of

18. Bettye Collier-Thomas, *Daughters of Thunder: Black Women Preachers and their Sermons, 1850–1979* (San Francisco: Jossey-Bass, 1998).

19. Deborah Gray White, *Ar'n't I A Woman: Female Slaves in the Plantation South* (New York: Norton, 1985; rev. ed., 1999).

the resurrection, the song tradition bore witness to their centrality, thus creating what I have elsewhere called a "biblical option for women."[20]

Within the slave community, mourning and seeking became prescribed spiritual practices that enabled the believer to be present with Jesus at pivotal moments. In seeking a vision and a conversion experience, one was expected to be carried away in the Spirit in a manner similar to the way Ezekiel and Philip (whose daughters were preachers) were carried away in the Spirit. Such visions allowed the believer to "come through" and be able to give a testimony.[21] Such testimonies answered the question sometimes sung, "Were you there when they crucified my Lord?" Not only did biblical consciousness in the slave community recognize and name the women whose voices were central to the formulation of the good news, but biblical consciousness also made the women's behavior as mourners, seeking to care for the body of Christ, the principal paradigm for conversion and spiritual practice. Such consciousness was extended by Baptist women and women in the Church of God in Christ who developed lists of named biblical women, highlighting their importance to salvation history.[22]

Freedom and the Rise of the Sanctified Church

The end of slavery fostered several conflicts within black churches over traditional spiritual practices. Northern missionaries descended on the South hoping to bring the light of the Gospel to contraband and former slaves. They discovered that these black communities were not only already Christian but had also been self-catechizing Christian communities since 1820.[23] What was apparent was that these communities'

20. Cheryl Townsend Gilkes, "'Go and Tell Mary and Martha': The Spirituals, Biblical Options for Women, and Cultural Tensions in the African American Experience," *Social Compass* 43.4 (1996): 563–82.

21. Clifton Johnson and A. P. Watson, eds., *God Struck Me Dead: Religious Conversion Experiences and Autobiographies of Ex-Slaves* (Philadelphia: Pilgrim, 1969).

22. Segments of a list developed by Baptist leader Nannie Helen Burroughs can be found in Jualynne E. Dodson and Cheryl Townsend Gilkes, "Something Within: Social Change and Collective Endurance in the Sacred World of Black Christian Women," in Rosemary Radford Ruether and Rosemary Skinner Keller, eds., *Women and Religion in America: Volume Three—The Twentieth Century* (San Francisco: Harper and Row, 1986), 80–128.

23. Albert J. Raboteau, *Slave Religion: The Invisible Institution in the Antebellum South* (New York: Oxford University Press, 1978).

worship practices were far too enthusiastic by puritanical (literally) New England standards. In one particularly dramatic incident, according to Leon Litwack, a freedwoman informed northern missionaries that her Bible told her "that if I were to hold my peace the very rocks would cry out and I don't want the rocks to speak for me."[24] After additional testimony, the congregation took a portion of her words, created a spiritual, and proceeded to sing in the traditional style until the Spirit descended. According to the missionaries' journals, they too were taken by the Spirit and did not demonstrate the restrained behavior they had been teaching.

Religious practices that encouraged the sustained presence of the Holy Spirit or Holy Ghost, such as sustained periods of communal singing, shouting, the ring shout, falling out, and "getting happy," were often derided as primitive elements of a "fist and heel" religion that needed to be "stamped out."[25] Adherents of such religion often argued that such behavior was necessary for the visitation of the Spirit and that failure to worship in such a way was a failure in one's relationship with God.[26] Although nearly everyone wanted the literacy that black and white northern missionaries brought to the rural South, many freed women and men did not want what they perceived to be the dead worship practices these missionaries also sought to impose. As these increasingly diverse religious constituencies acquired the theological fluency necessary to sustain their particular sides of the debates over worship, the Bible gained in importance. In response to those who admonished black people not to shout, church founders such as Bishop Charles Harrison (C. H.) Mason pointed to the biblical admonitions to shout, sing, and dance in order to defend such practices.[27]

These conflicts precipitated denominational and associational splits and the subsequent re-organizations of churches. For some

24. Leon F. Litwack, *Been in the Storm So Long: The Aftermath of Slavery* (New York: Vintage, 1979).

25. Daniel Payne, *Recollections of Seventy Years* (New York: New York Times, 1969).

26. Carter G. Woodson, *The History of the Negro Church* (1921; reprint, Washington, DC: Associated Publishers, 1972).

27. Charles Harrison Mason, "Is It Right for the Saints of God to Dance," in German O. Ross, J. O. Patterson, and Julia Mason Atkins, eds., *History and Formative Years of the Church of God in Christ with Excerpts from the Life and Works of Its Founder, Bishop C. H. Mason* (Memphis: Church of God in Christ Publishing, 1969), 36–37.

groups, the Holiness Movement became a vehicle for the defense of their ways of worship. Additionally, these new churches arose during the historical periods of Emancipation, where the problem of what West and Glaude described as "intense institutional terror" was paramount, and where urbanization and black religious pluralism were increasingly felt.[28] Women comprised half of the working class that founded congregations and built churches during this period.[29] Women provided both the money and the labor that developed these churches as they worked alongside men.

As preaching women faced discrimination in mainstream churches they responded in several ways. In some cases, particularly in the dominant Baptist and Methodist churches, women waged protracted battles over their roles utilizing the Bible. Women educated themselves by attending home Bible studies and denominational educational activities in order to argue in defense of their leadership.[30] As these conflicts grew, preaching women found their situations increasingly precarious. Where women could not maintain their leadership roles, especially as preachers, they formed powerful auxiliaries that raised money for missions, education, and other works. At other points, the women raised money and utilized their economic clout to shape policies, steer organizational direction, and to approve or veto men appointed to utilize or spend their money.[31] Church women also created their own secular organizations from which they sought to lead and "uplift the Race."[32] Women also devised several strategies to subvert the discrimination and subordination prescribed for them. These strong missionary societies not only raised money for missions and provided space for women's leadership and voices, but they also created semi-autonomous women's organizations within denominational bodies that exercised power similar to the military in many societies. Both within churches

28. West and Glaude, "Introduction," *African American Religious Thought*.

29. Tara Hunter, *To 'Joy My Freedom: Southern Black Women's Lives and Labors after the Civil War* (Cambridge: Harvard University Press, 1997).

30. See further Higginbotham, *Righteous Discontent*.

31. Jualynne E. Dodson, *Engendering Church: Women, Power, and the A.M.E. Church* (Lanham, MD: Rowman & Littlefield, 2002).

32. See Dodson and Gilkes, "Something Within," and also Deborah Gray White, *Too Heavy a Load: Black Women in Defense of Themselves, 1894–1994* (New York: Norton, 1999).

and in the larger community, women also took positions of leadership as educators.

Women in the Sanctified Church did all of the above and more. They not only carved out powerful roles for themselves through their economic support and roles as educators, but they also linked the theme of uplift to the elevating consequences of life in the Spirit to become "the women whom God raised up."[33] As missionaries and "church mothers" who were allowed to "teach" the Gospel, these women "dug out" churches, expanded the reach of new denominations out of the South, and educated generations of clergymen. Women in denominations that refused to ordain them managed to push against the boundaries that were imposed on them to establish very strong traditions within their churches.

Some women moved beyond the limitations of the more patriarchal denominations, leaving their churches to found new ones more accommodating to their sense of calling. Bishop Ida Robinson, for instance, established the Mt. Sinai Holy Church after leaving a church that ordained women for pastorates, permitted them to vote for the bishops, but banned them from seeking election as bishops.[34]

Women Whom God Raised Up: Biblical Role Models

Women enter any form of church leadership, in the words of Bishop Vashti Murphy MacKenzie, "not without a struggle."[35] Therefore biblical role models have been very critical to women's assertions of their rights to lead. The largest of the Sanctified Churches, the Pentecostal denomination Church of God in Christ, has been the site of a protracted struggle over the roles of women. Indeed, the *Official Manual of the Church of God in Christ* echoes this conflict by actually listing the scriptures that it does *not* recognize as a mandate to ordain women to the

33. Cheryl Townsend Gilkes, "'Together and in Harness': Women's Traditions in the Sanctified Church," *Signs: Journal of Women in Culture and Society* 11.4 (1985): 678–99.

34. See Harold Dean Trulear, "Ida B. Robinson: The Mother as Symbolic Presence," in Grant Wacker and James R. Goff, Jr., eds., *Portraits of a Generation: Early Pentecostal Leaders* (Fayetteville: University of Arkansas Press, 2002), 309–24.

35. Vashti M. McKenzie, *Not Without a Struggle: Leadership Development for African American Women in Ministry* (Cleveland: United Church Press, 1996).

roles of pastor, elder, or bishop.[36] The conflict has been long, protracted, and biblical.

Most people who wish to keep women out of roles of leadership appeal to texts that call for women's silence. Unfortunately for those arguing women's exclusion, women are able to appeal to a wide variety of texts within the Bible where women's leadership is clearly in evidence. Those women are biblical role models who appear in arguments for women's leadership and in women's writings. In addition to the previously mentioned roles of those women who were "last at the cross and first at the tomb" as carriers of the Gospel after their visit to the empty tomb of Jesus, other women in the Bible, both in the Old and New Testaments, figure prominently in women's sense that they have a right to play significant roles in the Church.

Within the Old Testament/Hebrew Bible, one of the most important women is the judge, Deborah. The role of "church mother," official in some denominations and honorific in others, is often tied to the text in Judges 5:7 where Deborah sings, "The inhabitants of the villages ceased . . . in Israel, until that I Deborah arose, that I arose a mother in Israel." Deborah is a particularly appealing role model. First of all, she holds the title judge alongside the men in this role. As a warrior, she anticipated the roles of African American women in their activist responses to the institutional terror and the rise of Jim Crow that characterized the period in which Holiness and Pentecostal churches were formed. For instance, even though women did not have the right to vote, black women actively participated in political meetings during Reconstruction, sometimes providing security for the meetings and threatening with public exposure those men who were fearful about voting.

Although the Sanctified Church has been viewed as the most dramatic example of the compensatory and other worldly model of the black church, the reality has been different. Women in the Church of God in Christ were particularly proud of their relationship with leaders such as Mary McLeod Bethune and their participation in the club movement. Women of the Church of God in Christ also saw themselves reflected in Deborah when they look at their history of maintaining

---

36. Church of God in Christ, *Official Manual of the Church of God in Christ* (Memphis: Church of God in Christ Publishing, 1973).

the organizational integrity of the Church of God in Christ in times of transition. Leaders such as Lillian Brooks Coffey utilized biblical models of military leadership and preparedness when she claimed that women held the church "in harness" between the death of founder, Bishop Charles Harrison Mason, and the election of his successor.

In addition to Deborah, both Vashti and Esther figure importantly among biblical women emphasized in African American churches. There are exegetical traditions that discount and disparage Vashti. However, Frances Ellen Watkins Harper, a nineteenth century writer, presented Vashti as a woman to be admired and as someone who sacrificed much to maintain her dignity. After reviewing Vashti's story in a poem that detailed the demand of the king that Vashti show herself to his drunken friends, Harper wrote:

> She heard again the King's command,
> And left her high estate;
> Strong in her earnest womanhood,
> She calmly met her fate,
>
> And left the palace of the King,
> Proud of her spotless name—
> A woman who could bend to grief,
> But would not bow to shame.[37]

Vashti represented a respectable woman who faced an important set of ethical choices in the context of powerlessness. Guided by the Holy Spirit, African American Christian women should be able to face similar choices and triumph in the face of adversity and disrespect. Vashti's actions anticipated the kind of thinking that sings, "Take this world but give me Jesus." Esther of course became a particularly important successor, especially as she calls a community to prayer and fasting. African American tradition enshrined her choices in song: "If I perish, let me perish! / I'm going to see the king." Esther provides a biblical anchor for women's roles as Prayer Warriors.

African American women were also able to appeal to Huldah, another Old Testament (Hebrew Bible) personage who reinforced the importance of women as educators and as prophets. In 2 Kings 22:14 //

37. Frances Ellen Watkins Harper, "Vashti," in *Poems: The Black Heritage Library Collection* (1895), available at "Poetry Archives," Online text © 1998–2007, Poetry X, all rights reserved [http://poetry.poetryx.com/poems/14219/].

2 Chronicles 34:2, Huldah is able to establish the authenticity of a scroll of Deuteronomy found in the Temple. Not only does she speak a word of judgment against Israel, she also brought a word of affirmation and redemption to Josiah. Huldah's authority came through the Spirit as she replied to her inquirers saying, "Thus saith the Lord."

In addition to the sisters, Mary and Martha, and Mary, the mother of Jesus, African American tradition placed the Samaritan woman in a place of prominence. When men preach on the text, they tend to dwell on her "five husbands," emphasizing that she is a loose woman who draws water from the well at noontime because of her shame. Women who preach or speak about the Samaritan woman, on the other hand, tend to emphasize her importance because Jesus moved against the norms and restrictions of that time to hold a serious theological conversation with a woman.

The theological conversation that Jesus held with the Samaritan woman placed the Spirit in the theological foreground. It is in John 4:24 that Jesus explicitly states that "God is a Spirit: and they that worship him must worship him in spirit and in truth." When the role of direct witness to the words of Jesus is taken into account, as contemporary exegesis increasingly does, then this is one of the most significant points in the Gospel, particularly in the case of a biblical theology of the Spirit. Jesus makes this very direct statement about the nature of God, "God is a Spirit," and the proper approach to worship, "in spirit and in truth," to a woman considered an outsider by those who defined themselves as the dominant culture.

This theological revelation also contains one of Jesus' "I Am" statements—statements that link him directly with God's revelation to Moses. The fact that God speaks to and reveals his nature to a woman provides an important argument for the inclusion of women's voices in the church leadership. Furthermore, the Samaritan woman's role in revealing Jesus and evangelizing her community is often stressed in women's interpretation of John 4; in the words of Nannie Helen Burroughs, the Samaritan woman "went to town" telling the world about Jesus.[38] Of course in John 11:25, Jesus makes an additional "I Am" revelation to Martha, saying, "I am the Resurrection and the Life."

---

38. See Dodson Gilkes, "Something Within," 125.

The Gospel of Luke and the Acts of the Apostles have women role models woven throughout. In Luke women are part of the crowd of disciples traveling with Jesus and "the twelve," women who "ministered of their substance." In Acts, there are important women leaders, especially in Philippi where Lydia, a single head of household and an entrepreneur, invites Paul to lodge at her house to begin the Philippian church. Later in the letter to the Philippians, the problem is conflict among women leaders—a fact that is not lost on contemporary women.

With all of these women in the Bible, simple doctrinal admonitions urging women to be silent, such as those found in Pauline and pseudo-Pauline biblical texts, generate resistance on the part of church women. These texts stand in contrast to the stories about Jesus and about prominent women. As Howard Thurman discovered when reading the Bible to his formerly enslaved grandmother, African Americans made active decisions about what aspects of the Bible would be canonized and enshrined within their daily lives and community.[39] Women are able to exploit the community's liberationist canon to challenge the more exclusionary uses of the Bible. Without using the word androcentric directly, bolstered by the preaching tradition and its centrality to African American Christianity, women in the Sanctified Church are able to engage in what Elisabeth Schussler Fiorenza calls "imaginative reconstruction" to raise an argument for their inclusion and the legitimacy of women's leadership.[40]

Conclusion: A Vital Tradition for All Women

Overall, women in the Black Church, including but not limited to the Sanctified Church, have developed vital and activist traditions around women in the Bible. These traditions are utilized on those days when women's voices are heard in the church, days such as Women's Days and Missionary Sundays, usually on fifth Sundays. In most churches such days represent a minimum of six Sundays each year when women ascend the pulpit or the lectern and utilize the women of the Bible to teach

39. See Howard Thurman's *Jesus and the Disinherited* (New York: Abingdon-Cokesbury, 1949), to review the story about his grandmother's refusal to listen to readings from Paul except for I Corinthians 13 where Paul emphasizes love.

40. Elisabeth Schüssler Fiorenza, *In Memory of Her: A Feminist Theological Reconstruction of Christian Origins* (New York: Crossroad, 1985).

the Gospel, "lift" Jesus (a reference to Mary Magdalene's intent in John 20:15), and counter patriarchal ideologies of exclusion and silence.

In reality, women's voices are heard far more often and in many more settings than is actually acknowledged. Over twenty years ago, when I first began my research on the Sanctified Church, I visited a jurisdiction in the Church of God in Christ. With the permission of their Bishop, the head of the Women's Department invited me to their Ministers' and Missionaries meeting. All the men were ministers and all the missionaries were women. At that particular meeting, one of the missionaries introduced the Church's new manual for teaching biblical studies. Not only did this meeting reinforce for me the importance of the Bible to the Church, but I was able to observe women teaching men and women together about the importance of the Bible. This occasion also made clear that fundamental agreement within the entire Church concerning the centrality of the Bible, and thus the willingness to engage in struggle utilizing the sacred text. One was able to observe the role of women as educators within the Church of God in Christ—educators of both women and men who were church leaders. Furthermore, the voices of women were an integral part of the process of shaping and affirming the Church's doctrines and practices.

Women in the Sanctified Church have, for nearly one hundred and thirty years, provided significant role models for African American women who have felt called to leadership in church and community. Holiness and Pentecostal women's ascendancy as leaders in the Black Church has been rooted and grounded in a tradition of biblical interpretation that takes women in the Bible very seriously and renders them visible through sermons, teachings, and argumentation. The larger religious culture has been shaped by these examples and has mutually reinforced the importance of these biblical women through literature and in naming traditions. The overall history of African American Christian women leaders, in both sacred and secular settings, has been greatly influenced by this biblical tradition where the visibility of women has been dramatically inscribed.

When W. E. B. Du Bois argued that "the freedom of womanhood," was one of the significant components of the "Gift of Black Folk," he pointed out that the role of black working women was liberating for all women. Du Bois went further to point to the clubs and missionary societies as the source of black women's ascendancy as "the intellectual leadership" of the black community.[41] Women's leadership enabled and uplifted the entire community. Furthermore, women connected people in a way that actualized community. The ability of people to be empowered and encouraged in their leadership is, perhaps, tied to the ability of the community to extend their voices back over two thousand years to encourage women who were witnesses to the resurrection as they claimed their right lift their voices with the Good News. When enslaved women and men sang, "Run, Mary, run . . . You've got a right to the tree of life," they trumpeted encouragement for women leaders in their struggle to raise their voice. In the process they crystallized a biblical foundation that fostered an attitude of empowerment in the face of powerful forces of exclusion and subordination. In the struggle for women's leadership, it is important to hear the echo across the century telling us, "I've got a right / You've got a right / We've all got a right to the tree of life."

41. Du Bois, *The Gift of Black Folk*.

10

Spirited Vestments

Or, Why the Anointing Is Not Enough

Cheryl Bridges Johns

Introduction

IN MANY WAYS PENTECOSTALISM IS NOT A CULTURE THAT OVERTLY suppresses women's abilities and gifts. From the early days of the movement women have been affirmed along with men as recipients of the same Spirit who distributes to them gifts and callings. As noted by Jenny Evert Powers, Pentecostals understood the outpouring of the Holy Spirit on the Day of Pentecost as signaling a new era prophesied by the prophet Joel wherein women were empowered to speak for God and to be vessels of ministry in the last days.[1] However, this is often where the theological reflection begins and stops. Pentecostals have failed to clearly enunciate the ontological and soteriological implications of the liberating power of the full gospel. As a result, they have created an environment characterized by ambiguity and confusion.

In regards to women, Pentecostalism is a culture of both exclusion and embrace. Within this tradition women experience the acceptance of God and a deep sense of his calling, but they quickly discover that women's ministry is often limited to what may be termed the prophetic realm. They may be encouraged to testify, exhort, and preach, but the more priestly functions of pastoral and denominational leadership are

---

1. See Janet Everts Powers, "Pentecostalism 101: Your Daughters Shall Prophesy," in this volume.

likely to be reserved for men. The emphasis on the prophetic gifting and calling of women has done little to change the all pervasive belief in the inherent inferiority of women. Pentecostals have not questioned the subordinate role of women; they have merely overlaid this assumption with an ideology of empowerment.

This paradox of exclusion and embrace is backed by a strong tradition that was woven into the fabric of twentieth century Pentecostalism. It is now time to examine closely how this came to be and to move forward into a new era. Moving forward will mean going beyond the prophetic model for women in ministry with its proof texts. It will mean going beyond the language of "power" into the deeper language of authority and identity. It will mean reconstructing the meaning of being human based upon Trinitarian reflection of the *imago Dei*. Pentecostals must face squarely the issues of personhood, asking the question, "What does it mean to be human—male and female?"

It is not my intention to belittle the strong historical precedent of the prophethood of believers within Pentecostalism. However, it is my intention to show that women are ghettoized into the prophetic while men are free to be both prophetic and priestly. Pentecostal women can no longer bear the burden of wearing a prophetic mantle as a covering over their inferior status. Prophetic mantles are colorful and lively attire, but they kill the human spirit when women are denied the right to be vested with priestly garments of authority. Personhood cannot be denied in favor of prophethood. Women are in need of full humanization, clothing them in an ontological identity that is grounded in the Triune life of God and that frees them to be full persons in Christ. This essay is a call for "Spirited vestments" that allow a full range of vocational identity, empowering women "to be" as well as "to speak."

Origins of the Prophetic Ghetto

During its early days, the Pentecostal movement provided free spaces for those who were marginalized by traditional cultural constraints. In particular, African Americans and women experienced the baptism of the Holy Spirit as liberation. The Azusa Street Revival serves as the paradigmatic heart of this third "Great Awakening." Boundaries that were long established by society—namely that blacks and whites should be separate, women should be silent, and the poor and the rich should remain apart—were broken down at Azusa Street and within the movement as a whole. Clearly God was doing a new thing. This new thing, however, was difficult to actualize in a world that did not regard the radical values of the fledging movement. The tension between the ideal and the pragmatic, what Grant Wacker calls the "primitive and the pragmatic,"[2] has remained within the movement. This is especially true in regards to the status of women.

Charles Barfoot and Gerald Sheppard's insightful article, "Prophetic vs. Priestly Religion,"[3] is helpful in understanding how women became ghettoized within the prophetic realm. Barfoot and Sheppard utilize Max Weber's premise that religion among the de-privileged classes often affirms the equality of men and women, but that as these movements institutionalize they come to embrace the male monopolization of priestly functions. The authors identify two distinct stages of Pentecostalism: prophetic and priestly. The prophetic period (1907–1930), was characterized by a strong belief in the "last days" and the calling of both women and men to fulfill the Great Commission. The emphasis during this time was on personal callings that were known through manifestations of the *charismata*. Yet, while women were given freedom to preach the gospel they were often forbidden from fulfilling priestly/governmental functions.

As the second phase of the movement took effect (after 1930), more formal actions were taken to prevent women from gaining full ordination. For example, in 1931 the Assemblies of God passed a resolution to ordain women only as "evangelists" and to prohibit them from administering the ordinances of the church. A clear example of the emerging distinctions between the prophetic and the priestly can be seen in the joint ministry of Robert and Marie Brown, who co-pastored during the 1930's. At the 1931 meeting of the General Council of the Assemblies of God, Robert Brown expressed the prevailing view regarding prophetic and priestly functions:

2. Grant Wacker, *Heaven Below: Early Pentecostals and American Culture* (Cambridge: Harvard University Press, 2001).

3. Charles H. Barfoot and Gerald T. Sheppard, "Prophetic vs. Priestly Religion: The Changing Role of Women Clergy in Classical Pentecostal Churches," *Review of Religious Research* 22.1 (1980): 2–17.

He could not help noticing that in the scriptures there was no woman in the priesthood and none in the apostolic ministry. God chose men. He stated that his wife always refrained from "acts of priesthood." He said he hated to see women put on a white garment and try to look like angels, and go into the baptismal pool to baptize converts.[4]

Agreeing with Brown, the General Council passed resolutions that banned women from priestly functions.[5] Although the Assemblies of God removed these restrictions in 1935, the disdain of women "who put on a white garment" remained deep.

The research of David Roebuck is also helpful in understanding the development of the culture of exclusion and embrace within Pentecostalism. Roebuck points out that within the Church of God there was never a "golden age" for women in ministry. Rather, from the very beginning of the denomination women's roles were limited to the prophetic realm.[6] Under the influence of A. J. Tomlinson, the denomination's first General Overseer, the Church of God made a clear distinction between the prophetic and the priestly functions. "Let the good sisters," wrote Tomlinson, "feel at perfect liberty to preach the gospel, pray for the sick or well, testify, exhort, etc., but humbly hold themselves aloof from taking charge of the governmental affairs."[7]

Throughout the twentieth century the prophetic model was the dominant image for women entering Pentecostal ministry. Following World War II this image was joined by a powerful domestic one wherein women were encouraged to remain at home and not to take to the fields of mission. The domestic image was a mirror reflection of the larger American culture and Evangelical ethos, and Pentecostals were anxious to be part of both of these worlds.

---

4. *Pentecostal Evangel* (1931): 5, quoted in Barfoot and Sheppard, "Prophetic vs. Priestly Religion," 12.

5. It should be noted that under the leadership of A. J. Tomlinson the Church of God made rapid movement to restrict the role of women in priestly/governmental affairs of the Church. As early as 1908 the decision was made to exclude women from being ordained as deaconesses.

6. David G. Roebuck, "Limiting Liberty: The Church of God and Women Ministers, 1886–1996" (PhD dissertation, Vanderbilt University, 1997).

7. A. J. Tomlinson, "Paul's Statements Considered," *Church of God Evangel* (September 1915): 4.

Today women desiring to enter ministry have few role models. The evangelists-prophets are almost extinct, and likewise, priestly images for women are largely limited to mainline Protestant churches. In addition, there is new wave of traditionalism and feminist backlash within American culture. Conservative Evangelicals continue to promote "biblical roles of men and women" that restrict the ministry of women. However, in spite of these obstacles toward full humanization and full ministerial authorization, there is still hope for a future wherein our daughters will live, in the words of Hollis Gause, "both magnificently and scripturally."[8] This hope is contained in the Triune Life of God, revealed in Scripture, and made possible by the power of the Holy Spirit.

Evangelicalism's Debate over Women's Identity and Pentecostal Responses

The current debate within Evangelicalism over women's roles interfaces with issues regarding the identity of the Trinity and with the meaning of the *imago Dei*. In recent decades there has been a turn by Evangelical theologians including Wayne Grudem, John Piper, and Andreas Kostenberger, among others, toward grounding women's identity not just in scriptural passages of submission, but also within the nature of God.[9] Their view of the Trinity includes what may be termed "functional subordinationism," in which the temporal role subordination of the Son seen in the incarnation is read back into the immanent Trinity.

The proponents of the functional subordination of the Son argue that the "differences between the divine persons should be understood entirely in terms of differing roles or functions. Within this school of thought are those such as George Knight who see an "ontological subordination" within the Trinity. Knight speaks of a "chain of subordina-

---

8. These terms are those which Hollis Gause uses to describe the biblical status of women. They convey the possibility of an authentic selfhood that is grounded in creation. See Kimberly Ervin Alexander and R. Hollis Gause, *Women in Leadership: A Pentecostal Perspective* (Cleveland, TN: Center for Pentecostal Leadership & Care, 2006), 45.

9. John Piper and Wayne Grudem, eds., *Recovering Biblical Manhood and Womanhood: A Response to Evangelical Feminism* (Wheaton, IL: Crossway, 1991), and Andreas J. Kostenberger, Thomas R. Schreiner, and H. Scott Baldwin, eds., *Women in the Church: A Fresh Analysis of 1 Timothy 2:9–15* (Grand Rapids: Baker, 1995).

tion" within the Godhead.[10] Robert Letham calls for "subordination in subsistence," making a case for the eternal subordination of the Son within the immanent Trinity because of the subordination of the Son in the incarnation. He writes, "the revelation of the economic Trinity truly indicates the ontological Trinity."[11]

It seems that contemporary Evangelicals who appeal to the doctrine of the Trinity to support their belief in the headship of the male are making great efforts to keep viable a patriarchal worldview. Knowing that to ground woman's subordination in her inferior nature, as has often been the case in history, would be problematic in a contemporary culture that emphasizes equality, they have emphasized "role" distinctions over "nature" distinctions. Kevin Giles makes clear the real intentions of this hierarchical-complementarian viewpoint and strategy:

> for the hierarchical-complementarian, the word *difference* is a code word. It means something that the hierarchical-complementarian cannot ever say or ever admit. In the truly historic position, exegetes and theologians said God made women inferior; the contemporary hierarchical-complementarian emphatically denies this. In our age this is an unacceptable idea for anyone to promulgate. The women's revolution has forced men to give up using the word *inferior* or even suggesting the idea. What hierarchical-complementarians say instead is that God made women "different" from men. But when we ask how they are different, they mention only one matter: men have been given the ruling role and women the subordinate role in the home and the church.[12]

Within Evangelical circles, the move toward the language of "roles" first appeared in the 1970's. During this time there was the push for the Equal Rights Amendment as well as a flourishing of Evangelical feminist literature such as Letha Scanzoni and Nancy Hardesty's *All We're Meant to Be*.[13] In the 1980's Evangelicals such as Aída Besançon Spencer

10. George Knight, *New Testament Teaching on the Role Relationship of Men and Women* (Grand Rapids: Baker, 1977), 56.

11. Robert Letham, "The Man-Woman Debate: Theological Comment," *Westminster Theological Journal* 52 (1990): 65–78.

12. Kevin Giles, *The Trinity and Subordinationism: The Doctrine of God and the Contemporary Gender Debate* (Downers Grove: InterVarsity, 2002), 185; italics original.

13. Letha Scanzoni and Nancy Hardesty, *All We're Meant to Be: A Biblical Approach to Women's Liberation* (Waco, TX: Word, 1974).

attempted to ground the equality of women in creation, noting that the subordination of women was a result of the Fall and the curse. Spencer made a case for redemption in Christ as reversing the curse.[14]

In response to "Evangelical feminists" those advocating the complementarian-hierarchical view of humankind attempt to counter-argue that the distinction between the sexes is grounded in creation and not the Fall. They move from a hierarchical view of the Trinity, with the Father at the top, to a hierarchical view of humankind with the man at the top. Just as God commands and the Son obeys, so too are men to command and women to obey. This chain of command is often referred to as "the divine order." There is a "divine order" in the Trinity, a "divine order" in creation, a "divine order" in the home, and a "divine order" in the church. As has already been noted, what drives the complementarian-hierarchical view is "an all-consuming concern to maintain the 'headship' of men"; it is a passion that has led, as Giles aptly observes, "to the most dangerous of all errors—the corruption of the primary doctrine of Christianity, the doctrine of God."[15]

Historically, the subordination of woman has focused more on her inferior nature. Augustine viewed subordination as intrinsic to original creation, while proposing that sin and death were not. For him the image of God referred to the soul in its rational nature and its representation of God's domination over the natural world. Men possess the capacity for dominion, but women, representing nature or the body, are to be under dominion. Women, therefore, lack the image of God and are related to God's image only by their inclusion under male headship.[16]

This understanding of the *imago Dei*, which has dominated the Western Church, is related to a view of God heavily influenced by neo-Platonic thought. In this world-view God is ontologically static, endowed with timeless characteristics of immutability, omnipotence,

14. Aída Besançon Spencer, *Beyond the Curse: Women Called to Ministry* (Nashville: Nelson, 1985).

15. Giles, *Trinity and Subordinationism*, 115.

16. Augustine, *De Trinitate* 7:7.10. See Rosemary Radford Ruether, "Christian Anthropology and Gender," in Miroslav Volf, Carmen Kreig, and Thomas Kucharz, eds., *The Future of Theology: Essays in Honor of Jürgen Moltmann* (Grand Rapids: Eerdmans, 1996), 241–52; cf. also Kari Elisabeth Børresen, *Subordination and Equivalence: The Nature and Role of Women in Augustine and Thomas Aquinas* (Washington, DC: University Press of America, 1981).

and omniscience. God is "pure being." Humans, on the other hand are messy, material, and full of passion.

Along with the understanding that God is ontologically static is the elevation of reason as the defining element of the *imago Dei*. Aquinas believed that men more fully bore the image of God, noting that "with reference to interior qualities, it can be said that man is more especially God's image according to the mind, since his reason is stronger."[17] Commenting on Genesis 1, Martin Luther writes, "Although Eve was a most extraordinary creature, similar to Adam with respect to the image of God . . . still she is a woman . . . She does not equal the glory and worthiness of the male."[18]

The view of women as ontologically inferior is based upon a belief that women are less rational, more emotive, and more sensual (material). Maleness equals rationality and maleness conveys most fully the *imago Dei*. Implications of this stereotype are abundant in Christian literature, even well into the twentieth century. In his essay in *Women in the Church,* Thomas Schreiner asserts that women should not teach because they are "less prone than men to see the importance of doctrinal formulations, especially when it comes to the issue of identifying heresy and making a stand for the truth."[19] Daniel Doriani echoes the same sentiment in his analysis of Paul's comment that "Adam was not deceived but the woman was deceived."[20] According to Doriani, Paul is teaching that "God created women with an orientation towards relationships more than analysis."[21]

The view of women as more relational and less rational severely limited women's roles in society and the church. Government was to be run by rational agents (men) whose emotions did not get in the way of their abilities to govern. Likewise, in the church, governing was to be

17. Quoted in Kari Elisabeth Børresen, "Is Woman Excluded? Medieval Interpretation of Gen. 1, 27 and I Cor. 11,7," in Kari Elisabeth Børresen, ed., *The Image of God: Gender Models in Judaeo-Christian Tradition* (Minneapolis: Fortress, 1995), 222.

18. Martin Luther, *Lectures on Genesis* chapter 1–5, quoted in Giles, *Trinity and Subordinationism*, 151.

19. Thomas R. Schreiner, "An Interpretation of 1 Timothy 2:9–15: A Dialogue with Scholarship," in Kostenberger, Schreiner, and Baldwin, eds., *Women in the Church*, 145.

20. Daniel Doriani, "History of Interpretation of 1 Timothy 2," in Kostenberger, Schreiner, and Baldwin, eds., *Women in the Church*, 258.

21. Ibid., 266.

in the hands of men. Today, the argument gets more nuanced with the insertion of the language of "roles"; however as pointed out above, this language is only a cloak for the deep and long held belief in the inherent inferiority of women.

Pentecostals did not fully address the issue of ontological identity during the early days of the movement. Instead, they took the prevailing view of the inferior ontological status of women and over-laid it with a pneumatology of power. God was pouring his Spirit out upon all flesh, including women. But this outpouring did not reflect an ontological status. Instead, it was intended functionally, to enable and authorize women to prophecy. After all, it was not the agency of the woman involved in prophetic ministry, but the agency of the Holy Spirit. Under the anointing of the Holy Spirit women could overcome their inferior status and thereby be effective in preaching the gospel.

By focusing on Joel 2:28, Pentecostals failed to adequately ground women's empowerment in creation. This failure led them to look to Evangelical theologians for their theology of the ontological status of women. The result was that during the twentieth century Pentecostals perpetuated an ideology of the ontological inferiority of women while at the same time advocating their liberty to preach. Few questioned this bipolar perspective.

Only recently have Pentecostal theologians begun to address the ontological status of women. Hollis Gause, in a recent book co-edited with Kimberly Alexander, grounds his view of women's leadership roles in creation:

> Rather than argue that woman is equal to man, we argue that in their humanity (i.e., being in the divine image), they are the same. We will also argue that while the fall defaced and obscured the divine, it did not destroy it because of God's grace. The aim of grace is the restoration of this image for humankind through Jesus Christ. The image of God is restored in His life, death and resurrection. Since this image *is* restored in Christ, no human hierarchal systems apply to the place and privilege of the redeemed in Christ.[22]

Gause's view is that leadership in the church should not be an issue of gender but of vocation. All offices of the church should be open

22. Alexander and Gause, *Women in Leadership*, 25; italics original.

to women. For Gause it is the nature of the Trinity and the restored creation in Christ that serve as the foundation for women's identity and calling. Asserting that "the church is a community of love patterned after the community of the Holy Trinity," Gause notes that, "the relationship between the Father, Son and Holy Spirit is a relationship of equal divine Persons (the same in substance and equal in power and glory) who commit Themselves to each other for the fulfillment of divine work in relationships with creation."[23] Furthermore, in regards to submission, Gause makes the following observation:

> Christ came to do the will of the Father (Hebrews 10:7–9). In the fulfillment of that mission, Jesus said, "My Father is greater than I" (John 14:28). In this pattern of operation, "the head of Christ is God" (1 Corinthians 11:3). The Holy Spirit comes into the world as the Comforter in Christ's place, because He has been sent by both the Father (John 14:16, 17) and the Son (John 15:26). He declares the things of the Father and the Son (John 16:12–16). The Father fulfills the desires of the Son. There is no greater example of this than the sending of the Holy Spirit: I will pray the Father, and He will send you another Paraclete/ Comforter" (John 14:16, 26). The point of these observations is that the submission of the members of the Trinity to the will of the others is a submission among equal divine Persons.[24]

Toward a Viable Future

In light of the resurgence of a hierarchical view of Trinity within Evangelicalism, Pentecostals need to offer their own counter-responses. The hierarchical view has become popularized with prominent figures such as James Dobson promoting its ideology in the media. In addition there are numerous books, seminars, etc., that keep the subordination message alive and well. Further, as previously stated, the prophetic-evangelistic model for women is dying out within North American Pentecostalism. Hence the future of women within the movement lies not necessarily in recapturing Joel 2:28 but in the direction of Gause's research. What follows is a brief overview of two of the main issues that need addressing: that regarding the relational identity of the Trinity and that regarding the image of God as being both male and female.

23. Ibid., 7.
24. Ibid.

Relational Trinitarian Identity

In regards to Trinitarian reflection, images of God as relational and dy-namic, existing in both co-inherence and unity but also otherness and distinctiveness, are important for Pentecostal theological reflection. For women, who traditionally define themselves in terms of a relational web or a matrix of relationships, it is liberating to image God as constituted and defined relationally. In this way the *imago Dei* becomes a mirror for women to see themselves reflected in the light of the Divine light. God is love, so much so that he emptied himself of the glory that was rightfully his and took upon himself the form of a suffering human. It is in the image of this God, the one who loves to the point of self-denial and suffering, that women and men are created.

It should be noted, however, that the alternative to envisioning God as Transcendent Rational Substance is not what may be termed "radical relationalism." In this latter paradigm there is the danger of God fusing with the creation in "pure immanence." Such a model of relationalism threatens "difference." There is the need to maintain a sense of divine immutability and sovereignty on the part of God, while at the same time imaging God as the one who opens himself to the mysterious and messy dynamics of relationships.

For women's development it is crucial to understand "difference" within the *imago Dei,* just as it is important to understand the dimen-sions of personal relationality. There is the need for imaging humankind and God in ways that maintain the dialectic of otherness-transcendence and relatedness-immanence.[25] Miroslav Volf observes that the notion of pure relationality eliminates the soteriological dialectic between "I" and "not-I." As a consequences the "I" dissolves in its relations and becomes the "not-I."[26] To express the "I"—"not-I" dialectic Volf proposes the category of personal interiority. It is his assessment that "this category

25. Jürgen Moltmann, *The Spirit of Life: A Universal Affirmation,* trans. Margaret Kohl (Minneapolis: Fortress, 1992), esp. 5–8, calls this dialectic "immanent transcen-dence" and uses it as the lynchpin of his pneumatology. See also Andrew M. Lord, "The Pentecostal-Moltmann Dialogue: Implications for Mission," *Journal of Pentecostal Theology* 11 (April 2003): 271–87.

26. Miroslav Volf, *After Our Likeness: The Church as the Image of the Trinity* (Grand Rapids: Eerdmans, 1998), 187. In this text Volf examines Cardinal Ratzinger's (now Pope Benedict) definition of "ecclesiastical subjects," in which believing people are able to be persons within a comprehensive collective subject.

is originally at home in the doctrine of Trinity, where it describes the mutual indwelling of divine persons. The one person is internal to the other persons without suspending their personhood."[27]

Volf's assessment of the notion of pure relationality is of particular importance in regards to issues of female identity. Historically women have been inculturated into an existence of pure relationality, dissolving the "I" into the "not-I," often suspending their personhood for the sake of relationships. It is important that women develop and retain the "I." Only then can they be in the joyful but painful dialectic of true relationality.

Elizabeth Moltmann-Wendel seemed to have this necessity in mind when she remarked: "A new community can mature and become fruitful only if women remain their own persons. Only if their singularity, their special character, their uniqueness are preserved can the contribution that they make to society remain alive"; furthermore, "[o]nly if they continue to make *their* concern the life that they lack and have now discovered, can it be the common concern of all."[28] I would agree that it is imperative that women make *their* concern the "life that they now lack." For until they do so this lack of vital life will not become a concern in a greater sense.

It can be concluded that a relational Trinitarian theology is a fruitful place for Pentecostals to begin assessing the identity of women and men as created in the image of God. Questions remain about the relational character of women and the rational character of men. However, these questions are best put into a full spectrum of the *imago Dei* rather than in a dichotomizing and subordinating system. When differences are placed on a continuum rather than polarized, women are freed to move toward the rational side and men are free to move into the relational domain. This imagery is reflected in the Trinitarian life, where there is freedom to direct, freedom to submit, freedom to love, and freedom to judge. No one person of the Trinity bears the burden of judging and no one Person bears the burden of love. No one Person of the Trinity bears the burden of directing and no one Person bears the burden of submitting. Mutual life is reflected in the freedom to be both the "I" and the "not-I."

27. Ibid.

28. Elizabeth Moltmann-Wendel and Jürgen Moltmann, *God—His and Hers* (New York: Crossroad, 1991), 11; emphasis original.

Male/Female Elements of Being in the Image of God

Another issue for Pentecostals is the task of imaging God as masculine/ feminine. Just as there cannot be a stark separation in the operations, works, and functions of the three Divine Persons, there should not be a stark separation of masculine versus feminine imagery.[29]

There is a rich history of locating the feminine in the Holy Spirit. Although Pentecostals may be tempted to take up the Holy Spirit as feminine, in the long run such imagery is not helpful in the construction of women's identity. It eventually leads to another "subordinating" paradigm, locating the work of the Holy Spirit as being sent by the Father and Son as indicative of the subordinating role of women. Feminizing the Holy Spirit also leaves us open to image the Father in rational terms and the Holy Spirit in emotive imagery. This split has been part of the problem within Pentecostalism. The prophetic image available to women retained the emotive side of Pentecostal faith, while the rational, judicial side was made available only to males. In a very real sense, when women were ghettoized into the prophetic realm, the Holy Spirit was also ghettoized away from the governmental and administrative functions of the church.

The other possibility in imaging God is to neuter the Godhead. While it is true that God is Spirit and above any anthropomorphic images, neutering God leaves us without a full-blown image of being human—male and female—as created in the image of God. The alternative is to image God as masculine and as feminine and to locate masculinity and femininity within the fullness of the Godhead. In doing so, we avoid the divine image being split and can speak of "the female element of being" and "the masculine element of being."[30]

29. When confronted by the image of subordination of the Son (male imagery) as paradigmatic for women (female imagery), it is difficult to see how the "role" distinctions between the sexes take the leap into the life of the Trinity or vice-versa. To look to the economic role of the Son as a mirror for women offers little in terms of femaleness. It is clear that the complementarian subordinationists care little about gender identity. What they are more concerned about are issues of power and authority.

30. Object relations theory is helpful toward understanding the mysterious depth of our subjective-objective God images. Object relations theory assists us in understanding how God is both public and private, transcendent and immanent. We see how God-images function both positively and negatively. God can be imaged through culture, family, church, and tradition. These images of God are necessary and provide the basic "stuff" of our theology. Object relations theory is helpful in seeing the power of con-

Augustine helped turn the feminine role over to the church. For Augustine, it was the arms of mother church that received the baptized infant, nurturing the infant into the faith and life. Further development of the doctrine of Mary located the feminine in her role as mediator and intercessor. Both of these developments—feminizing the church and highlighting the role of Mary as mother—have done little to empower women as bearers of the image of God. Moreover, they have further separated the feminine from the Godhead.

If we retain the female element of being within the life of God we highlight the state of unity and co-inherence of the Trinity. Furthermore, the female element of being is seen in God as source of life and the ground of all being. "God's thriving, self-communicating gift of life"[31] is seen in the feminine element of being.

The male element of being accents the disparateness of I and other. We may identify with the other but we do not become the other. Our ability "to stand back from relationships, explore potentialities and limits" and to "abstract from our experience of the other, generalize, compare, contrast our experiences," are part of the male element of being.[32] Furthermore, the male element of being is found in the Trinitarian life as otherness and distinctiveness. It is found in the divine immutability and sovereignty of God.

Both the female and male elements of being are crucial in understanding the meaning of being made in the image of God. God is large enough and mysterious enough to contain both masculine and feminine identities without having to define these identities too tightly. The language of "Father" and "Son," while helpful in reading a text written in a patriarchal world, do not limit us to the fullness of God. These images reveal an aspect of God that is helpful and necessary for salvation. But for women to know that they are created in God's image, a fuller picture has to be developed.

struction held within human hands. See Ann Belford Ulanov, *Finding Space: Winnicott, God and Psychic Reality* (Louisville: Westminster John Knox, 2001).

31. Ibid., 74.

32. Ibid., 70.

The Way Forward

A Pentecostal ontology has yet to be developed. Without this, Pentecostals will continue to hold an operative theology that focuses on Spirit empowerment as an overlay upon human finiteness rather than as a transformative sign of God's re-creating and restoring power. As mentioned at the beginning of this essay, Pentecostals need to develop a theology that images God's life as paradigmatic for our life. This means looking carefully at the doctrine of God and the meaning of the *imago Dei*. Furthermore, it means examining our life together in light of this reflection.

11

The Spirit, Nature, and Canadian Pentecostal Women

A Conversation with Critical Theory

Pamela Holmes

Introduction

The involvement of ministering women in the early years of American Pentecostalism, followed by the subsequent decline in their numbers, has been noted time and again and explained in various ways.[1] Within Canada, women's active involvement has been less well documented. However, from my research,[2] it is evident that women were actively and significantly involved in the emergence and the establishment of the movement. For example, Ellen Hebden with her "Canadian Azusa Street" in the form of the Hebden Mission in Toronto influenced many within the early years in Canada before the establishment of the male dominated Pentecostal Assemblies of Canada (PAOC).[3] The first

1. Pamela Holmes, "The 'Place' of Women in Pentecostal-Charismatic Ministry Since the Azusa Street Revival," in Harold D. Hunter and Cecil M. Robeck Jr., eds., *The Azusa Street Revival and Its Legacy* (Cleveland, TN: Pathway, 2006), 297–315.

2. Pamela Holmes, "Ministering Women in the PAOC: A Feminist Exploration," in Michael Wilkinson, ed., *Canadian Pentecostals* (Montreal: McGill/Queens University Press, forthcoming).

3. See Ellen Hebden, "How Pentecost Came to Toronto," *The Promise* 1 (May 1907): 1–3; William Seymour, *The Apostolic Faith* 1.6 (1907): 4; George C. Slager, letter to W. E. McAlister, 24 Mar 1954 (Pentecostal Assembly of Canada Archives, Mississauga, Ontario); and Roger Nelson, "And Your Daughters Shall Prophesy: The Impact of Dominant Ideology of Canadian Society on the Role of Women in the PAOC," (in-

official PAOC historian was a woman, Gloria Kulbeck.[4] Aimee Semple
MacPherson, the Canadian farm girl turned evangelist, and Zelma
Argue, evangelist and writer, actively ministered on both sides of the
Canadian/U.S. border.[5] While in 1908 Alice Wood pioneered in Swift
Current, Saskatchewan,[6] in 1911 Alice Belle Garrigus started the Bethesda
Mission in St. Johns, Newfoundland, eventually forming the Pentecostal
Assemblies of Newfoundland,[7] and in 1923 the Davis sisters, Carro and
Susan, established congregations throughout New Brunswick, Nova
Scotia and Prince Edward Island.[8] Even after the PAOC formed in 1919,
it was not unusual for the numbers of ministering women to be greater
than the numbers of ministering men. The only major difference is that
the men would only ordain other men and not the women as "ministers" with full privileges including the right to govern the movement
and to vote.[9] Until 1984, Canadian Pentecostal women had to settle for
lower designations on the male-established hierarchical organization
under the men as "Licensed Ministers," "Deaconesses," "Evangelists," and
"Missionaries."[10] Even then, they had to wait until 1998 for all positions

---

dependent inquiry, School of Social Work, Carlton University, 1992), 2; cf. Thomas
W. Miller, *Canadian Pentecostals: A History of the Pentecostal Assemblies of Canada*
(Mississauga, Ontario: Full Gospel Publishing, 1994), 39–44. Hebden's husband, James,
was a contractor who was also involved in this ministry, oftentimes in a supportive role
to his wife's work.

4. Gloria Grace Kulbeck, *What God Hath Wrought: A History of The Pentecostal
Assemblies of Canada*, rev. ed., eds., Walter E. McAlister and Rev. George R. Upton
(Toronto: The Pentecostal Assemblies of Canada, 1958).

5. Edith L. Blumhofer, *Aimee Semple McPherson: Everybody's Sister* (Grand Rapids:
Eerdmans, 1993), 3.

6. Ron Kydd, "Canadian Pentecostalism and the Evangelical Impulse," in George
Rawlyk, ed., *Aspects of the Canadian Evangelical Impulse* (Montreal: McGill-Queen's
University Press, 1997), 289.

7. Burton K. Janes, *The Lady Who Stayed: The Biography of Alice Belle Garrigus,
Newfoundland's First Pentecostal Pioneer*, vol. 2 (St. Johns, Newfoundland: Good
Tidings, 1983).

8. Fred H. Parlee, "Carro and Susie Davis," *The Pentecostal Testimony* (December
1987).

9. Women credentialed with the "Ministerial License for Women" were not al-
lowed to vote within the PAOC until 1950. Randy Holm, "A Paradigmatic Analysis of
Authority within Pentecostalism" (PhD dissertation, Faculté de Théologie Université
Laval, Quebec, 1995), chap. 7, "Ordination of Women," esp. 276.

10. Letter to Rev. J. Roswell Flower, General Secretary, Assemblies of God, from Dr.
C. M. Wortman, General Secretary, PAOC, 22 June 1949, and "Report of the General

within the organization of the PAOC, including the national General Executive, to become open to them.[11]

This essay will explore the dialectical phenomena of both the affirmation and denial of women's active involvement within Canadian Pentecostalism as typified by the PAOC as the largest national Pentecostal denomination within Canada, and attempt to analyze it by placing aspects of Pentecostal women's experiences in a self-reflective, critical dialogue with the intentionally multi-disciplinary insights of critical theorists Max Horkheimer and Theodore Adorno. This critique is intended to be radical, as befits both critical theory and Pentecostalism,[12] in the sense of getting to the root of the problem. The hope is to illustrate that the problem of patriarchy and the domination of women within Pentecostalism is part of a much deeper problem embedded within Western enlightenment thinking, which oftentimes creates conflict with the will and work of the Spirit in empowering and calling Pentecostal women.

Critical Theory

Critical Theory is a multidisciplinary discourse that highlights the importance of both theory and empirical studies in its attempt to construct a comprehensive social theory confronting key social and political problems. As such, Critical Theory includes critiques of traditional or

---

Conference Committee, Re: Ordination," 1978. For mention of women "Evangelists," see *Canadian Pentecostal Testimony* 2.13 (1923): 3; *Canadian Pentecostal Testimony* 8 (September 1921): 4; *Canadian Pentecostal Testimony* 1 (December 1920): 1; and *Canadian Pentecostal Testimony* 4 (March 1921): 1, 4. For women "Missionaries," see *Canadian Pentecostal Testimony* 1.11 (1921): 3; *Canadian Pentecostal Testimony* 8 (September 1921): 4; *Canadian Pentecostal Testimony* 5 (April 1921): 2; *Canadian Pentecostal Testimony* 2.12 (1922): 1; *Canadian Pentecostal Testimony* 2.6 (June 1922): 1; *Canadian Pentecostal Testimony* 2.13 (1923): 5; *Canadian Pentecostal Testimony* 6 (May 1921): 3; and *Canadian Pentecostal Testimony* 2.6 (1922): 4. In 1984, the organization voted to allow the ordination of women (*Minutes of the 34th Biennial General Conference of the Pentecostal Assemblies of Canada* [1984], 10–20, and photocopied note overlaid on page 20). See also Randy Holm, "Ordination of Women," in *The Pentecostal Testimony* (May 1992): 2.

11. "36 Resolutions," appended to the *Minutes of the 41st Biennial General Conference of the Pentecostal Assemblies of Canada* (1998), 3–5; compare 5, 7, 16–17.

12. I have argued elsewhere in an unpublished paper that Pentecostalism was a radical reformation movement; see Holmes, "A Crisis/A Call: An Exegesis and Contextualization of Jeremiah 2:1–13."

mainstream social theories, philosophy, science, and technology as well as a range of ideologies, including religious ones.[13] This paper focuses primarily on the work of two early critical theorists, Theodor Adorno and Max Horkheimer, whose interest in the role of enlightenment rationality in both liberating and dominating humanity[14] as it sought to differentiate and free humanity from the contingencies of nature, may assist Pentecostals in understanding the challenge they face in following the lead of the Spirit in freeing the women in their midst.

Critical Theory draws on Marxist thought, which in the nineteenth century had challenged and critiqued the inequalities stemming from industrialization. In Karl Marx's and Friedrich Engel's opinion, the need for constant expansion in a capitalist, patriarchal economy mandated that both nature and people become resources to be dominated.[15] While Marx viewed humanity and nature as essentially interdependent, nature was submitted to humanity's service in that it was "the primary source of all instruments and objects of labour."[16] However, nature's value, even though it historically preceded all human societies, lay in its potential economic realization through human labour.[17]

Refusing to view Marxism as "a closed body of received truths,"[18] critical theory significantly revises Marxist thought through an

---

13. For an overview of the history and interests of Critical Theory, see Rolf Wiggershaus, *The Frankfurt School: Its History, Theories and Political Significance*, trans. Michael Robertson (Cambridge: Polity, 1994), and Martin Jay, *The Dialectical Imagination: A History of the Frankfurt School and the Institute of Social Research 1923–1950* (Boston: Little, Brown, 1973).

14. Horkheimer and Adorno were using "man" in the sense of male humans as representatives of humanity.

15. Ariel Salleh, *Ecofeminism as Politics: Nature, Marx and the Postmodern* (New York: St. Martin's Press, 1997), 72–73; Howard L. Parsons, "Marx and Engels on Ecology," in Carolyn Merchant, ed., *Ecology: Key Concepts in Critical Theory* (Atlantic Highlands, NJ: Humanities Press, 1994), 28–43.

16. See Alfred Schmidt, *The Concept of Nature in Marx* (London: NLB, 1971), 15–16, 27, with quotes and references from Karl Marx and Friedrich Engels, *Critique of the Gotha Programme* and *Capitol*, printed in *Selected Works of Marx and Engels*, 2 vols. (Moscow: Foreign Language Publishing, 1962), 2:17, and 1:177. See also Marx's *Economic and Philosophic Manuscripts of 1844*, trans. Martin Mulligan (Moscow: Progress Publishers, 1959), 112, 180–82, and Marx and Engels, *The German Ideology*, as quoted in Merchant, *Ecology*, 30, 32.

17. Schmidt, *The Concept of Nature in Marx*, 15–16, 27, 30, 33.

18. Jay, *Dialectical Imagination*, 256.

inter-disciplinary and contextual research methodology. As historical circumstances change, so does critical theory's approaches and emphases. After the events of the Second World War, which had necessitated the immigration of the predominately Jewish scholars of the Early Frankfurt School from Germany to America, Max Horkheimer and Theodore Adorno moved beyond their earlier focus on economic matters to a broader and more comprehensive analysis of the relationship between humanity and nature within modern Western societies.

In their book, *The Dialectic of Enlightenment*, Adorno and Horkheimer insist that the Enlightenment as a process of rationalization was part of the civilizing of humanity. In their argument, "the Enlightenment" refers to a particular mode of enlightened thought, rather than the Enlightenment as an historical era. The Enlightenment and enlightened thinking is oftentimes understood to free humanity from some sort of primitive, earlier way of being involving magic and myths which were used to control the aspects of life and nature over which humanity seemingly had little control. However, in the critical theorists' opinion, that understanding is wrong. Magic and myth were already enlightened thought, as they were part of humanity's first step toward separating itself from nature. As humanity started to differentiate itself from the rest of the natural world as a species which could consciously reason in a cause and effect manner and reflect upon its own existence and, thus, attempt to free itself from the uncertainties and dangers of nature, humanity was already using enlightened thinking. Progressing from magical rituals and myths, humanity ended up viewing nature as an impersonal object which could be exploited. Consequently, and ironically, Horkheimer and Adorno argue that while enlightened thought, even today, assumes that it has destroyed myth from some "outside" position, it was, nevertheless, from an inside stance that humanity attempted to master nature.[19]

As a result, while enlightenment thinkers may believe themselves to have destroyed myths with rational thought, they have simply adopted a new myth, that is, that enlightenment destroys myth and is indeed strictly rational.[20] Furthermore, Horkheimer and Adorno argue

19. Theodore W. Adorno and Max Horkheimer, *The Dialectic of Enlightenment*, trans. John Cumming (1944; reprint, New York: Continuum, 1998), 10–12, 27, 41.

20. Wiggershaus, *Frankfurt School*, 329.

that enlightenment, like myth, is making ultimate mythic truth claims.[21] They insist that the enlightenment has legitimated those ways of think-ing and methods of verification, whether rationalist or empiricist, that allowed humanity to master nature. Systems such as the scientific method, mathematics, physics, and formal logic are esteemed, while approaches such as religion, aesthetics, and speculative philosophy are ridiculed and devalued.[22]

Nevertheless, in both cases identity-thinking (that is, the belief that one's concepts completely explain objects and are identical with reality) and mathematical-like logic and calculation are methods of control and domination governed by the drive for self-preservation. Reason, accord-ing to Horkheimer, has become an "absolute" and "final truth" against which everything else is judged and found wanting.[23] Abstraction, in Horkheimer and Adorno's opinion, has become a tool of Fascist-like domination. With the more recent advances in technology, domination has only increased.[24]

The role of Christian religious thinking is brought into the dis-cussion with the mention of Martin Luther, the so-called Father of the Protestant Reformation, who is implicated in the process of domina-tion, and along with him the Protestant church.[25] In Horkheimer's and Adorno's understanding, supposedly enlightened human culture op-erates from a secularized religious core belief. This belief allows men to view nature as an inferior, lifeless, external, exploitable "other." The religious core belief is that God controls and dominates the world for "His" own purposes. The secularized version is that man controls and dominates nature for "his" own purposes.

In addition, not only has outward nature been dominated, but also man's inner nature. As Horkheimer and Adorno deepen their analysis even further, they draw upon what they consider to be classic work

21. Adorno and Horkheimer, *Dialectic of Enlightenment*, 6–10, 25.

22. Ibid., 4–7, 25–26, 71–72, 248. Frances Bacon, the "father of experimental phi-losophy," is criticized for having negatively defined the enlightenment's motives.

23. Max Horkheimer, "Beginnings of the Bourgeois Philosophy of History," in Horkheimer, *Between Philosophy and Social Science: Selected Early Writings*, trans. G. Frederic Hunter, Matthew S. Kramer, and John Torpey (Cambridge, MA: MIT Press, 1995), 313–88, esp. 358.

24. Adorno and Horkheimer, *Dialectic of Enlightenment*, 6, 11–13, 26–31.

25. Ibid., 3–5, 19–20.

within Western cultural history, the *Odyssey*.[26] Through this Homeric epic and the adventures of Odysseus, they illustrate how man overcomes both threats from the natural world and from within his own nature on his voyage toward being the master of himself, his own house, and domain. This, they insist, is the fundamental principle of all human culture with its enlightenment rationality—the domination of nature, both man's inner nature, those parts of himself that he associates with animal instincts, and the outer natural environment. Both are rejected and repressed as "other" than man and as a threat to "man. Furthermore, not everyone embarks on a journey in the same way as Odysseus. Male servants and women are placed under the domination of the master ruling male, Odysseus, rather than being granted the privilege of directly attempting to control themselves or their environment.

Significant to this discussion, Adorno and Horkheimer link the domination of nature and the domination of women, stating, "As a representative of nature, woman in bourgeois society has become the enigmatic image of irresistibility and powerlessness. In this way she reflects for domination the pure lie that posits the subjection rather than the redemption of nature."[27] Through the examples of Odysseus' interaction with the Sirens and their songs, with Circe and her sexuality and ability to turn men into animals, and with Penelope his faithful wife, and her riddle of the marriage bed carved out of a live tree,[28] Horkheimer and Adorno demonstrate that women are associated with the weaker, seductive, sexual, and animal-like aspects of nature. It is these aspects within himself that Odysseus must dominate and control in order to rejoin the civilized world and take his rightful, ruling place within it.

Horkheimer and Adorno also recognize the precarious position in which women oftentimes find themselves when they remark, "where the mastery of nature is the true goal, biological inferiority remains a glaring stigma, the weakness imprinted by nature as a key stimulus to aggression."[29] In their schema they do not view patriarchy as a family arrangement, but rather a societal form of domination, one that both a male dominated culture and church have encouraged and from

26. Ibid., 43ff.
27. Ibid., 71–72.
28. Ibid., 32–36, 58–59, and 69–75.
29. Ibid., 248.

which both have profited through co-opting the work and efforts of women as their own.[30] While Adorno and Horkheimer's critique of this domination of women is insulting to women, as illustrated by the statement that the "last vestiges of female opposition to the spirit of a male-dominated society are engulfed in a morass of paltry rackets, religious sects, and hobbies,"[31] their point is well taken. Women, in being identified with nature, are understood by both church and society to be "other" than man and naturally, inherently subject to men. The Church adds a divinely ordained legitimacy to this domination when it teaches "male headship" and "female submission" supported by the "order of creation," along with God giving man dominion over the earth, including the right to name other creatures.[32]

In summary, in Horkheimer's and Adorno's understanding, the crisis of contemporary culture is deeply embedded, as enlightenment rationality or enlightened thinking has included the principle of domination from time immemorial. This domination involves nature in all its various forms by ruling men like Odysseus. As a result, such dominating enlightened thinking, rather than civilizing and freeing humanity from the vicissitudes of nature, has led to disaster. Humanity is now dominated both psychically and culturally,[33] and nature, which has been seriously damaged while being repressed and exploited, is noticeably responding in a manner oftentimes disastrous to human life. While Mother Nature may be able to survive without humanity, humanity can't survive without its Mother Earth.

According to Adorno and Horkheimer, enlightenment, or at least enlightened thinking, does not have to be dominating.[34] While the goal of enlightened thinking has been the self-preservation of man, which was unfortunately pursued through attempts to dominate nature, within enlightenment thinking is also to be found another, more liberative goal, which opposes such domination and the misuse of power in any way. The implication is that, while the enlightenment has been

---

30. Ibid., 21, 71–72, 109–11, and 248.

31. Ibid., 250. See also Marsha Hewitt, *Critical Theory of Religion: A Feminist Analysis* (Minneapolis: Fortress, 1995), for a feminist critique of their work.

32. Adorno and Horkheimer, *Dialectic of Enlightenment*, 247–53.

33. Ibid., xi, 3, 31–32.

34. Adorno and Horkheimer seem to waver between more radical breaks with enlightenment rationality and attempts to defend a form of critical reason against current forms of irrationalism.

destroying itself, truly enlightened thought could bring about a change. Unfortunately, as far as they were concerned up through the 1940s, the most powerful model of enlightenment rationality was the dominating one, which has been preventing the second, more liberative one from expressing itself.[35] Domination had won out, and disaster could only result as men were not likely to change their way of being in the world until it was too late.

God, Nature, and Canadian Pentecostal Women

One place to start in determining whether the dominating heritage of the enlightenment described by Horkheimer and Adorno evidences itself in Canadian Pentecostalism would be to examine the work of Canadian Pentecostals. A comparison of different writings from three periods in Canadian Pentecostal history indicates that within the movement both the destructive enlightenment dilemma and a more mutual God/nature/humanity affirming understanding was evident. Canadian Pentecostalism seems to have its own "dialectic of enlightenment."

The first example is from the early years, when women were ministering in large numbers, but relegated to a second class position when the PAOC instituted itself and refused to allow women to be ordained or to vote. A sermon by Evangelist Zelma Argue, recorded in her work *Contending for the Faith* in 1923, presents a striking image of God, nature, and human beginnings. The biblical images Argue draws upon reflect a somewhat mutual, inter-connected relationship between God, creation and humanity. She writes,

> From Eden to paradise!
> From Genesis to Revelation!
> From Eternity, to Eternity, the River of God flows on!

> Throughout the pages of the wonderful Word there flows the river, crystal clear. Adam beheld its streams. Moses partook . . . Christ plunged beneath its flow at Jordan. Then He cried of the river that should flow from within believers, when the Spirit should come . . .

> Life-giving current! The river of God!

---

35. Adorno and Horkheimer, *Dialectic of Enlightenment*, 40.

Crystal-clear! Cleansing! Refreshing! Healing! Oh, every need may be met, to those who plunge into its stream . . .

Sin came, and with it expulsion from the Garden . . . They now tasted the waters. The river of Marah, it was. But the waters now were bitter. Moses cried to the Lord, saying, "What shall we drink?" God showed him a tree, which, when thrown into the waters, the waters were made sweet.

For the tree, the Old Rugged Cross, alone could sweeten that which sin had sullied . . .

AH! At the smiting of the rock the waters gushed forth. Abundant! Free! Ever flowing! They had but to partake. And the smitten Rock was Christ.

"Ho, every one that thirsteth, come ye to the waters!" . . .

At Jordan Christ insisted that He be plunged beneath the waters of the river at the hand of John, that all righteousness might be fulfilled in Him. Blessed river, where we may step in, leave our sins and sorrows, leave our old nature for ever, and rise to walk in the newness of life with Christ . . .

Sweet mystery! When we come for salvation we are drinking of the living waters. But when we partake of the Spirit, the living waters flow out from within our inmost souls carrying life to the parched ground around. Wherever the Spirit-filled child of God goes, an oasis is formed. New life springs up.

Pour it out in floods, Lord,
On the parched ground,
'Til it reaches the earth around.

In the beautiful Paradise of God it stills flow on . . .
Blessed River, life-giving stream—Flow on![36]

The second example is an excerpt from curriculum being used in Canadian Pentecostal Sunday Schools from the 1970's until the late 1980's, when the ordination of women was being hotly debated within the PAOC.[37] The *Adult Teacher* guide on the topic "The Christian Family," designed for use in the summer of 1982, states,

36. Zelma Argue, *Contending for the Faith* (Winnipeg: The Messenger of God Publishing House, 1951), 100–102.

37. In 1974 the General Conference of the PAOC held its first formal vote on the motion to ordain women; *Minutes of the 29th Biennial General Conference of the*

When God had completed the six days of creation, He set about the task of custom-making the man He would designate the custodian of His handiwork. From the dust of the earth God formed the body of man, the highest form of His creative genius ... Adam, the man created by God, lived for some time in the Garden of Eden. He tended the garden and classified all of the creatures that lived there ... God had created man a social creature, and it was necessary for him to have someone with whom to share his life. So God met Adam's need for companionship by creating Eve ... Woman was made to be the "completer" of man. She was designed to be a helper who would make him complete. Since loneliness was a primary need in Adam, Eve was designed to provide someone with whom he could communicate openly and intimately. This communication was to be both verbal and nonverbal. It involved intellectual, spiritual, emotional, and physical dimensions of communication ...[38]

The student copy of this same curriculum, *Insight for Young Adults: The Christian Family*, goes on to link God with the masculine and creation with the feminine in defending hierarchical roles between men and women within marriage. In answer to the question "In what ways are the sexes fundamentally different?" Elisabeth Elliot answers,

It's in Genesis 2 that we really get into the differences between men and women ... God caused a deep sleep to fall upon Adam and He took a rib out of his side and made a woman ... From this, I find four truths that indicate the difference between men and women.

First of all, the woman was made for the man. Secondly, she was made from the man. Third, she was brought to the man, and fourth she was named by the man. The authority to name indicated the acceptance of responsibility ...[39]

Pentecostal Assemblies of Canada (August 23rd to 27th, 1974), 4–6. This motion and those following continued to be defeated until 1984. Even then, a motion was introduced in 1988 to overturn the 1984 decision to ordain women; see *Minutes of the 36th Biennial General Conference of the Pentecostal Assemblies of Canada* (1988), 42.

38. Raymond T. Brock, and Ronald G. Head, "Study 1: Foundation for the Christian Family," in *Adult Teacher: The Christian Family* (Springfield, MO: Gospel Publishing, 1982), 6–12.

39. In Hardy W. Steinberg, et al., *Insight for Young Adults: The Christian Family* (Springfield, MO: Gospel Publishing, 1982), 8–10.

As it was through the use of the "symbols of masculinity and femininity," such as husband and wife, bride and bridegroom, that God described His relationship with Israel, and the New Testament described the relationship between Christ and the Church, Elliot insists that "sexuality is not merely a biological difference but a theological one." She then answers the question "What is the essence of femininity?" in the following manner: "Eve was made for Adam. Fit, suitable, adaptable. The fact that the female body is made to receive, to carry, to bear, to nurture, to go down into death to give life to another person all indicates the essence of response. C. S. Lewis said *God is so masculine that all creation is feminine by comparison.* Our role is to respond."[40]

A third example was written in 1997, thirteen years after the PAOC's 1984 decision to finally ordain women,[41] but one year before the decision to allow women to hold any position in the government of the organization, including the national elected General Executive.[42] Cecily Gillespie authored an article in *The Pentecostal Testimony* entitled "Getting Past our Prejudices: Can You Be an Environmentalist and Christian Too?" In it, she attempts to persuade Pentecostal Christians to "set aside stereotypes" she has encountered in her own experiences including the following:

> . . . A commonly held belief in the environmental community places the blame on Christianity for the ecological crisis . . . Christianity encouraged fear and domination of nature, establishing the reason why the Western world has embarked on exploiting the earth for all it has . . .
>
> Although it appears that Christians are becoming more aware of environmental issues, prejudices about environmentalists remain. Many Christians think that all environmentalists worship the earth. All are New-Agers, Gaians, or pantheists, praying to "Nature" or "Mother Earth" instead of the God that created "her."[43]

40. Ibid., emphasis added.

41. *Minutes of the 34th Biennial General Conference of the Pentecostal Assemblies of Canada* (1984), 10–20, and photocopied note overlaid on page 20.

42. See *Minutes of the 41st Biennial General Conference of the Pentecostal Assemblies of Canada* (1998), 3–4, 5–7, 16–17, and "36 Resolutions," appended to the *Minutes of the 41st Biennial General Conference of the Pentecostal Assemblies of Canada* (1998), 4–5.

43. Cecily Gillespie, "Getting Past Our Prejudices: Can You Be an Environmentalist and Christian Too?" *The Pentecostal Testimony* 78.4 (1997): 13–15, esp. 13–14.

Nevertheless, based on her own interpretation of the Scriptures, Gillespie insists that "If God loves this earth, then we cannot justify exploiting it for our own personal gain. Like Adam, God has called us to care for the earth"; she even goes so far as to state that, "The present state of the world, with forest destruction, ozone depletion, smog warnings, and so on, is a reflection of how far we are from God. As we come to know the Lord, we can come to see the beauty of His creation, the importance of protecting it, and our place in it. So saving souls results in saving the creation."[44] Gillespie recommends that, like David, the prophets, John the Baptist, Jesus, Celtic monastics and Franciscans, Pentecostal Christians should "spend time with God in nature," in order "for God to test our dependence upon Him, as well as the opportunity for spiritual growth and renewal"; Christians need to "learn how to relate lovingly to God's creation."[45]

While all three examples tended to reflect, perhaps even legitimate, the prevailing practices of their time in regards to the limitations and freedoms afforded women, the third example, written only ten years ago, not only echoes the concerns of critical theorists above, it also illustrates Canadian Pentecostalism's dialectical dilemma quite clearly. While acknowledging that stereotypes exist that Pentecostals would recognize, such as, the Western world believes, partly based on Christian teaching, that nature, which is often labeled "female," is to be dominated and exploited, Gillespie argues, based on her interpretation of the Scriptures, that God loves creation and Pentecostals could benefit from being part of nature.

I would argue that the second example, the Sunday School curriculum, unwittingly drew upon the dominant and dominating enlightenment rationality so scorned by Horkheimer and Adorno as it attempted to follow the rules for sound doctrine, including an appeal to an "objective" foundation and authority for its position.

In comparison, the first example, Argue's sermon, not bound by the prescriptions and limitations of academic, enlightened rationality, which prides itself on an insistence upon and assumption of being "objective," was able to side step much of that dominant and dominating ideology and practice through her own interpretation of readily

44. Ibid., 14–15.
45. Ibid., 15.

available biblical images, which was both christocentric and pneuma-tological. It also, in comparison with the sample from the curriculum, which started with God and then proceeded hierarchically downward to man and then nature and women, began on a more mutual note with "Eden," the Scriptures, Eternity, and God's River before proceeding to major male figures from the Scriptures. No longer is there an opposi-tional and dominating relationship to be found. While God's provision in Christ was deemed necessary "[f]or the tree, the Old Rugged Cross, alone could sweeten that which sin had sullied," it was offered to all, "every one that thirsteth," and offered abundantly and free of charge. While clearly reflecting a patriarchal world view in that it mentions only male figures from the Scriptures and omits the many female ones, in Argue's work the relationship between God, nature, and humanity is relational and interconnected. As one of the early, great evangelists of the Pentecostal movement, Argue's presentation of the Gospel was not only non-dominating, it was effective. She introduced many people to Pentecostal Christianity.[46]

A Provisional Way Forward

While Horkheimer and Adorno's critique includes the various religions of the world, their own work contains a distinctly religious component, that is, that a truly humane world is totally different than anything hu-manity has ever known. Similar to Marx,[47] they insist that religions, including Christianity, contain protests against injustices and the status quo as well as the hopes and longing for a more humane existence, of-tentimes in a utopic form in their teachings on heaven and an other-worldly existence.[48]

---

46. Argue's name and articles are sprinkled throughout early copies of the Canadian *Pentecostal Testimony*.

47. Karl Marx, "Contribution to the Critique of Hegel's *Philosophy of Right*: Introduction," in Robert C. Tucker, ed., *The Marx-Engels Reader*, 2nd ed. (New York: Norton, 1978), 53–56.

48. See for instance, Horkheimer, *Dawn and Decline: Notes 1926–1931 and 1950–1969*, trans. Michael Shaw (New York: Seabury, 1978), 58, and Horkheimer, "Theism and Atheism," in his *Critique of Instrumental Reason: Lectures and Essays since the End of World War II*, trans. Matthew J. O'Connell and others (New York: Continuum, 1984), 34–50, esp. 50.

Reflecting their Jewish heritage, which refuses to name God or the sacred,[49] Horkheimer and Adorno insist that the only way to work toward such a humane world is to constantly negate, through a comprehensive, radical, and multi-layered critique, the world which humanity has created, a world which could never measure up to the nameless other of God. The method of sustained negativity they utilize was derived from a revision of the Hegelian dialectic, whereby a synthesis is never reached as such a synthesis would be considered premature.[50] A truly humane world is never attainable within the context of what humanity has created for itself and experienced. It is completely "other," an observation of which is only expressed within religion. Hence the need for a sustained negative dialectic, with any supposed synthesis or constructive suggestions remaining provisional and suspect. "Heaven" may be hoped for, but never achieved in this world.[51] Horkheimer and Adorno have also critiqued the churches for capitulating to the status quo in their own attempts at institutional self-preservation, thereby oftentimes muting their potentially liberating message.[52]

This, I would suggest, is the radical root of the problem within Canadian Pentecostalism, which manifests itself in many ways, including, but not limited to, the hierarchical domination of women within its midst by privileged Caucasian men. Dominating enlightened rationality and enlightened and civilized ways of being within the world that humanity has created for itself within the West have been adopted, thereby suppressing the operation of the Spirit, including the empowering of women to minister and lead. Pentecostalism, even with its denial of this world's ways and thinking, nevertheless has been enculturated to think within the modern world's value systems. That's all we know apart from God. Therefore, recognizing that domination as part of enlightenment and our own way of thinking is essential, since our enlightenment enculturation has had an adverse effect on the women within our midst

49. Michael R. Ott, *Max Horkheimer's Critical Theory of Religion: The Meaning of Religion in the Struggle for Human Emancipation* (Lanham, MD: University Press of America, 2001), 10.

50. See Theodore Adorno, *Negative Dialectics*, trans. E. B. Asthon (New York: Continuum, 1966), for an in-depth discussion of this approach.

51. See for instance, Horkheimer, *Dawn and Decline*, 148.

52. Hewitt, *Critical Theory of Religion*, 207ff.

who continue to receive mixed messages concerning who they are and
how they should respond to God's calling and leadings.

Although an important part of the project due to the authority
granted various interpretations, analyzing the causes and results of this
adverse effect must go beyond an appeal to various Scriptures interpreted in different ways by various scholars. It must also go beyond recapturing and communicating the enormous and diverse contributions
women have made to the Pentecostal movement both at home and
around the globe. Again, while important in that it situates the question of women's involvement clearly within a social-historical framework rather than some abstract, eternal proposition, it is not sufficient.
Pentecostals must go back to the beginning and rethink their doctrines
and assumptions of the relationship between God and creation, including humanity, male and female, in order to deconstruct the concept of
domination within its midst. Until a comprehensive analysis of this
"myth of man," including the influence of enlightenment rationality on
Pentecostalism, has been undertaken, no ecologically aware theology or
answer to the "woman question" will prove adequate.

Countering the influence of enlightenment rationality will not be
easy. Nevertheless, I would suggest that it is possible for Pentecostals to
begin to do so for several reasons. First, many Pentecostals would agree
with the negative judgement of human history and this world. Only
heaven is understood to be truly humane and completely other-worldly,
even as the promise of heaven begins in the here and now, amidst the
"now but not yet" tension within which Pentecostal Christians live.

Second, within Pentecostalism nature has never been "disen-
chanted." There is no dualistic understanding of the spiritual and material. Instead, the spiritual and the material are understood to be parts
of a larger whole. The enlightenment, with its empirical and rational
worldview, is understood to promote a deficient, fragmented view of
reality. As more than one Pentecostal has pointed out,[53] "knowing" is
not limited to the realm of reason alone but also is deeply experiential
and affective, thereby collapsing false, hierarchical dichotomies such as
object/subject, mind/body, emotional/rational, human/nature, man/
woman, scholarly/confessional, etc. As such, Pentecostalism has within

53. See for example, Robert O. Baker, "Pentecostal Bible Reading: Toward a Model
of Reading for the Formation of Christian Affections," *Journal of Pentecostal Theology*
7 (1995): 34–48, esp. 35.

it the possibility of developing a holistic, nonhierarchical understanding of the relationship between God, humanity and nature.

Third, Pentecostalism stresses the need to discern what the Spirit of God is doing on an ongoing basis. The Spirit has oftentimes operated in a fashion directly counter to the prevailing modes of interaction of our enlightened culture, with its assumption of a multi-layered, hierarchical, and repressive domination as a norm for civilized humanity. Perhaps it's time that Pentecostals, as people of the Spirit, start paying more attention to what the Spirit has been saying and doing, rather than the cultural status quo. The Spirit has consistently empowered and called women.

Fourth, in spite of the co-existence of hierarchical and dominating, along with egalitarian and mutual, assumptions about how God, nature, men, and women relate to each other, there also exist within Canadian Pentecostalism indications that some are moving beyond this dialectical way of thinking. In an article in *The Pentecostal Testimony* in April 2007, long after the dust over the roles and ministries of women has seemingly settled, Karen Reed speaks eloquently regarding "a number of helpful insights for evangelism in this postmodern culture." These insights include the following:

> The Celtic movement emphasized the image of God in all humanity. Although sin distorts and blurs that image, the Celtics acknowledged the noble efforts of all people groups as a way to affirm God's image in *human nature*. Instead of a focus on human depravity, they encouraged the honouring of individuals who made achievements in science and culture, even if they were not Christian.
>
> Celtic believers also stressed God's immanence and dynamic activity, and sought ways for people to experience *God's presence* and power. History shows that they also adapted well to each *culture*, not isolating themselves from it, but effectively engaging and serving humanity ...
>
> They invited "outsiders" to belong to the community of faith *before* they believed. Also, all people were valued and freed to use their gifts and abilities regardless of ethnicity and gender. Women were given the same opportunities to lead a church as men. An atmosphere of inclusiveness, warmth and depth of community marked the movement ...

The final insight from the Celtics was their call to give attention to humanity's kinship with *nature,* honouring the earth
and creation . . . [54]

Reed is suggesting that "humanity's kinship with nature" be hon-
oured, the image of God in human nature generally be recognized, all
people, including women, be valued, and God be experienced in our
midst. Perhaps Adorno and Horkheimer were wrong. Perhaps the dominant form of enlightenment rationality has not had the last word or
completely repressed and overpowered a more egalitarian and affirming one.

Come, Holy Spirit, we need you . . .

54. Karen Reed, "The Old Story in a New Era," *The Pentecostal Testimony* 88.1
(2007): 18; emphases original.

12

Changing Images

Women in Asian Pentecostalism

Julie C. Ma

Introduction

WHILE CONTEMPLATING THE ASSIGNED TOPIC, PAUL'S WORDS TO THE Corinthian Church came to mind: "For man did not come from woman, but woman from man; neither was man created for woman, but woman for man" (1 Cor 11:8–9). These words invite a fresh reconsideration of the relationship between men and women in our twenty-first century context.

The image of women has been changing rapidly in most societies, except in some closed Muslim and communist countries. Yet surprisingly, women are now able to fill prominent positions in many professions. Even less than a decade ago, most Asian countries were primarily male dominated, and to a certain degree, this still continues. However, what we see today could never have been envisioned in previous decades. The image of the fragile woman is gradually vanishing. Women are portrayed as important figures in the media and appear in all forms of advertising. In fact, attracting the attention of women and children is a crucial part of contemporary business.

The purpose of this essay is to discuss images of women from biblical and contemporary cultural perspectives, and to explore the changing roles of women in society, especially in Asia. An underlying question I will be exploring is: to what degree can we expect the roles of women to be transformed and expanded in the church today? This question brings with it unique challenges and opportunities for the churches in Asia.

Changing Images of Women

Change marks our society, and this is seen at the social, political, and economic levels. Likewise, images of woman today differ from the prevalent image in former times, clearly showing that cultural perceptions are not static but dynamic.

Images of Women in the Biblical World

During the Second Temple period, Jewish women were separated from men in the synagogues.[1] This symbolized male authority over, and superiority to, women. For the same reason, women were not allowed to study the Torah, and it was assumed either that women were not expected to learn, or that they were incapable of learning. Even if some women were literate, they were not permitted to read aloud during public gatherings. Furthermore, women were not permitted to pray, neither in public places nor at home (e.g., at meal times). Their role was confined solely to the home, caring for the family and the children. Precisely because such discrimination against women was widespread in the first-century Jewish diaspora, it may well have been inherited by the early church.[2]

Granted that Hellenistic culture in the first century may have been less restrictive than Jewish culture, there was also clearly discrimination against women in Hellenistic perceptions and practices. An ancient saying is attributed to Aristotle: "Woman is an embarrassment to man, a beast in his quarters, a continual worry, a never-ending trouble, a daily annoyance, the destruction of the household, a hindrance to solitude, the undoing of a virtuous man, an oppressive burden, an insatiable bee, a men's property and possession."[3] Along these lines, the Babylonian

---

1. Flavius Josephus, *Antiquities of the Jews in the Words of Flavius Josephus*, (Edinburgh: Brown & Nelson, 1828), 15.11.431.

2. Elaine Pagels, *The Gnostic Gospels* (New York: Vintage, 1989), 140–41.

3. Emma T. Healy, *Women according to Saint Bonaventure* (New York: Georgian, 1956), 46. See also Ruth A. Tucker, *Woman in the Maze: Questions and Answers on Biblical Equality* (Downers Grove, IL: InterVarsity, 1992), 156.

Talmud reminds its readers, "The woman, says the Law, is in all things inferior to the man. Let her accordingly be submissive, not for her humiliation, but that they may be directed; for the authority has been given by God to the man."[4]

The New Testament depiction of the early church portrays a male dominated culture that provided little opportunity for women to take leadership roles in public worship and life. Paul lived amidst a cultural milieu which viewed women as intellectually inferior and subordinate to men. He argued that women should be silent in public worship (1 Cor 14:34–35), and stated, "I do not permit a woman to teach or to have authority over a man" (1 Tim 2:12). Paul also asked Timothy to instruct women "to dress modestly with decency and propriety, not with braided hair or gold or pearls or expensive clothes, but with good deeds, appropriate for women who profess to worship God" (1 Tim 2:9–10). It was understood that prostitutes wore such worldly dress. Therefore, it is plausible that such restrictions discouraged women from participating in church gatherings and activities. A byproduct of this restriction may have been that the majority of church members were male.[5]

What then is Paul's intent? It should be remembered that his epistles are ad hoc literature, as Gordon Fee argues.[6] Most likely Paul's intent was not to offer a universal prohibition on women in ministry, but rather to address specific congregational situations.

In spite of the cultural tendency to limit the opportunities of women, Paul elsewhere affirms their role in ministry. If we read the New Testament carefully, we see that the early church challenged its social and religious cultural norms. Women are found teaching (Acts 18:26) and prophesying (Acts 21:9 and 1 Cor 11:5). Phoebe is called a "deacon"

4. Babylonian Talmud VII 18, 16. See also G. F. Moore, *Judaism in the First Centuries of the Christian Era, the Age of the Tannaim*, 3 vols. (Cambridge: Harvard University Press, 1927–30), 1:128. See also what Tertullian said about women, "You are the Devil's gateway. You are the unsealer of that forbidden tree. You are the first deserter of the Divine law. You are she who persuaded him whom the Devil was not valiant enough to attack. You destroyed so easily God's image of man. On account of your desert, that is death, even the Son of God had to die"; Tertullian, Concerning the Dress of Women 1.1, quoted in Rosemary Radford Ruether, *Sexism and God-Talk: Toward a Feminist Theology* (Boston: Beacon, 1983), 167.

5. Josephus, *Antiquities*, 15.11.431.

6. Gordon D. Fee and Douglas Stuart, *How to Read the Bible Book by Book* (Grand Rapids: Zondervan, 2002), 315.

(Rom 16:1–2), while Priscilla was Paul's fellow co-worker (Rom 16:3). I will not try to portray Paul as being larger than life, as he was also a man of his own culture and times. But, it is possible to understand Paul is "inclusive" with respect to the role of woman in the church to the extent that some women were his partners in the work for God's kingdom. His actions thus did not conform fully to the prevalent cultural conventions regarding women (Rom 16:1–2).[7]

Modern Images of Woman

Modern images of women span the "traditional" to "liberated" spectrum. On the one hand, the traditional understanding of women has been tied with their ability to produce children. Their roles as homemaker and caretaker of the family are a natural outgrowth of this responsibility. In various parts of the world, this traditionalist view continues to significantly restrict the social roles of women. For example, in traditionalist Korea, most married women have perennially been housekeepers, doing household chores and rearing children. If a woman lived with her parents-in-law, her domestic obligations increased drastically. In spite of improvements in many developing countries, traditional male dominance remains entrenched, especially in regions where patriarchal structure is deeply rooted.[8]

Yet on the other hand, around the contemporary world, this traditional image of women has changed. Since the Enlightenment, there have been arguments against the traditional subordination of women to men that insists on "the ontological identity of all human beings (all human beings are equal because all partake universally in human nature)."[9] As a result, women have emerged as leaders in prominent positions. The traditional image of women as only being good housekeepers no longer

---

7. Cullen Murphy, *The Word according to Eve: Women and the Bible in Ancient Times and Our Own* (London: Lane, 1999), 178.

8. Christine Battersby, *Gender and Genius: Towards a Feminist Aesthetics* (London: Women's Press, 1989), 10.

9. Ursula Le Guin, "Bryn Mawr Commencement Address," in Ursula K. Le Guin, *Dancing at the Edge of the World: Thoughts on Words, Women, Places* (New York: Grove, 1989), 155. See also Steven Connor, *Theory and Cultural Value* (Oxford: Blackwell, 1992), 159, and Jane Flax, "Postmodernism and Gender Relations in Feminist Theory," *Signs: Journal of Women in Culture and Society* 12 (1987): 625.

holds, and the exercise of their capabilities within the wider community is now respected. There is always the possibility of change.[10]

The Contributions of Women in Contemporary Asian Societies

Some of these changes have been quite dramatic, resulting in the ascent of women to positions of authority and power. Just as there have been various examples of women in the highest political positions in the West—e.g., Catherine the Great brought Russia out of feudalism; Joan of Arc united the dispirited troops of France, pulling along a frightened crown prince into battle and victory; and Queen Elizabeth I ended the bloodbath of religious persecution, and her long reign allowed for a golden age of new ideas and exploration[11]—so also has this been the case in Asia. In the following, I highlight two contemporary women who serve as exemplars of change in the Asian context, and discuss other changes related to the role of Asian women in the public sphere.

Corazón Aquino: Former President of the Philippines

People remember Aquino as "the bespectacled woman in her trademark yellow dress."[12] She acknowledges that she never imagined becoming the political figure that she is today, although her family has a long history of political involvement. Aquino was born into a wealthy and politically prominent family on 25 January 1933. Her parents—Jose Cojuangco, a three-term congressman, and Demetria Sumulong, a pharmacist and daughter of a senator—were among the most influential names in Central Luzon. She achieved her education in the United States: elementary and high school at Saint Scholastica's College and Notre Dame Convent School in New York, and a Bachelor of Arts in French and mathematics at Mount Saint Vincent Convent, New York. In 1956, she

---

10. Jaynie Anderson, *Giorgione: The Painter of Poetic Brevity* (Paris: Flammarion, 1997), 20.

11. Loren Cunningham, "Your Gifts and Destiny," in Loren Cunningham, David J. Hamilton, and Janice Rogers, eds., *Why not Women?* (Seattle: YWAM Publishing 2000), 45–56, esp. 55.

12. This is what Filipinos express about Aquino's image as a woman.

was planning to take up law at the Far Eastern University when Benigno Servillano Aquino Jr. (1932–1983) came into her life.[13]

Not too long after her husband was assassinated in 1983 by government agents—he was, after all, the chief political opponent of then President Ferdinand Marcos—Aquino decided to run for the Presidency. After the election (1986), she, as well as Marcos, claimed to have won. When Marcos refused to step down, Aquino planned strikes. With the country on the edge of civil war, Marcos fled to the United States as a refugee, and Aquino assumed the presidency. She became the first woman president of the country, and served until 1992.

Some of Aquino's achievements have been summarized as follows: "The movement led by Cory against the dictatorial rule resulted in the 'People Power Revolution' that overthrew the Marcos government in February 1986. Once in power, Cory ordered all political prisoners freed and built the machinery for democracy."[14] Yet while Aquino promised changes and improvements, most did not materialize during her term in office. The nation was plagued by economic hardships and incompetent leadership. The continual political struggles and natural calamities that ensued endangered the gains made by her administration. Her presidency survived seven military revolts, typhoons, drought, an energy crisis, a major earthquake, and a volcanic eruption. However, Aquino gained the attention of the world as she "received several international awards including Time Magazine's Woman of the Year, the Eleanor Roosevelt Human Rights Award, the United Nations Silver Medal and the Canadian International Prize for Freedom. She was cited for setting the example of a nonviolent movement for democracy which was later tested in Burma, South Africa, Poland and Chile."[15]

Myoeng Sook Han: Prime Minister of South Korea

Myoeng Sook Han, born on 24 March 1944, served as Prime Minister of South Korea (April 2006–March 2007). She completed her B.A. in French literature and M.A. in women's studies in Ewha Women's University in

13. Who's Who 1997: An Annual Biographical Dictionary (London: A. & C. Black, 1997), 47.

14. "Aquino, Corazon," in The Columbia Electronic Encyclopedia, 6th ed. (2006) [http://www.infoplease.com/ce6/people/A0804461.html].

15. Ibid.

Seoul. Han was the first Minister of "Gender Equality" (2001–2003), and also served as the Minister of Environment (2003–2004).

In March, 2006, following the resignation of Prime Minister Lee Hae Chan, President Roh Moo Hyun nominated Han to become the first female Prime Minister of South Korea. Han is only the second woman to be nominated for the Prime Minister's position. In the following month, she was officially sworn in. Han focused on building international relationships, and she has traveled to the United Arab Emirates, Kazakhstan, and Uzbekistan. Korea is a conservative society that hardly acknowledges women in leadership roles. Hence, Han's appointment has been considered to be rather radical in the Korean context, and she has been under close and constant scrutiny by the public.

Tong Kim, former senior interpreter at the U.S. State Department and now a visiting scholar at Johns Hopkins School of Advanced International Studies, has suggested that Han's work may influence the prospects of the Grand National Party woman leader, Park Geun-hye, in Park's candidacy for the 2007 presidential election. On the one hand, some observers contend that the idea of a woman president is a bit too premature for Korea. On the other hand, Korea's ancient history includes three queens ruling the Silla kingdom: SunDuk (632–47), JinDuk (648–54), and JinSung (887–897). For this reason, Han's performance may have profound implications for the future of women's leadership in Korea.

Women in the Public Square

Growing up in Korea, I hardly saw any married women working in prominent public positions, except teaching in schools. The majority of companies hired single women, and once married, they would lose their jobs. But in recent years, spaces have often been created for Asian women, both single and married, to actively participate in public positions. One example is Indra Nooyi. Born, raised and educated in Chennai, India, Nooyi became CEO of PepsiCo in 2004. Her management studies at Yale prepared her to be the first "desi" (native Asian Indian) to head an American company of this size. PepsiCo is one of the two largest U.S. companies run by a woman.

Besides women like Aquino and Han, others are also increasingly found in leadership positions in politics today. The "First Asia-Pacific

Congress of Women in Politics" was held in Manila, Philippines in June 1994 under the theme "Why Women, What Politics?" The conference was attended by 250 Asian politicians from 23 countries who discussed their plans to transform politics in Asia. Senator Leticia Shahani, the convener of the Third World Conference on Women held in Nairobi, Kenya, in 1985, was the keynote speaker on the first day of the conference. She emphasized it was imperative for more women to get involved in the electoral process. This would be one way for women to gain access to primary decision-making positions where they could help shape a better and more sustainable world. A guest of honor at the concluding ceremony was President Fidel V. Ramos of the Philippines, who shared his administration's promise to include more qualified women in leadership positions. He was reported to have "challenged the Philippine delegation in the Congress to come up with names of women whom he could include in his short list of nominees to key positions in his administration."[16] Discussions focused on two major concerns: 1) to declare the rightful place of women in the public square, and 2) to redefine the notion and exercise of politics and power.

Challenges and Opportunities for Asian Pentecostalism

The preceding examples of the outstanding Asian women show that women are capable leaders in their own right. The myth of women's incapacities in the public arena has been broken. With this trend in view, I now want to issue a challenge to my own Pentecostal movement.

The Pentecostal tradition has been generally inclusive with regard to women's roles in ministry. This has to do with their central doctrine of baptism in the Spirit and Peter's use of Joel 2 as a theological explanation of the Spirit's advent on the day of Pentecost (Acts 2:17–20). The "democratic" outpouring of the Spirit is the main feature of Joel's prophecy: the Spirit will be poured out upon everyone regardless of gender, age, or social status. This egalitarianism has freed the typically marginalized to serve in their churches, resulting in women being as, if not more, active than men in early Pentecostal ministry and mission settings. However, it is also noted that in recent years among Pentecostal

16. "First Asia-Pacific Congress of Women in Politics: Why Women, What Politics?" [http://www.capwip.org/actirities/a-p-congresses/a-plcongress.htm] (last accessed 26 Oct. 2000).

communities, a "glass ceiling" has remained for women who have felt the call to ministry.

The Ordination of Women

In the West, Pentecostal churches regularly ordain women as ministers. Often the criterion for evaluation is not qualifications, but the evidence of a divine call for service. For this reason, the ordination of women in the early Pentecostal movement was not an issue. However, this seemingly revolutionary concept was tested severely during the process of Pentecostal institutionalization. It has also been challenged when Western Pentecostal missionaries arrived on Asian soil. Can Pentecostal women receive equal treatment in ministry and have the same opportunity as men to receive ordination? Could this be applied to all Pentecostal traditions, including those in Asia?

For example, in the first thirty years of the Korean Assemblies of God, there were less than three ordained women ministers throughout the country, while the ordained men numbered more than one thousand. (Even now, some large Korean Presbyterian churches still do not allow women's ordination). Although its constitution provided for the ordination of women, the Korean Assemblies of God placed an unusual number of restrictions on women, including requirements to be single or widowed. It was not until recently that many of these restrictions have been removed. In other Asian countries, the ordination of women is simply not permitted. Women ministers, possessing the same divine call to serve the church as men, still live as second-class ministers. The male dominant culture of most Asian contexts has suppressed the freedom that is found in Christ and in his Spirit.

Women as High-Level Decision-Makers

Paul had a high regard for Priscilla and Aquila in Corinth. Although the structure of the church had not yet reached a level of sophistication during that period of early Christianity, Pricilla's role was definitely that of a leader, not only in her local congregation but also in leadership training (e.g., Acts 19). Pricilla and Aquila assisted Paul in planting the church in Ephesus and Rome. Paul strongly commended their leadership qualities and counted them among his most trusted co-workers.

Paul listened to their suggestions and valued their input (Acts 18:18–19, 24–26; Rom 16:3–5; 1 Cor 16:19; and 2 Tim 4:19).

Can Pentecostal churches accept women as members of its national level executive bodies? Such positions would include top-level denominational officers, district-level leaders, or national mission committee members. Most of the national-level leadership posts are occupied by men, and only rarely are women to be found. This suggests the existence of a glass ceiling for women's leadership development. Most women remain involved only at the level of local church ministry, missionary service, or education. This is a general trend among Evangelical churches as well.

Through their close attention to details and relational sensitivity, women can contribute significantly to the decision-making processes of their churches and denominations. What was suggested in the "First Asia-Pacific Congress of Women in Politics" (noted above) remains a challenge for Pentecostal churches. If women can now be found in positions at the highest levels of government, why should they not be found in similar positions in the church?

What would it take for Asian Pentecostal churches and denominations to elect or appoint women as denominational heads, or as heads of various departments of their denomination? Although it is rare to see a woman denominational leader, one surprise comes from an extremely young Pentecostal church, the Mongolian Assemblies of God, which elected a woman general superintendent. But these exceptions prove the rule: that the highest position in any organization is still reserved for males. Thus, the glass ceiling remains in place.

Women in Mission Leadership

A quick glance at mission organizations reveals, unsurprisingly, that the highest leadership responsibilities are still in the hands of men. This is the case even though women exceed the number of men in missions and missionary training programs. Women should be encouraged to take up leadership roles in preparing missionaries, providing missionary care, and establishing mission policies.

Returning to St. Paul and the New Testament, the involvement of women in ministry training is well attested. Priscilla most likely took a leadership role in teaching Apollos by inviting him to her home and expounding on God's Word (Acts 18:18–19, 24–25). Under her tutelage, Apollos became an effective preacher in Corinth and other places. Priscilla's role was elaborated on by John Chrysostom of the fourth century:

> Paul has placed Priscilla before her husband. For he did not say, "Greet Aquila and Priscilla," but "Priscilla and Aquila." He does not do this without a reason . . . . What I said is not guesswork, because it is possible to learn this from the Book of Acts. [Priscilla] took Apollos, an eloquent man and powerful in the Scriptures, but knowing only the baptism of John; and she instructed him in the way of the Lord and made him a teacher brought to completion.[17]

David Hamilton, a missionary to South America, notes Paul's admonishment: "Women likewise must be serious, not slanderers, but temperate, faithful in all things" (1 Tim 3:11). When Paul called on women with leadership roles, he used the term "likewise," which serves as a literary identical sign, i.e., "in the same way." Therefore, he did likewise in 1 Tim 2:9, and this word connects both texts, moving his discussion from men to women.[18] Without doubt, Paul handled men and women equally as fellow workers in the gospel.

I wonder if women themselves were reluctant to be equal partners with men in responsibility and authority. With an abundance of women field missionaries, mission organizations, and denominations will never lack potential candidates for women mission leaders. An interesting study could investigate how many male missionaries later became mission leaders in comparison with women missionaries who later took leadership positions.

Leadership in Academia

The academic world is where women have advanced furthest in leadership roles in Pentecostal circles. A significant number of women scholars are active in colleges, universities, and seminaries throughout the world. Yet in higher education settings, women's participation, not to

17. John Chrysostom, "First Homily on the Greeting to Priscilla and Aquila," trans. Catherine Clark Kroeger, *Priscilla Papers* 5.3 (1991): 18; emphasis in the original.

18. David Hamilton, "Women Leaders Too," in *Why not Women?* 227–30, quotation from 229.

mention leadership, is still lacking in comparison to men. This is especially the case in non-western and international contexts. My experience tells me that at various international conferences, for example, the role of women is significantly less than that of men. Often, only a token number of women participate in any given international conference. Further, most of the time, men's voices are heard and women keep silent. Finally, it seems that we have still a long way to go before women are elected to leadership positions in international societies. It goes without saying that this is also the case with regard to positions of leadership at Bible colleges or theological seminaries in the Pentecostal tradition. I would encourage female academicians to join such societies, participate in them, and even organize conferences when the opportunities arise.

Conclusion

My intention in this study is not to downgrade men or belittle their abilities. Rather, I seek to encourage and empower women to exercise their God-given talents and gifts for the kingdom. I have never placed myself among feminists nor sought to fight for or insist on women's rights.

It is time for Asian Pentecostal churches to contribute to the paradigm shift in our society, and do so by living out Pentecostalism's inherent theological valuation of women. I hope our discussion may encourage women to envision the possibilities regarding their contributions to God's kingdom, and also encourage men to empower women in expressing their God-given gifts and talents.

I close by mentioning the courageous life of Huldah Buntain, the wife of Pentecostal missionary Mark Buntain. Even after her husband's death, she is continuing the feeding program for children in India which her husband carried on during his life. In an endorsement of a book on their ministry, Ken Dobson writes, "I wondered what life would be like for Huldah now in India, so far from family, and alone. Surely, if anyone deserves to retire from ministry, it is Auntie Huldah."[19] But authentic leaders do not just retire, and this applies to women just as well as it does to men.

19. Hal Donaldson and Kenneth M. Dobson, *Woman of Courage* (Springdale, PA: Whitaker, 1989), 18.

13

Spiritual Egalitarianism, Ecclesial Pragmatism, and the Status of Women in Ordained Ministry

Frederick L. Ware

Introduction

CONFLICTING TENDENCIES EXIST IN PENTECOSTALISM. IN HIS BOOK *Heaven Below*, Grant Wacker argues that the "genius of the Pentecostal movement lay in its ability to hold two seemingly incompatible impulses in productive tension."[1] He names these impulses the "primitive" and "pragmatic." The primitive impulse is stirred by Spirit baptism, seeks to restore the "apostolic faith," and is fueled by the desire to be guided by the Holy Spirit in all aspects of one's life. The pragmatic impulse concerns itself with practical matters, such as the exercise of prudent judgment in the face of everyday realities, the deliberate pursuit of self-interest, routinization of spirituality and worship, social organization, and institution-building. Wacker claims that these dual impulses compensate for each other's excesses and accordingly compliment each other.[2]

My use of the terms "spiritual egalitarianism" and "ecclesial pragmatism" correspond respectively to the impulses that Wacker names the "primitive" and "pragmatic." By "spiritual egalitarianism," I am referring primarily to the belief that all persons are equal before God and that spiritual gifts are bestowed impartially by God. By "ecclesial pragmatism," I am referring to thought and actions undertaken, as well as beliefs

---

1. Grant Wacker, *Heaven Below: Early Pentecostals and American Culture* (Cambridge: Harvard University Press, 2001), 10.

2. Ibid., 12–14.

formulated, in the process of institution-building. Ecclesial pragmatism is a covering term for the ways that Pentecostals have organized social-ly, built institutions, and articulated values and underlying rationales for these social structures. The beliefs, values, and practices developed through ecclesial pragmatism are not always compatible with the core values and theological distinctives of Pentecostalism. However, ecclesial pragmatism is not necessarily antithetical to spiritual egalitarianism. At its best, ecclesial pragmatism seeks to implement the faith commitments of Pentecostalism, one of which happens to be spiritual egalitarianism. It is imperative, not only for the issue of women's ordination but also for other matters of concern facing Pentecostal churches, that ecclesial pragmatism be informed, challenged, and accountable to the core val-ues and theological distinctives of Pentecostalism.

In order for Pentecostals to maintain a sense of the integrity of the church as an autonomous social institution, women's full ordination and service in chief positions of leadership should occur as a result of the movement's internal consistency and adherence to its core values and theological distinctives. While some Pentecostals accept women's ordination, there are other Pentecostals who reject it. Mark Chaves' study of women's ordination in the United States reveals that Protestant denominations that allow women's ordination have done so mostly as a result of external pressures caused by organized women's movements and social expectations of gender equality throughout the society.[3]

This essay deals with the internal problem of reconciling ecclesial pragmatism to spiritual egalitarianism, both of which are valued, in varying degrees, in the history of Pentecostalism. The focus is limited to my social location, which is that of an African American Pentecostal within the Church of God in Christ. Three areas of discussion covered in this essay are: (1) the status of women in African American Pentecostal churches, (2) the Church of God in Christ's statement on women's or-dination, and (3) dialectical tensions indicative of core values and theo-logical distinctives of Pentecostalism. The discussion presupposes that Pentecostal churches must evaluate the history and status of women within their institutional boundaries and scrutinize their assumptions about women's ordination in light of their core values and theological distinctives. I suggest that these core values and distinctives, of which

3. Mark Chaves, *Ordaining Women: Culture and Conflict in Religious Organization* (Cambridge: Harvard University Press, 1997).

spiritual egalitarianism is but one, emerge from Pentecostal spirituality, biblical hermeneutics, and eschatology.

Women in Pentecostal Churches: Sometimes Free, More Often Restricted

Though not all Pentecostal denominations trace their origins to the Azusa Street Revival (led by William J. Seymour), that revival figures preeminently in the history and doctrine of the Church of God in Christ (COGIC). In the spring of 1907, three COGIC leaders, Charles H. Mason, John A. Jeter, and D. J. Young, attended the revival in Los Angeles. While there, Mason and Young each had a "Pentecostal" experience of baptism in the Holy Spirit accompanied by tongue-speaking. Their pilgrimage set in motion a series of events that resulted in COGIC's transformation from a Holiness to a Pentecostal denomination.

Women of Azusa Street

The Azusa Street Revival is said to have begun with a small group of African American domestics employed by white families.[4] The work of these women consisted of tasks such as washing clothes, cooking, and caring for the children of their white employers. At the revival and mission, these women prayed and preached. Miracles of healing were wrought through them. They guided many persons into the experience of Spirit baptism. Leaving the revival, they went out and planted churches.

Though African American women formed the core of the membership of the Azusa Street Mission, other persons found place and space in the leadership of the mission and revival. The leadership of the mission and revival was an interracial group of men and women. William J. Seymour's leadership team consisted of ten persons, six of whom were women. The credentials committee, which would commission persons

4. Estrelda Alexander, *The Women of Azusa Street* (Cleveland: Pilgrim, 2005), 23, 122; *The Apostolic Faith* 1.1 (1906): 1. Alexander tells the stories of prominent African American women in the Azusa Mission and Revival, namely Lucy Farrow, Julia Hutchinson, Jennie Evans Moore Seymour, Sister Prince, Neely Terry, and Ophelia Wiley. Seymour acknowledges only that the mission was predominately African American. See William J. Seymour, *Doctrines and Discipline of the Azusa Street Apostolic Faith Mission* (Los Angeles: Azusa Mission, 1915), 12.

to further the work of the revival, consisted of nine persons. Of these nine, five were women. Only two African American women, Jennie Evans Moore and Sister Prince, served on the leadership team. Jennie Evans Moore would later marry Seymour. When Seymour died, in 1922, Jennie assumed leadership of the mission. She would pastor the mission for 14 years until her death in 1936. Sister Prince's role was equivalent to that of a "church mother" or "spiritual mother," whom persons at the mission and revival held in high esteem and would seek out for prayer and council.[5] Sister Prince was the only African American woman to serve on the credentials committee.

In a 1907 issue of *The Apostolic Faith* newsletter, an article bearing Seymour's name as author reads:

> Before Jesus ascended to heaven, holy anointing oil had never been poured on a woman's head; but before He organized His church, He called them all into the upper room, both men and women, and anointed them with the oil of the Holy Ghost, thus qualifying them to minister in His Gospel. On the day of Pentecost they all preached through the power of the Holy Ghost. In Christ Jesus there is neither male nor female, all are one.[6]

The article makes clear that baptism in the Spirit and the Spirit's non-discriminatory bestowal of gifts results in equality between women and men in the work of God. The article is an expression of belief in spiritual egalitarianism.

Seymour later retracted his initial openness to women in ministry and church leadership. In his *Doctrines and Disciplines*, published in 1915, Seymour placed limitations on both women's leadership and white participation at the mission.[7] He stated that "women can be ministers but not elders or bishops," insisting that only a "colored man" can serve as bishop.[8] Women could not hold positions that placed them in

5. Alexander, *The Women of Azusa Street*, 182; Cecil M. Robeck Jr., *The Azusa Street Revival and Mission: The Birth of the Global Pentecostal Movement* (Nashville: Nelson, 2006), 103.

6. *The Apostolic Faith* 1.10 (1907): 3.

7. Seymour, *Doctrines and Discipline*, 49–50, 91. According to Seymour, women can be ministers (i.e., deaconesses and elders) but not bishops.

8. Ibid., 3, 49. Whites are welcome to join the mission but they cannot hold the highest leadership positions.

authority over men. While women could participate in the ceremony of ordination, they could not "lay hands," that is, confer holy orders, on a man. Seymour's wife Jennie was the only woman allowed to serve on the mission's board of trustees.[9]

The values to which Seymour juxtaposed spiritual egalitarianism and gave the greater priority were social order and black leadership. In his effort to legally incorporate the mission, Seymour was not seeking to institutionalize the value of egalitarianism. His ecclesial pragmatism was informed by a history of distrust of whites who had undermined his authority as pastor of the mission and leader of the revival.[10] Seymour sought to stave off what he thought would be a "race war" of sorts, an ongoing conflict between blacks and whites. He defined black leadership in terms of patriarchy. The need and privilege of blacks to lead their own organizations was satisfied by African American men only. He assumed that women are, by nature, subordinate to men, and are fulfilled in support roles to men.[11]

Separate and Unequal Spheres for Women

In 1910, three years after its establishment as a Pentecostal denomination, the Church of God in Christ formed a women's department. COGIC's Women's Department has become the largest such auxiliary of any African American denomination.[12] Charles H. Mason, COGIC's

9. Ibid., 48.

10. Ibid., 12. The hurtful experiences to which Seymour alludes are Florence Crawford and Clara Lum's taking the mailing list for the mission's newsletter, leaving Seymour without ways of contacting his supporters, and William H. Durham's introduction of new teachings and self-declaration as leader of the mission and revival. Durham taught what became known as the "finished work" doctrine which declares that persons are sanctified at the moment of conversion and that holiness is a life-long quest. Durham's teachings, not to mention his usurpation of authority, undermined Seymour's teaching that Pentecostal experience is a three-step process of conversion, sanctification, and baptism in the Holy Spirit.

11. For further discussion of the role of women in ministry at Seymour's mission, see Barbara Cavaness' essay, "Leadership Attitudes and the Ministry of Single Women in Assembly of God Missions," in this volume.

12. For information on COGIC's Women's Department, see Adrienne M. Israel, "Mothers Robeson and Coffey—Pioneers of Women's Work, 1911–1964," in Ithiel C. Clemmons, *Bishop C. H. Mason and the Roots of the Church of God in Christ* (Bakersfield, Calif.: Pneuma Life Publishing, 1996), 101–21; and Anthea D. Butler, "A Peculiar Synergy: Matriarchy and the Church of God in Christ" (PhD dissertation, Vanderbilt

founder, sought out Lizzie Robinson to organize this auxiliary.[13] Today, the Women's Department has multiple levels of organization in local churches and jurisdictional and national settings.

As COGIC reads Scripture, there exists a "distinct order" for women separate from that of men.[14] Women are restricted to separate and unequal spheres for participation and leadership. Because women's call to ministry is not validated with ordination, women's departments become alternative paths for involvement, recognition, and leadership. As in the case of COGIC's Women's Department, women are limited to work and interaction among themselves and work and supervision of children and youths.

Several organizations and activities constitute the Women's Department. The department includes: Prayer and Bible Band (women's prayer and Bible study), Sunshine Band (work with children), Purity Class (work with teenagers), Nurses Unit (emergency care for persons suddenly ill at church gatherings), Usher Board (directing and seating persons at church gatherings), Hospitality Committee (serving as greeters, hosting receptions, etc.), Sewing Circle (making clothing, quilts, and other handicrafts), Young Women's Christian Council (for women in their 30s), Christian Women's Council (for women 40 & over), Ministers' Wives Circle, and Business and Professional Women's Federation. Jurisdictions maintain Examination Boards that train and license "missionaries" (i.e., women ministers) on the recommendation of their pastors. The Women's Department is involved also in missions and evangelism. Women play a vital role in growing the membership of the church and extending and supporting its operations financially. Most local churches have a Mothers' Board that gives formal recognition to women of the congregation that exemplify faith, leadership, and moral integrity.

Women are organized hierarchically. The "evangelist missionary," who may work within several local churches or outside the local church where she is member, is thought to have a higher status than the "deaconess missionary," who is authorized only for work within the local

University, 2001), recently published as *Women in the Church of God in Christ: Making a Sanctified World* (Chapel Hill: University of North Carolina Press, 2007).

13. In some publications, her last name appears incorrectly as "Robeson."

14. *Church of God in Christ Official Manual* (Memphis: Church of God in Christ Publishing, 1973), 158–59; hereafter cited as *Official Manual 1973*.

church of her declared membership. District missionaries, jurisdictional women's supervisors, and international supervisor of the Women's
Department oversee the activities of missionaries.

The highest denominational leadership position that a women can
reach is that of the supervisor of the Women's Department or a mostly
female division such as the Music Department. With the ordained ministry restricted to males and organized hierarchically, women will never
reach the highest positions of leadership in the church. The track for
males starts at the lowest level of licensed minister (local preacher), and
moves upward to that of ordained minister (elder), pastor, superintendent, jurisdictional bishop, and to the highest rank of a bishop on the
General Board. The presiding bishop of the denomination is selected
from the General Board. Every ordained minister (elder) in good standing is eligible for participation (voice and vote) in the General Assembly,
COGIC's policy-making, and doctrine-establishing body as well as
highest decision-making authority.

Women are grossly under-represented and without a significant
voting block to influence the formation of church policy and doctrine
in the General Assembly. Few seats in the General Assembly are available for women. The Church of God in Christ's Constitution allows
each jurisdiction in the United States to send to the General Assembly
four women delegates: the women's supervisor, two district missionaries, and one lay delegate.[15] While most woman pastors are admitted to
the General Assembly as lay delegates or district missionaries, some
bishops insist that women pastors from their jurisdictions be admitted
as pastors. The number of delegates varies for jurisdictions in foreign
countries. In November 2000, the General Assembly reached its highest
record of registered delegates—5,495 persons, of which 923 were wom-
en.[16] At this record breaking level, women comprise close to seventeen
percent of the voting delegates.

15. *Church of God in Christ Official Manual*, 1991 ed. (Memphis: Church of God in
Christ Publishing, 1991), 9.

16. The number of registered delegates was reported by the General Secretary upon
the Chair's call for certification of the General Assembly for business. I was a delegate
present and voting for this meeting of the General Assembly. These figures as well as
voting results are reported in the *Whole Truth Magazine* 6.1 (2001).

African American Pentecostals and Women's Ordination

Formal Rules and Actual Practices

African American Pentecostalism has only a few stellar examples of denominations with policies of full ordination for women. Bishops Ida B. Robinson and Mary Lena (Magdalena) Lewis Tate are pioneers that put ecclesial pragmatism into the service of spiritual egalitarianism. Each of these women established small denominations wherein women may become elders, pastors, and bishops. Tate formally established, in 1908, the Church of the Living God, the Pillar and Ground of the Truth. Robinson established, in 1924, the Mt. Sinai Holy Church of America. Though Tate and Robinson were seeking to provide a place for themselves and other females, men have participated and held significant leadership positions in these denominations since their inception. All of the current national officers of the Mt. Sinai Holy Church are male.

Historically, The United Holy Church of America has ordained and formally recognized women as pastors. The United Holy Church currently has three women serving as bishops. The Fire Baptized Holiness of Church of the Americas ordains and recognizes women as pastors. However, in the Fire Baptized Holiness of Church, only men are accorded the titles of elder and bishop. The titles given to women are "Reverend," "Pastor," and "Reverend Sister."

COGIC, the largest African American Pentecostal denomination, does not ordain women. Yet in spite of their official statement prohibiting women's ordination, for several decades women have "acted" as pastors without appropriate title or official public recognition.[17] In the absence of a pastor and with official approval, a woman can "act" in the

---

17. Women pastors, past and current, in the Church of God in Christ include: Emma Cotton, Crouch Temple (Los Angeles), Alleyne Gilmore (Patterson, NJ), Ruth Jordon (Columbus, OH), Irene Oakley (Philadephia), Lee Ella Smith, Southside Church (Memphis), Mable Smith, Rescue Temple (Greensboro, NC), Maria Gardner Thomas, B.M.O. Memorial Temple (Philadelphia). Lee Ella Smith is the niece of Presiding Bishop J. O. Patterson Sr. (1968–89), and sister of Presiding Bishop Gilbert E. Patterson (2000–2007). For profiles on COGIC women pastors see Felton O. Best, "Breaking the Gender Barrier: African American Women and Leadership in Black Holiness-Pentecostal Churches, 1890–Present," in Felton O. Best, ed., *Black Religious Leadership from the Slave Community to the Million Man March: Flames of Fire* (Lewiston, NY: Mellen, 1998), 165–66.

role of pastor. Official approval may come from the pastor who designates which woman will serve while he is absent from his church. In the event of a vacancy of the pastorate, a district superintendent or jurisdictional bishop may authorize a woman to act in the role of pastor until a permanent appointment can be made. But, then, she can not assume the title of "pastor."[18] She may be called by other titles, such as, "missionary," "mother," or "shepherdess." If the woman pastors, she must use the "covering" of a man—a husband, father, brother, uncle, son or nephew—in order to carry out pastoral and other chief leadership roles. Several women are reputed as the source for the success enjoyed by male clergy.[19]

This apparent contradiction between official statement and actual practice may be attributable to three factors. First, COGIC has never had total episcopal control and centralized operation. COGIC's episcopacy functions more as a structural framework for ranking among men than as a powerful executive branch for the execution of denominational policy. Given the looseness in organizational structure (i.e., more precisely COGIC's congregationalist tendency), local churches and certain jurisdictional bishops will recognize women as pastors. Secondly, COGIC responds to the external pressure of recognizing the actual history of women's contributions to African American churches and communities. African American women have been equal partners (and sometimes principal actors) in the advancement of African American people. It has not been the work of men alone, but also that of women that has been responsible for building strong social institutions. Thirdly, there is very little distinction between men's "preaching" and women's "teaching." Women are supposed to "teach" not "preach." However, there is little difference between women's religious speaking and men's religious speaking. It is increasingly difficult for COGIC to deny women ordination and recognition as pastors when several women excel not only in the so-called "women's work" but also outperform males in

18. *Official Manual 1973*, 159–60.

19. Elizabeth J. Dabney's prayer ministry and role as "national evangelist" contributed to her husband's success and advancement in COGIC. For autobiographical information on Dabney, see E. J. Dabney, *What it Means to Pray Through* (1945; reprint, Memphis: Church of God in Christ Publishing, 1987). A biography and information on Dabney's ministry is found in LaVerne Haney, "Praying Through: the Spiritual Narrative of Mother E. J. Dabney," *Journal of the Interdenominational Theological Center* 22.2 (1995): 231–40.

religious speaking. Through women's "teaching" and missionary activities many persons are brought to belief and spiritual maturity in Jesus Christ.

The Church of God in Christ on Women's Ordination

COGIC's statement on women's ordination is as follows:

> The Church of God in Christ recognizes that there are thousands of talented, Spirit-filled, dedicated and well-informed devout women capable of conducting the affairs of a church, both administratively and spiritually . . .
>
> I Tim. 5:9–10 suggests that there was a "distinct order" for women . . .
>
> The Church of God in Christ recognizes the scriptural importance of women in the Christian ministry (Matt 28:1; Mark 16:1, Luke 24:1; John 20:1), the first at the tomb on the morning of Christ's resurrection; the first to whom the Lord appeared (Matt 28:9; Mark 16:9; John 20:14), the first to announce the fact of the resurrection to the chosen disciples (Luke 29:9; 10:22) and etc., but nowhere can we find a mandate to ordain women to be an Elder, Bishop or Pastor. Women may teach the gospel to others (Phil. 4:4; Titus 2:35; Joel 2:28), have charge of a church in the absence of its Pastor, if the Pastor so wishes (Romans 16:1–5) without adopting the title of Elder, Reverend, Bishop or Pastor. Paul styled the women who labored with him as servants or helpers, not Elders, Bishops, or Pastors.
>
> Therefore, the Church of God in Christ cannot accept the following scriptures as a mandate to ordain women preachers: Joel 2:28; Gal 3:28–29; Matt. 28:9–11.
>
> The qualifications for an Elder, Bishop, or Pastor are found in I Tim. 3:2–7 and Titus 1:7–9.
>
> We exhort all to take heed.[20]

There are three assumptions made in the above statement that require examination. First, the statement assumes that men alone are representative of God (and Christ). Only men are thought to be elders, pastors, or bishops. Priestly and leadership functions are performed by men. If a woman "acts" as a pastor, she must do so with the pastor's approval and only in his absence. Secondly, the statement assumes that all differences between the sexes are a natural part of the created

20. *Official Manual 1973*, 158–60.

order. The statement does not distinguish between biological function and social roles. Gender determines what position a person will have in the church. By nature, women are subordinate to men. Women are "servants" or "helpers" to men. Thirdly, it assumes that texts frequently cited in arguments for women's ordination are not univocal statements that stand as a clear, unambiguous mandate for women's ordination. The assumed idea raises questions. Does the assertion of oneness in Christ and record of women's involvement in Christian ministry justify the full ordination of women? No biblical texts refer explicitly to women in the roles of pastors, elders, or bishops. When the qualifications of deacons and elders are discussed, the persons who are expected to fill these offices also are male.

The statement makes no allusion to the pressures exerted from inside and outside of the denomination that affect its understanding and positions on women's ordination.[21] The internal pressures arise from fears of the feminization of the membership of the church, the possible dissolution of the women's department, confusion over sex roles, and the inability of women to act freely and without influence of significant males in their lives. The denomination's membership is overwhelmingly female. Will the few males remain under women's leadership? The Women's Department is the largest, best organized, and most financially supported auxiliary of the denomination. Will the creation of a policy of ordination of women result in a mass exodus of women from participation and support of the Women's Department? Would it mean the end of the Women's Department? Women are stereotyped as being subordinate, standing in or behind some man's shadow of influence. If presented with a dilemma, the choice to execute church policy or obey her husband, would a woman act in defiance of her husband?

The external pressures being exerted upon the denomination include the construal of black liberation in terms of black patriarchy, the construction of social roles around reproduction, stereotypes of men and women, and the women's liberation movement. Historically, black

21. Mark Chaves, *Ordaining Women*, 5–6, 12, 139, argues that it is external pressure more so than internal problems that influence women's ordination. The external pressures are caused by organized women's movements and social expectations of gender equality throughout the society. The internal organizational factors include clergy shortage, the presence or absence of autonomous women's society or women's department, and congregationalist polity that permits local congregations to institutionalize or resist gender equality without reprisal from the denomination.

liberation has been defined as a struggle to gain manhood.[22] The rights of free citizens were understood as men's rights to defend their wives and children. Traditional gender roles assign to men work outside of the home. Men are expected to battle, to lead and to be "bread winners" for the family. Women are assigned to work within the home. They are expected to stay at home and care for children. Women are stereotyped as being passive and emotional. Men are stereotyped as being aggressive and rational.

As more women enter the labor market, delay or forego child-bearing, and balance career and family, men often feel threatened by this newfound liberation of women. Black matriarchy is erroneously portrayed as a threat to black manhood. In actuality, black womanism is characterized by assertiveness in the interest of advancing the entire African American community.[23] The quest for black patriarchy is difficult to justify and fulfill. Black men have faced obstacles posed by white racism.[24] African American women have rarely been dependent completely on black men. Black women have suffered the same abuses of black men and have been equal partners (and sometimes principal agents) in the preservation of the black family and development of other social institutions. With respect to the level of responsibility, power, and influence, relations between black men and black women have not been as disparate as those between white men and white women.

22. Classic illustrations of this practice of construal of black liberation in terms of black patriarchy are Frederick Douglass, "Appeal to Congress for Impartial Suffrage," *Atlantic Monthly* (January 1867): 112–17, and Martin Luther King Jr., "The Birth of a New Nation" (April 1957), sermon at Dexter Avenue Baptist Church, Montgomery, Alabama, reprinted in Clayborne Carson, Kris Shepard, and Andrew Young, eds., *A Call to Conscience: The Landmark Speeches of Dr. Martin Luther King Jr.* (New York: Intellectual Properties Management and Warner Book, 2002), 13–42. Critical interpretations of this practice are found in Laura Frances Edwards, "The Politics of Manhood and Womanhood: Reconstruction in Granville County, North Carolina" (PhD dissertation, University of North Carolina at Chapel Hill, 1991), and Laura F. Edwards, "Sexual Violence, Gender, Reconstruction, and the Extension of Patriarchy in Granville County, North Carolina," *North Carolina Historical Review* 68 (July 1991): 237–60.

23. Delores S. Williams, "Womanist Theology: Black Women's Voices," in James H. Cone and Gayraud S. Wilmore, eds., *Black Theology: A Documentary History, Volume Two: 1980–1992* (Maryknoll: Orbis, 1993), 269–71.

24. Lewis T. Tait, Jr. and A. Christian van Gorder, *Three-Fifths Theology: Challenging Racism in American Christianity* (Trenton, NJ: Africa World Press, 2002), 119–20. Tait and van Gorder discuss the religiously supported racial prejudice against African American men.

African American women's leadership is not the mere consequence of African American male weakness but of African American female contribution.

The assumptions underlying COGIC's official statement on women's ordination are not self-evidently true and therefore are open to contestation. The first assumption does not square with the denomination's affirmation of God as Trinity. As Trinity, the Godhead is perfect community, a unity found in inclusion and diversity. God creates humanity as both male and female. Man and woman together are created in the image of God and together represent God. The persons of the Trinity are beyond the sphere of gender, which is fundamental only to humankind. Trinity helps us to understand the inherent worth of each member that composes the whole. As no member of the Trinity is inferior or subordinate, a humanity that reflects the triune God is without inferior and subordinate classes of persons.

The second assumption fails to grasp the power of God's transformation of human life and proleptic creation of a new heaven and a new earth. It is unlikely that the subordination of women to men is an inherent feature of creation. Even if it is, the work of God is to bring forth a new creation. Biological difference is real, a part of nature, but gender differences (i.e., sex roles) are socially constructed. A great deal of how men and women behave is rooted in social norms more so than in biology. Jesus Christ is the image of the new humanity, which is inclusive of men and women. As an eschatological community, the church lives in this new being in Christ. The church is the model of the kingdom of God on earth. While Jesus Christ is incarnated as male, masculine language communicates a message other than biological inferiority and superiority; it is used to describe the mystery of the triune God. Though a male best fulfills the role of Messiah in ancient patriarchal society, Jesus' masculinity as well as his messiahship did not conform to conventional expectations of his day. As Messiah and male, Jesus weeps, is moved by compassion, suffers, and dies for the benefit of others. Jesus' messiahship focused on righteousness, servanthood, and redemptive suffering rather than on domination, control, and violence.

The third assumption is suspect, not because it is totally false but because it is partially correct. While it is correct to point out that no single passage (or set of passages) can be quoted for the ordination of women, an equal emphasis must be placed also on the absence of a single passage that is explicitly against women's ordination. The Bible does not speak clearly either in favor of or against women in ordained ministry. All texts cited by the proponents and opponents of women's ordination are interpreted.

If biblical literalism is consistently maintained and carried to its logical conclusion, then black men (as other Gentile people) are not qualified for ordained ministry (i.e., to stand in the tradition of the Apostles). In the Bible, there is no record of a woman named and numbered among the first twelve apostles. Yet, there was no Gentile (non-Jewish) male named and numbered among them. Why allow alteration of the apostolic tradition to accommodate Gentile (especially black) men but make no allowance for black women? If women are excluded by this literal reading of the Bible, then so are all Gentile males.[25] It is not by the text itself, but by a freedom taken in interpretation and logical inference, that non-Jewish Christian males have affirmed their representation in the Bible and thus rationalized about their place in ordained ministry.

The arguments that black men now make to exclude black women from ordained ministry are structurally similar to those of white Protestant churches, during the antebellum period, which excluded black men from ordained ministry. During this period of exclusion, black men could only aspire to be "preachers" or "exhorters" and serve only black congregations, and then often under the supervision of a white clergyman.[26] African American males were recognized as "gifted" but unqualified for ordained ministry. Black ministers were stereotyped as lacking ability and courage necessary for leadership. Rarely were black ministers accorded the same or similar liberties enjoyed by white ministers. Those who were enslaved lacked freedom to function as Christian clergy. It was not unusual for black ministers to have to

25. Some Afrocentric biblical scholars will argue that blacks are present in the Bible. However, the construction of race is more of a modern practice than an ancient convention. Constructions of race are unique to modern culture and are not designations used for classification of persons in biblical literature. For a brief historical overview of the development of the concept of race, see Cornel West, *Prophesy Deliverance! An Afro-American Revolutionary Christianity* (Philadelphia: Westminster John Knox, 2002), 47–68.

26. Albert J. Raboteau, *Slave Religion: The "Invisible Institution" in the Antebellum South* (New York: Oxford University Press, 1978), 136, 138.

request permission from their white masters in order to engage in ministerial work.

Negotiation of Tensions in Deliberation on Women in Ordained Ministry

That tensions exist in Pentecostalism are indications of core values in Pentecostalism. In addition to the tension between ecclesial pragmatism and spiritual egalitarianism, other tensions which are (and which might be more) fundamental to Pentecostalism are a dialectical tension between the Bible and human-divine encounter and between the present state of the world and the future reign of God.[27] It is only because Pentecostals have a collective memory and valuation of equality that ecclesial pragmatism, at times, seems problematic. Biblical literalism seems problematic because of the liberty that Pentecostals have taken in the interpretation and application of the Bible to spirituality.[28] Pentecostals bear witness to a life-altering encounter with God. The freedom, empowerment, and the wisdom derived from human-divine encounter makes biblical literalism appear restraining and uncomfortable. Belief in and anticipation of Christ's return lead to discontent with the state of affairs and social conditions of our world.

Values and Theological Distinctives of Pentecostalism

Values are central to the process of decision-making and institution-building. Flexibility is needed in dealing with new and changing situations. Policy once formed, resolutions once made, or structures once created are subject to change. It is through values that consistency is maintained in theological tradition.

---

27. See also Cheryl Bridges Johns, "The Primitive and the Pragmatic," a review of *Heaven Below: Early Pentecostalism and American Culture* by Grant Wacker, in *First Things* 123 (May 2002): 48–50, who suggests that the tensions that are most likely at the center of Pentecostalism are between Word and Spirit and between the "now" and "not yet."

28. In addition to Bible, there is mutual influence between human-divine encounter and Christian doctrine. Believers adopt and regard as authoritative statements of faith. Many Pentecostals regard their constructions of doctrine to be biblically-based. They willfully disregard (and denounce) constructions of doctrine that they believe are incompatible with their interpretation of the Bible and/or experience of God.

A "value" is something highly important, so much so that it influences our behavior. A value is something that we seek to obtain or preserve. A value is something that we admire and respect. A value is something for which we long. A value is something that is indivisible, that is, something that we are rarely content about if we may have it only partially.

What do Pentecostals value and believe? They value immediate experience of God, freedom in the Spirit, and equal opportunity of participation in the work of God. Elsewhere, I have maintained that the theological distinctives of Pentecostalism include: (1) interracial, ecumenical, egalitarian fellowship, (2) ecstatic worship, (3) tongues as the biblical sign of baptism in the Holy Spirit, (4) divine healing, and (5) premillennialism.[29]

Pentecostalism is a movement in Christianity marked by a dialectic between religious experience and biblical hermeneutics. Pentecostal witness to encounter with God influences reading and interpretation of the Bible, and vice versa. The God whom believers encounter also inspires the writing and formation of the Bible. The Spirit of God who inspires enables believers to understand and appropriate what has been written in the sacred texts. Pentecostalism cannot be based on a simple or rigid biblical literalism. The Bible is a document made alive and meaningful by virtue of the dynamic encounter with God in the Holy Spirit. In the dialectic between Bible and spiritual experience, the human-divine encounter remains fundamental, as ought to be the case with all of Christianity.[30]

29. Frederick L. Ware, "The Church of God in Christ and the Azusa Street Revival," in Harold D. Hunter and Cecil M. Robeck Jr., eds., *The Azusa Street Revival and Its Legacy* (Cleveland, TN: Pathway, 2006), 243–57.

30. On the centrality of divine encounter in Christianity, see Adolf von Harnack, *The History of Dogma*, vol. 1 (New York: Dover, 1961), 16, 72. Harnack identifies encounter with God (or Jesus Christ and his gospel) as the constant in Christianity. Religious faith is dynamic, arising from lived experience marked by encounter with God. Testimony (i.e., self-reporting, witness, or narrative) is offered in response to the encounter. It is testimony and not dogma that is fundamental in the propagation of faith. Stories of individual encounters with God hold forth the possibility for other persons to encounter God. Lived experience is prior to theological reflection and must continue to inform theology, in order for theology to be a study that is representative of actual religious traditions. The encounter with God (Christ), that is, the witness to it, varies between social groups and from one generation to the next. Theology, reflection on the experience, yields multiple images of God (Christ).

The Holy Spirit gives gifts to whomever S/He chooses (1 Cor. 12).[31] It is quite presumptuous to claim that the freedom of the Holy Spirit is restricted to conventional social understandings of gender. Early Pentecostals believed that persons of all ages, both genders, different economic classes, and various races and ethnic backgrounds could be used by the Holy Spirit.[32]

Pentecostal premillennialism's emphasis, which is shared by other forms of Christian millennialism, is belief in a positive outcome of history. Not all Christians are certain or in agreement about how and to what extent the future reign of God can be lived out in any present social situation. Yet, there is some intuition, on the part of most Christians, that the Christ-event has ushered in or begun a significant change.[33] Early Pentecostals linked eschatology with ethical conduct; they were not fixated on predicting the precise moment of the end of the world. Their focus on the imminent return of Jesus Christ infused them with a sense of seriousness and urgency about life and faith.[34] Anyone genuinely concerned about his or her salvation was not only preparing to meet a soon-coming Lord but also involved in God's work of salvation.

31. Why use "S/He"? This word may be interpreted either as a gender-neutral alternative to use of "he" only or "she" only or as an indication that both "he" and "she" are acceptable pronouns to use when talking about God. In the biblical texts both masculine and feminine images are used in talk about God. The Hebrew word for spirit, *ruach*, is feminine. In New Testament Greek, though the neuter word *pneuma* is used for spirit, the pronoun "he" is used rather the pronoun "it." While God transcends gender, the use of personal pronouns and implied-gender metaphors are means of nurturing close relationship between ourselves and God. Human talk about personhood is overlaid and inseparable from gender. Interpersonal relationship is not with an "it."

32. Robeck, *Azusa Street Revival and Mission*, 14–15; Douglas Jacobsen, *Thinking in the Spirit: Theologies of the Early Pentecostal Movement* (Bloomington: University of Indiana Press, 2003), 79–80.

33. To indicate that he and other Christians are living in the end times, Paul uses phrases like "the fullness of time" (Gal 4:4), the "beginning of the resurrection of the dead" (Rom 1:4), and "new creation" (Gal 6:15; 1 Cor 5:17). In response to questions about the end times, the writer of the Gospel of Luke attributes to Jesus the saying the "kingdom is in the midst of you" (Luke 17:21).

34. Jacobsen, *Thinking in the Spirit*, 80–84.

Prioritizing Values and Theological Distinctives

Is radical equality only for revival, that is, for gathering persons into churches for ecstatic worship? Is the justice of the reign of God only for the future? Is the record of women's involvement and leadership in the history of Pentecostalism unrelated to the issue of women's ordination? These questions are answered correctly, by Pentecostals, from critical reflection on their distinct religious heritage.

It is only with difficulty or by denial that Pentecostalism is disassociated from belief in freedom and equality. Focus and priority on life in the Spirit, the "not yet" as experienced in the "now," will influence greatly deliberation and policy formation on women's ordination. Early Pentecostal self-representations (what they thought of themselves and their movement) took as a clear sign of the revival of the Church the conformity of their spiritual experiences to those mentioned in the Bible (mainly, the Book of Acts) and the gathering of God's people across the barriers by which contemporary society had divided them. The color line was "washed away in the Blood [of Jesus]."[35] The gender line was washed away also. As they began creating institutions, they aligned social structures with a number of their beliefs. However, beliefs about spiritual egalitarianism have not been realized fully in Pentecostal social structures and denominational policies. A clear articulation and prioritizing of values is needed in order for effective organization to be done in concert with core values and theological distinctives. Ecclesial pragmatism is not necessarily antithetical to spiritual egalitarianism. Actually, ecclesial pragmatism can (and should) be in the service of spiritual egalitarianism. The source of the problem with respect to women's ordination is in the failure of Pentecostal churches to articulate and assign priority to their core values and theological distinctives.

Conclusion

It is likely that full ordination of women will come in Pentecostal churches as a result of increasing external social and cultural pressures for social organizations to demonstrate gender equality. A woman, Nancy Pelosi, is now, for the first time, Speaker of the U.S. House of Representatives and second in line of succession to the President. Her

---

35. Frank Bartleman, *Azusa Street: the Roots of the Modern-Day Pentecost* (Gainsville, FL: Bridge-Logos, 2006), 24.

election as speaker is celebrated as a grand achievement of American democracy, founded upon the principle that all persons are created equal. In responding to external pressures, churches engage in actions that appear to be "trendy" and "token gestures." However, churches need not be merely reactionary; they can be proactive and initiate change leading to profound reform of the society at large. Pentecostals have a unique history of experimentation (sometimes failing, sometimes succeeding) with the ideas of freedom and equality. They have a moral foundation that compels them, without external pressure, to strive for the equality of men and women in ordained ministry and church leadership.

Contributors

Estrelda Alexander PhD (The Catholic University of America) is Assistant Professor of Theology, Regent University School of Divinity, Virginia Beach, Virginia.

Barbara L. Cavaness PhD (Fuller Theological Seminary) is Visiting Professor of Intercultural Studies, Assemblies of God Theological Seminary, Springfield, Missouri.

Karen Kossie-Chernyshev PhD (Rice University) is Associate Professor of History, Texas Southern University, Houston, Texas.

Deidre Helen Crumbley PhD (Northwestern University) is Associate Professor of Africana Studies, North Carolina State University, Raleigh, North Carolina.

Gastón Espinosa PhD (University of California at Santa Barbara) is Associate Professor of Religious Studies, Claremont McKenna College, Claremont, California.

Cheryl Townsend Gilkes PhD (Northeastern University) is John D. and Catherine T. MacArthur Professor of African-American Studies and Sociology, Colby College, Waterville, Maine.

Pamela Holmes ThD cand. (Wycliffe College) is director of the Field Education Program and adjunct faculty at Queen's Theological College, Queen's University, Kingston, Ontario, Canada.

Cheryl Bridges Johns PhD (Southern Baptist Theological Seminary) is Professor of Discipleship and Christian Formation, Church of God Theological Seminary, Cleveland, Tennessee.

Julie C. Ma PhD (Fuller Theological Seminary) is Research Tutor in Mission Studies, Oxford Centre for Mission Studies, Oxford, England.

Janet Everts Powers PhD (Duke University) is Associate Professor of Religion, Hope College, Holland, Michigan.

David G. Roebuck PhD (Vanderbilt University) is Director, Dixon Pentecostal Research Center, and Assistant Professor of Religion, Lee University, Cleveland, Tennessee.

Susie C. Stanley PhD (Iliff School of Theology/University of Denver) is Professor of Historical Theology, Messiah College, Grantham, Pennsylvania.

Frederick L. Ware PhD (Vanderbilt University) is Associate Professor of Theology, Howard University School of Divinity, Washington, DC.

Amos Yong PhD (Boston University) is Professor of Theology, Regent University School of Divinity, Virginia Beach, Virginia.

Select Bibliography

Alexander, Estrelda. *The Women of Azusa Street*. Cleveland: Pilgrim Press, 2005.

———. *Limited Liberty: The Legacy of Four Pentecostal Women Pioneers*. Cleveland: Pilgrim, 2008.

Alexander, Kimberly E., and Hollis R. Gause. *Women in Leadership: A Pentecostal Perspective*. Cleveland, TN: Center for Pentecostal Leadership & Care, 2006.

Andrews, William. *Sisters of the Spirit: Three Black Women's Autobiographies of the Nineteenth Century*. Bloomington: Indiana University Press, 1986.

Billingsley, Scott. *It's a New Day: Race and Gender in the Modern Charismatic Movement*. Tuscaloosa: University of Alabama Press, 2008.

Bendroth, Margaret Lamberts, and Virginia Lieson Brereton, editors. *Women and Twentieth-Century Protestantism*. Urbana: University of Illinois Press, 2002.

Brusco, Elizabeth E. *The Reformation of Machismo: Evangelical Conversion and Gender in Colombia*. Austin: University of Texas Press, 1995.

Butler, Anthea. *Women in the Church of God in Christ: Making a Sanctified World*. Chapel Hill: University of North Carolina Press, 2007.

Chaves, Mark. *Ordaining Women: Culture and Conflict in Religious Organizations*. Cambridge: Harvard University Press, 1997.

Collier-Thomas, Bettye. *Daughters of Thunder: Black Women and Their Sermons, 1850–1979.* San Francisco: Jossey-Bass, 1998.

Gilkes, Cheryl Townsend. *If It Wasn't for the Women: Black Women's Experience and Womanist Culture in Church and Community.* Maryknoll, NY: Orbis, 2001.

Goodman, Felicitas D. *Maya Apocalypse: Seventeen Years with the Women of a Yucatan Village.* Bloomington: Indiana University Press, 2001.

Griffith, R. Marie. *God's Daughters: Evangelical Women and the Power of Submission.* Berkeley: University of California Press, 1997.

Pope-Levison, Priscilla. *Turn the Pulpit Loose: Two Centuries of American Women Evangelists.* New York: Palgrave Macmillan, 2004.

Ross, Rosetta E. *Witnessing and Testifying: Black Women, Religion, and Civil Rights.* Minneapolis: Fortress, 2003.

Lawless, Elaine J. *God's Peculiar People: Women's Voices and Folk Tradition in a Pentecostal Church.* Lexington: University Press of Kentucky, 1988.

———. *Handmaidens of the Lord: Pentecostal Women Preachers and Traditional Religion.* Philadelphia: University of Pennsylvania Press, 1988.

Scanzoni Letha, and Nancy Hardesty. *All We're Meant to Be: A Biblical Approach to Women's Liberation.* Waco: Word, 1974.

Soothill, Jane E. *Gender, Social Change and Spiritual Power: Charismatic Christianity in Ghana.* Studies of Religion in Africa 30. Leiden: Brill, 2007.

Stanley, Susie. *Holy Boldness: Women Preachers' Autobiographies and the Sanctified Self.* Knoxville: University of Tennessee Press, 2002.

Sutton, Matthew Avery. *Aimee Semple McPherson and the Resurrection of Christian America.* Cambridge: Harvard University Press, 2007.

Warner, Wayne E. *Kathryn Kuhlman: The Woman behind the Miracles.* Ann Arbor: Servant, 1993.

Wessinger, Catherine, ed. *Women's Leadership in Marginal Religions: Explorations outside the Mainstream.* Urbana: University of Illinois Press, 1993.

————, editor. *Religious Institutions and Women's Leadership: New Roles Inside the Mainstream.* Columbia: University of South Carolina Press, 1996.

Author Index

Subject Index